Ohana
Delhi

PENGUIN BOOKS
SLUMMING INDIA

Gita Dewan Verma is a professional planner. She studied architecture
and planning from the School of Planning and Architecture (SPA), New
Delhi, and did postgraduate research at the IHS, Rotterdam. A former
Senior Fellow at HUDCO-HSMI and Visiting Faculty at SPA and the
TVB School of Habitat Studies, Gita has also been a consultant to numerous national and international habitat agencies. After quitting mainstream planning—The System—in 1997, she currently engages herself
as an independent planning researcher and writer, and as a planning
consultant to citizens' groups.

Gita lives in New Delhi with her husband and son.

Slumming India

A Chronicle of Slums and Their Saviours

Gita Dewan Verma

PENGUIN BOOKS

Penguin Books India (P) Ltd., 11 Community Centre, Panchsheel Park, New Delhi 110 017, India
Penguin Books Ltd., 80 Strand, London WC2R 0RL, UK
Penguin Group Inc., 375 Hudson Street, New York, NY 10014, USA
Penguin Books Australia Ltd., 250 Camberwell Road, Camberwell, Victoria 3124, Australia
Penguin Books Canada Ltd., 10 Alcorn Avenue, Suite 300, Toronto, Ontario, M4V 3B2, Canada
Penguin Books (NZ) Ltd., Cnr Rosedale & Airborne Roads, Albany, Auckland, New Zealand
Penguin Books (South Africa) (Pty) Ltd., 24 Sturdee Avenue, Rosebank 2196, South Africa

First published by Penguin Books India 2002

Copyright © Gita Dewan Verma 2002

10 9 8 7 6 5 4 3

Typeset in Minion by Mantra Virtual Services, New Delhi
Printed at Saurabh Print-O-Pack, Noida

For

The Little People in this book
They are the People of India and I hope they see the importance
of becoming the majority in the city.

The Big People in this book
They fabricated the stories it tells and I hope they see it is their
responsibility to write happier endings.

The Other People in the city
They wonder about what is happening and think it is not their
doing and I hope they see it is still their tragedy.

The Whistle-blowers
They understand what is happening and feel helpless and lonely
and I hope they do not throw away their whistles in despair.

Contents

Foreword

Keep 'em scratching, Gita!

Will someone please tell me why am I writing this foreword? Usually the more distinguished, better-established writers, get to write them. Whereas my sole claim to writing is that several times in the past I have thought of writing books, and have sometimes gotten as far as writing their prefaces! You could say, therefore, to an extent I am a practised—perhaps even an inveterate—preface writer. It was in early 2001, when I thought I was coming down with a fit of book writing, that Gita had magnanimously lent me her laptop to help me through the crisis. Sadly, once again, no book emerged despite the prefatory exertions. But, we are still an explanation short here, I think. I couldn't be writing a foreword to this book just because I could never write a book to my prefaces…

Before talking about either Gita or myself, I would like to tell you why I have chosen 'Keep 'em scratching' as the title of this foreword. Why, in cheering Gita on to do something she does with such consummate skill, use a verb which most often denotes an action that is too uncouth to even talk about? I have borrowed the verb from the biography of another woman from another age and another country, but with the same admirable spunk. Some may think she fought against greater odds. But I would not underestimate what Gita is up against. You can judge for yourself.

In 1799, a slave named Isabelle was born in New York. After being freed in 1827, she chose the name by which she has been remembered long after her death—Sojourner Truth. Truth was a preacher, an abolitionist and an activist for the rights of both blacks and women. Although she couldn't read, she could quote the Bible word for word, and was a powerful speaker. An imposing 6 feet tall, with a profound faith in God's love and a deep rich voice, she stirred audiences around the country until her death in 1883.[1] Sojourner's fame and stature as an abolitionist and feminist with wit and wisdom had spread across the countryside. Even her opponents had to respect her.

Once a heckler in an Ohio town shouted out that the constitution didn't say a word against slavery. 'Are you against the constitution, old woman?' asked the heckler.

'Well, children,' Sojourner began in her usual way, 'I talks to God and God talks to me. This morning I was walking out and I climbed over a fence. I saw the wheat holdin' up its head, lookin' so big. I goes up and take hold of it. Would you believe it, there was no wheat there! I says, "God, what's the matter with this wheat?" And He says to me, "Sojourner, there's a little weevil in it."'

'What's that got to do with the constitution?' the heckler yelled back.

Sojourner held up her hand to let him know she wasn't finished. 'I hears talk about the constitution and the rights of man. I comes up and takes hold of this constitution. It looks mighty big. And I feels for my rights. But they not there. Then I says, "God, what ails this constitution?" And you know what he says to me? God says, "Sojourner, there's a little weevil in it."'

This was something the Ohio farmers of 1852 could understand, because their wheat crop had been ruined by a tiny beetle called a weevil.

On another occasion a man asked, 'Do you think your talk about slavery does any good? Do you suppose people care what you say? Why, I don't care any more for your talk than I do for the bite of a flea.' Sojourner laughed. 'Lord willing, I'll keep you scratchin'.'

Now Gita is not 6 feet tall. She is not a preacher, but a professional planner. Not only can she read, she even makes her own multimedia documents and writes especially well. And what's more, for an English-educated elitist writer in India she writes with enviable fluency in two languages. Her Bible and her constitution is the master plan. And she has found a little weevil there. She may not be a celebrity—in fact I suspect she would consider becoming a 'Page Three regular' a fate worse than death. And she is very much alive. But I am sure, after having known her for some time, like Sojourner Truth, she will never let up. She will keep 'em scratchin'. So, I say, keep 'em scratching, Gita!

A dozen years ago, my family and I had moved house and begun living in Vasant Kunj, a residential neighbourhood in South Delhi. A close friend who taught at the School of Planning and Architecture had often mentioned that a former student of his, Gita, also happened to live in the same colony. Every time he mentioned his student, I noticed my friend always spoke in that tone teachers reserve for the *les enfant terrible* among their pupils—a tone composed of equal parts of pride and awe, with a tinge of fear and concern. She was something of a gadfly and a crusader, I gathered, someone who enjoyed challenges (taking *pangas* as we say in local lingo). Despite my mild curiosity, however, I never actually met her at the time. I was curious, I don't mind admitting, because I suspected what my friend had shrewdly guessed, that were she and I to meet, we would hit it off well. He knew me for a long time, and well enough, I think. I had just moved to Delhi after having chucked a good job, because the price that apparently had to be paid for economic security and academic advancement had seemed a bit steep to me at the time. He must surely also have known that sometimes I am a little less fascinated with the beaten path than I might be for taking the occasional panga myself.

It was years before I actually met Gita. Years during which much happened, as often happens with years. Soon, however, Gita and I began to talk intermittently—mostly on the phone—for long periods of time and became good friends. Then in early 2001 she gave me a manuscript to read. The catch (though I couldn't see it at the time) was that I would have to say what I thought about it. As I told Gita after I had read her typescript, given the choice, I would have perhaps preferred a kick in the groin.

Now don't get me wrong. Reading the book was and is a pleasure, as I am sure you will find out for yourself before long. I really, really, enjoyed Gita's style. As a long-standing admirer of the power of parables to make points, it reminded me of when I had first read about Hialy, who, 'accused of "using a sword to sever a thread", had said: "Shall I rather use honey to drown a camel?"'[2]

It was *responding* to the book, which, as you might already have noticed in my case at any rate, was causing problems. Now it certainly wasn't because the book was about something that did not concern me. Of the four categories of people—going by her dedication—for whom Gita has written the book, I think I belong to at least three. The only category to which I know I do not belong is that of 'the Big People, the people who fabricate the stories'. The Lord of Contemporary

Urban Development has never seen it fit to invite me to any special meetings of 'senior officials, representatives of friendly political parties, NGOs and donors'. (Must be because I have nothing to donate or be friendly or officious about I suppose.) And alas, not being of the Big People, it is not in my power to write endings, happy or otherwise. So, forewords it will have to be.

Of the other three categories, I know I belong to the first—the Little People who are in the majority in the city. However poor, small, weak and fragmented, we are among the citizens of India. I am also sure I am among the 'others who wonder about what is happening and think it is not their doing' but who can still 'see that it is their tragedy'. And finally, I think I do fancy myself—from time to time at any rate—as some sort of a 'whistle-blower', someone who has tried in the past to raise a feeble pen against some intolerable state of affairs. I did 'understand what was happening', but not why, and I felt 'helpless and lonely'. My whistle had currently fallen silent, even if I had 'not thrown it away in despair'. So the book was obviously of great concern to me as a poor, helpless urban citizen caught in a tragedy, with or without the inevitable feeling of loneliness and despair, irrespective of whether I was a whistle-blower (aspiring, active, or retired) or not. The question however is not whether the book is enjoyable reading or whether it is about something of concern to me or not. The question is, what does one *do* after reading it.

Here is a professional planner with impeccable credentials who has chosen to opt out of The System that seemed to her 'to be hurtling at breakneck speed on the path to sustaining rather than solving the problems of cities in general and slums in particular'. If she is proud of her professional credentials, she is even more justifiably proud of the fact that she has not become one of those forever alien, globalized, jet-setting, outside experts of popular standards. Like Fidel Castro, who pointed out the need—in view of the history of global economic development—to have a transitive verb 'to underdevelop', Gita too would like to go into the transitive aspects of slumming. Intransitive slumming—visiting slums, as for study—she has clearly done enough of. Now, through her one-year chronicle of events in the life of some slums and slum saviours, she would like to describe for us some dimensions of how the Big People, the powers that be, go about slumming our cities, transitively and merrily.

Gita is not like the devout at the Wailing Wall, who pray with folded hands, facing only one wall. She prays with both her hands, not by folding them meekly, but by trying to push back two walls at the same time, so to speak. Her praying thus may look rather more like parrying—with pen, video camera and banner. She holds them all with a sure touch and handles them equally deftly, even if they are sometimes shaken in rude encounters with the real world outside her door. With one hand she would like to depict and document, pushing back further our understanding of the contemporary reality of the urban world in India. With the other she would like to engage with that world and change it to become a better place. In the throes of this even-handed contest—between interpreting on the one hand and changing the urban world on the other—she is intimately familiar with the rough and tumble of the public arena. Her research, advocacy, public action and media coverage is largely focussed on the immediate real world around her at her doorstep. And if she is familiar with the heat and dust and scents of the parks, markets and slums of this real world, she is also a familiar figure there. She has faced the naked power of the state (or rather of the forces that have hijacked it) near her doorstep, because she has combined her global vision with determined local action in her own neighbourhood. She has been pushed around and threatened by goons of elected representatives as well as by public servants.

How perilously close to bitterness, frustration and supercilious cynicism her experiences have left her is something that the vitriol which drips from her pen will tell you and for you to decide. 'Perhaps all that people like me can hope to do in these maddening times is chronicle them,' she says. To her credit, she has done precisely that in this book, without pulling any punches. She leaves us in no doubt that our boat is leaking and that our captain is lying. She has also admitted that though it could be her bias, she is convinced what this state of affairs needs is not virtuous charity and kindness; it might be too late for that sort of thing already. She has challenged an injustice and is willing to fight it 'with vicious intolerance'. And she challenges all of us when she asks at the end: 'What are we waiting for? A bloody revolution?'

So what *are* we waiting for? Definitely for this bloody foreword to end I suspect, so that you can begin grappling with the real book, the ending of which is in your hands. Read on, and find an answer. For silence is not and should not be an option.

As for me, I am always game to hold up the other end of the banner, perhaps chip in with the odd stroke of the old pen, when it comes to fighting neighbourhood battles for upholding what is right by the law. I can help with odd jobs, perhaps even take the wheel if necessary. But just because I am older and greyer, don't look to me for 'The Bhagwat, Gita'! I cannot show the way, because I myself am unsure of how you can keep your sanity and use it too, having perhaps been caught short on both counts! Kenneth Keniston had published two studies of my cohorts when my generation was studying at university during the 1960s. They were called *The Uncommitted: Alienated Youth in American Society* and *Young Radicals: Notes on Committed Youth*. Well, some of us survived all these years by alternating between those two roles—without however being too sure of either having kept, or used, what we had always known was our sanity—even after we were no longer young. Perhaps some of us eventually even became too used to flipping channels!

Be that as it may, the reality of today's—and tomorrow's—ugly megalopolis cannot unfortunately be switched off though. There is no other channel. So, keep 'em scratching, Gita, till we can all decide what we should be doing and can do.

New Delhi   Kashyap Mankodi
December 2001

Introduction

The Plot

I'd like to begin this book with a story. Once upon a time there was a large family that lived in a large house and had a large income. Family elders ran the family in old-fashioned style. Some members commanded a greater share of the family's resources, but everyone's needs were met, no one was denied. The family prospered. Newcomers contributed to earnings and the house was expanded, but life became just a little 'tighter'. The elders realized their informal style of housekeeping would have to change. They engaged some professionals to suggest ways to ensure long-term well-being of the family. These people came up with a Plan, which spelled out how the house and earnings should be expanded and then allocated equitably so that every present and future member of the household was adequately taken care of.

The elders delegated responsibilities for implementing various Plan tasks to different people. They however did not assign the all-important function of monitoring the Plan to anyone. Those In Charge (TIC) of expanding the house did so, but no one noticed they were not distributing newly acquired space equitably. Those In Charge of expanding earning opportunities did so, but no one noticed that decided shares of earnings were not being pooled into the household kitty. Most importantly, TICs saw their roles not in terms of responsibility but in terms of power. Instead of becoming *custodians,* TICs became *owners* of household resources and used them to improve their own lifestyles (and those of their friends). 'Others' in the family did not get their due share and were left to fend for themselves in ways not envisaged in the Plan—to live and work in poor conditions, to make do with sub-standard services, to somehow survive.

Obviously, TICs were the *culprits* and the 'others' *victims* in all this, but since it was the TICs who wielded the brush, the 'others' got painted as offenders for not living in the house according to the Plan. It was projected that these 'others' were in the house with the deliberate intent of slumming it. As the house became slummier, the TICs turned all pious and said they would be kind to these wretched 'others' and *resettle* them with 'leftover' family resources. This in effect meant those who had never been settled were to be resettled with less than what was initially put aside for them in the Plan—and that too as a favour by the very TICs who had usurped what was meant for them. Having thus condoned their own errors, TICs resumed the pursuit of their own betterment. They continued to devour a considerable share of the household resources by shortchanging the 'others', and soon there were no 'leftovers' for resettlement and 'others' formed majority of the household.

Now, the patience of the 'others' began to run thin and they began to protest. The cleverest among the TICs then came up with the idea of blaming the Plan. They noisily and piously argued that the Plan was anti-people for not allowing the 'others' to live and work wherever they wanted. They demanded the Plan be changed so that even the subhuman conditions the 'others' were living and working in be considered as 'planned'. They argued that old-fashioned planning itself must go to make way for more 'progressive' planning that allowed people to remain unsettled. They demanded that such progressive planning be considered the 'right' of the 'others'.

Slowly but surely contemporary progressive planning became a 'global paradigm' and the 'others' were persuaded not just to accept but expect and even demand shortchanging. Even as they continued to contribute to the household kitty, they lost their right to be settled, and gained instead the dubious 'right' to remain unsettled with minimal services till they were resettled. And TICs gained the 'right' to do whatever gave them greater choice and greater control over resources.

■

This then is the saga of the slumming of India's cities in a nutshell. It is the story of how a large and growing number of 'others'—urbanites living on pavements or in jhuggis or shanties, running or working in squalid and risky shops, godowns and factories, going to schools that do not teach and hospitals that do not treat—came to be slum-walas. It is the story of how a small but increasing number of TICs—urban development-walas in government and non-government agencies, in the corporate and donor sectors, among professionals and activists and celebrities—are letting our cities slowly die. It is also the story of the lives of all those who are not obviously TICs or 'others' but are, nevertheless, caught in it for being city-walas.

Slumming India chronicles this continually unfolding story through a few urban events with a beginning, middle or end in just one year in the lives of slums and their saviours. The choice of the year 2000–2001 is based on two rather mundane reasons of what can be called 'relatability'. The first reason is that in our perceptual mindscapes years like these, marking as they do 'the turn of the millennium' and 'half a century of contemporary urban planning in India', are round-figure milestones that we relate to as moments to pause, contemplate, introspect and refresh. Two, by pure chance in telescoped time frame or perhaps by inevitable certainty in a longer spanning trend, this was a year in which most of the events chronicled here became 'news' on account of well-known personages engaging in them, making them at once easy to chronicle for the writer and easy to relate to for the reader. For less or more mundane reasons any other year could have been chosen, with no difference to the intent of this book—which is *not* to provide an account of particular events but, rather, to explore through them the larger story of which they are but small parts.

It is in the pursuit of this intent that this book stays clear of painting a static overview of the slum problem through statistics, assuming (quite safely) that consciously or subconsciously every urbanite realizes that the slumming of our cities is a growing reality. It also stays clear of profiling slums and their saviours, since roles are sufficiently stereotyped in literature, media and the movies. The stereotype slum-walas work in the informal sector where they may or may not be treated well. Their children may or may not go to a municipal school that may or may not have a building or a board or even a teacher who teaches. Their homes may or may not have electricity and their colonies any street lighting. The handpumps may or may not work. The public toilets, if they exist, may or may not be usable. They may or may not get drunk at night and fight with their neighbours or rob or kill. The stereotype kothi-walas keep clean homes (with or without help from one or more slum-wala) and may or may not be driven to work in fancy cars by some slum-wala. Their children go to schools with furniture, playgrounds, libraries, computers, extra-curricular activities and teachers who teach. They have municipal services and telephones, numbers which they can call in case of a breakdown or shortage, besides personal back-up mechanisms like inverters, generators and bore wells. They go to multiplex cinemas, to exclusive shopping arcades, to ticketed amusement parks and fair grounds and to clubs and restaurants in the city's prime areas, driving on flyover-studded wide roads made just for them. They also may or may not get drunk at night, have a fight or kill someone. In the stereotype good relation, the kothi-wala pays the slum child's school fee or the slum-wala looks after the kothi-wala's child devotedly. In the stereotype bad relation, the kothi-wala rapes his maid from the slums or the slum-wala murders his employer. In other stereotype relations, the kothi-wala is a politician who shows up at the slum-wala's door before elections and arranges public taps and brick paving, but cannot be reached when the bulldozer comes. Or the kothi-wala is a public servant who gets all the perks of a public job and provides facts and figures about slum-walas in departmental reports and fancy seminars and in answer to questions in parliament. Or the kothi-wali is a woman who, in cotton sari, kolhapuri chappal and kajal, does social work among the slum-walas. At times her husband or father or friend heads a department that funds NGOs and she registers or joins one. Or the kothi-wala or wali is a famous personality who picks up a slum baby on Children's Day or World AIDS Day or any other such day and smiles into news cameras.

No, this book does not dwell on these stereotypes and their numbers. It dwells, rather, on the underlying processes through which these stereotypes have come to be, on the reasons for their persistence in our minds and (albeit less starkly) in reality. It explores the fundamental question of how, in the world's largest democracy, committed not only to equality but also to the notion of a welfare state, a large and growing section of its urban population is less equal and not faring well.

There are many theoretical explanations for why the poor stay poor. But these do not fully explain the slumming of our cities. This is first because urban poverty and slums are only largely and not *entirely* coterminous. (All those who live and work in slums are not always poor in terms of income and some of the latter are fortunate enough not to live in slums.) More importantly, living and working in slum conditions itself contributes to poverty. Resources of time and money that could be spent more productively are spent on gaining access to basic services (such as time spent in fetching water or money spent on illicit protection payments). Expenses on health are higher because of poor environment and expenses on education are often dead investments or at best provide little value for money. And bulldozers and removal vans cause serious economic reversals. From this perspective, slumming causes—or at least exacerbates—urban poverty. The cyclic relation between urban poverty and slumming calls for identifying other independent factors that cause slumming in the first place. In place of the equation between urban slums and urban poverty, therefore, this work explores the equation between urban slums and urban inequity.

It is widely accepted that inequitable land distribution is a major factor in the emergence of slums. If too many sprawling farm houses are allowed to come up in the city for a few, then too many others will have to huddle in huts on some tiny piece of land because there is only so much urban land to go around. If fancy cyber parks used by a few are developed in the middle of cities on land suitable for local commercial use, then shops needed by many others will come up on roadsides. If a few industrial houses are allowed to occupy large sites in the city (even though they could be located elsewhere), many other small factories needing propinquity to ancillary establishments will come up in residential areas. The end result will be and is the slumming of our cities. Seen thus, the root cause of urban slumming seems to lie not in urban poverty but in urban wealth.

The first part of this book has, in black and white, long shots of two dominant trends in the overall plot of the slumming of our cities as seen from this vantage. The first of these is how the notion 'less is more' has been made the norm by the rich for the poor—TICs in the story benevolently shortchanging the 'others'. It is about the growing penchant for pilot projects, model projects, best practices, policy announcements, new policy announcements, etc., being continually published, discussed, debated, celebrated, replicated and extrapolated to create the illusion of constant activity with little regard to impact. In this book I have called this 'The Emperor's New Clothes' and illustrated it by the story of a citywide slum improvement project in Indore—one of the most celebrated projects in the world but also one of the most terrible tragedies on the ground. From faking success and globally celebrating the misery of the people in Indore, the tale moves to Delhi, where most of those associated with implementing and celebrating the 'success' in Indore extrapolated it into national policy. Done with the making, a set of these actors immediately moved on to unmaking the policy. The next act of this drama was played out in Indore again when lead actors returned to press the reset button and start a new game of urban improvement from scratch in a city they had declared slum free and adequately improved as a result of their earlier 'successful' effort.

The second dominant trend is about the growing power the TICs have given themselves—to make madness out of sense, to paint their implementation failures as planning failures and their victims as culprits, to corner an ever-increasing share of urban resources. This I have called 'The Great Terrain Robbery' and have illustrated it by the fracas surrounding polluting industries in Delhi. In 1962 the Master Plan for Delhi set aside land in various places for different types of industries. Most of that land was not developed or allotted to industries. A lot of it was also lost to other 'priorities' such as regularizing unauthorized colonies out of *humaneness*. And industrial units crucial to the city's economy were forced to come up in non-industrial areas. As all this was happening, TICs did nothing—in the garb of humaneness. Forty years later, the apex court, hearing a simplistic public interest litigation, castigated them for non-action and the TICs, having used up the land meant for industries, could only grab the Plan and start clamouring for its amendment—in the name, yet again, of humaneness.

The stories used to illustrate these trends are by no means unique. No astute observer of urban development could have missed the fact that for the urban poor less and less is being offered, accepted and celebrated more and more. Normative plot sizes for low-income housing are declining steadily. Poor children going to schools not in buildings but in tents or in small rooms within squalid slums or even in open streets is becoming progressively acceptable. In place of a proportionate share in public facilities (such as healthcare) on public land, separate landless options (such as health outreach) for the poor are becoming not just the accepted but the expected norm. Nearly every honour, acclaim and award bestowed in the name of the poor in recent years is really a celebration of the creativity of the rich—the tailors in the classic *Emperor's New Clothes*—in getting away with giving the poor very little space so as to have more for themselves. And nearly every urban development-wala has his or her own favourite awful story of blatant urban land grabbing and every city-wala is well aware of the 'land mafia' (ubiquitously featuring in 'The Great Terrain Robbery'). Indeed, these twin trends make up the black-and-white leitmotif of inequitable urban land distribution.

But while urban land inequity, quite separately from urban poverty, does explain the emergence of slums, what explains their persistence? Why is it that slums—despite their sheer numbers and the numbers of slum saviours and the fairly clear understanding of what causes them—continue to be? Why doesn't the majority in the democratic city stake its claim to its legitimate share of the city's land? Some of the answers must, obviously, lie in what makes inequity continue even though it has no place in a democratic society. It is posited in this book that just as fundamental rights enshrined in the constitution are meant to ensure equity, a *shadow charter of rights* has emerged in urban development practice to ensure inequity. The second part of this book offers, in shades of grey, close-ups of this shadow charter of rights.

The close-ups begin with the 'Little People Rights' (the 'others' in the story), generously bestowed on them by the development-walas. The first is the Right to Stay: the holiest of holy wars that slum saviours are constantly fighting is for slum-walas not to be evicted from their slums. The second is the Right to Resettlement—in handkerchief-sized plots in tight layouts in faraway locations and in lieu of settlement—if, and only if, the vacation of the land occupied by the slums is needed for some other greater common good directed by the courts or the land markets. The third (and the only one when not faced with eviction, which is most of the time) is the Right to Minimum Services—the operative word being 'minimum' and not 'services'. Obviously, these dubious 'rights' are no privilege for slum-walas. It is a sobering thought that they are, however, all that is on offer to them. It is an even more sobering thought that the Little People themselves have come to expect no more.

Next in focus are the 'Big People Rights'. Slum saviours have bestowed these upon themselves so that the dubious rights they have bestowed upon the 'others' continue to look righteous. Here, the first is the Right to Define and Redefine. The Big People decide who is poor and how poor they are and if, when and what they need. They decide which slums can stay and which need to be resettled and when. They decide what constitutes minimum services. And on all these and more they reserve the right to change their minds any time. They claim this right on grounds of inherent 'qualities'—power in the case of politicians, money in the case of donors, government status in the case of government and non-government status in the case of NGOs. These 'qualities' do not necessarily come with a vision (either of the larger problem or for appropriate solutions). As a substitute, saviours build 'consensus' through the Right to Align and Realign. The development sector seems to be experimenting with a mind-boggling range of odd and changing alliances among government, non-government, corporates, donors, celebrities, etc. The 'development dialogue' has become quite a cacophony, with room for the voices of real people getting rather crowded, especially as slum saviours have also assumed a most elegant Right to be Ostrich with Pet Red Herring. Reservations, criticism or protests are handled with stunningly simple silence. It is as though there is a 'do not disturb' sign outside the door behind which developmental decisions are taken. If the dissent gets large or persistent, the 'do not disturb' sign is replaced with a diversion sign and a red herring let loose. Development, after all, is so complex, it is always possible to find some other 'real issue' to talk about.

■

The events of just one year described in this book show how these utterly unequal, undemocratic and unconstitutional 'rights' actually characterize contemporary urban development. The real problem about the slumming of our cities is not the manifest pervasive urban squalor that offends us or moves us, oppresses us or confounds us, enrages us or engages us. That can be dealt with. The real problem is the moral and intellectual bankruptcy that is driving contemporary urban development in the direction of sustaining the problem rather than towards finding and implementing sustainable solutions, towards chaos and anarchy rather than towards orderliness and sanity.

This book does not provide yet another 'original solution' to the manifest problem of urban slumming, because the whole point is that to throw another 'original' hat into the ring only fuels the chaos in the circus (and it is the chaos that needs fixing!). The quest for the right answers to the wrong question is a self-defeating exercise. This book only posits that what needs to be done is to abandon the shadow charter of rights, rewind a little to the past to see that logically derived solutions are already implicit in our policies and plans, end the freestyle free-for-all jamboree that lets anyone assume the licence to sustain the problem out of vested interest or self-seeking indulgence and develop a clear definition of development roles so that everyone gets down to getting the job done.

The book does not offer any answers as to how this can be made to happen. It ends with a collage—of the writing on the wall, of glimpses of twists yet to come in the tale of our cities—that confirms however that this needs to be done and done urgently.

■

This book has no answers... because I have not been able to find any. In 1997 I opted out of The System which seemed to me to be hurtling at breakneck speed on the path towards sustaining rather than solving the problems of cities in general and slums in particular. The idea was to introspect and seek wider introspection, to pursue and seek wider pursuit of some limited but durable alternatives which would impact across all levels of intervention—from policy to grassroots. My work since then has covered professional research and writing and directly informing people, so that they ask for rights instead of favours. It has also covered not-so-professional 'protests'—through writing against governmental and non-governmental actions, lending support to petitions in courts and protests on streets. But all these, in retrospect, seem home remedies that cannot possibly cure the terminal ailment afflicting The System—the incurable urge to conform to itself. Perhaps all that people like me can do in these maddening times is to chronicle them. This book then is just a chronicle.

No chronicle is entirely objective, and this one reflects my biases as a cynical, conservative development thinker. It also carries the bias of my belief that urban slumming is not about poverty to be fought with virtuous charity and kindness, but about injustice to be fought with vicious intolerance. Many who know me will, in all probability, also read it (if they read it) with their own varying biases about my professional arrogance or honesty, my personal badtamizi (rudeness) or forthrightness, my disregard for authority or quest for systemic sanity, my negativity or lateral vision. Many of those featured in this book will, in all probability, read it with their own biases about themselves and what they are doing (besides their biases about me if they know me). Some of them, I am sure, will say I have not understood their actions or their motives and should have left space for their views. Indeed, I could have, except that my intention was not to describe each little piece in detail but, rather, to broad stroke the larger picture into which all of us (myself included since I, being a planner by profession, am positioned alongside TICs) willy-nilly fit. I have no hesitation in offering unconditional apologies in advance to all those who might be offended by this book, because this book is not meant to offend or belittle anyone. Our individual motives and actions are of little consequence in comparison with the larger reality to which they contribute. With the same logic, I request the reader to ignore my motives and biases and disregard the tone (at times intemperate) as well as inadvertent errors in describing particular events. Instead, pay heed to the big picture that we are all sketching but not quite seeing, like the blind men around the elephant. This book is written with a fervent hope that it will be read by those who are able and willing to change the contours of that, to reverse the slumming of our cities and to stop the maddening chaos in urban development.

PART ONE

BLACK AND WHITE— LONG SHOTS

The Emperor's New Clothes

The Lord of Contemporary Urban Development (CUD) was home. His little boy, blowing gum bubbles, said, 'India is Sovereign. People of India are Supreme. Does that not make the People Emperor?' The Lord nodded. 'But,' continued His baby, 'this Emperor has no clothes.' The Lord exclaimed, 'What do you mean? Are the officials who visit me naked?' Bursting a gum bubble, the little boy said, 'That's just the shiny crown, the rest of the Emperor is nangu (naked).'

The Lord switched on his computer, input Scenario and pressed 'Enter'. The screen flashed the default Old-fashioned Urban Development Option—'sell the crown and buy reasonably priced outfit from cap to sock'. The Lord shook His head and clicked Next. The screen flashed the CUD Option—'do nothing if the Emperor has not noticed'. The Lord was not sure and clicked Else. The screen flashed 'Get the Emperor outfitted by a minimalist high-fashion tailor through some global grant facility'. The Lord issued the necessary directions. A grant was negotiated and a High-fashion Outfitter and Tailor of All-India and International Repute (HOTAIR) was appointed. HOTAIR made a flamboyant presentation of his curriculum vitae to a large assemblage of officials, politicians and other representatives of civil society. He said he would do a need assessment, a client assessment and a resource assessment. (An assessment of how the Emperor came to be naked was not part of the Terms of Reference.)

First HOTAIR went to measure the Emperor, who was very surprised when assistants started measuring his body instead of his head. HOTAIR explained, 'I have been commissioned to make you an outfit that will make your crown look good.' The Emperor, who knew nothing of high fashion, was overwhelmed and cooperated fully, lifting and bending and turning and standing as instructed. Next HOTAIR went on a little trip for client assessment. He separately met all the important people who would have anything to do with his project to get an idea of what they expected from this important commission. Finally, HOTAIR returned to his hotel to begin resource assessment. From the gross resource amount he deducted his fees and allowances and expenses for equipment (some important people he had met wanted to sell something top-of-the-line that he wanted) and overheads, etc. Eventually he arrived at the net resource position.

HOTAIR then input the Emperor's measurements into his computer and clicked Output. The screen flashed only one option—a close-fitting plain tunic with a fashion score of 0. HOTAIR went to Options and enabled Shredding. He could generate a looser tunic with cutouts and a fashion score of 1. HOTAIR kept working with options on fabric and shredding till he had an option with a fashion score of 10—a net of thin ribbons of latest Lycra with broad gaps. It did not cover much, but looked very good. Indeed, his clients were electrified and his design was immediately approved. HOTAIR then sent high-quality printouts to international fashion institutes along with an explanatory text about the process, acknowledging everyone's participation. The execution of the design had barely started when a communication arrived to say it had won a prestigious fashion award. A date was set for completion and a parade was announced. The media waxed eloquent on the internationally acclaimed design and the build-up to the parade met the standards of the most exacting event managers. On the appointed day the excited Emperor waited to be clothed. (Actually he waited even after he was clothed but that was only because he knew nothing of high fashion and thought there was more to the dress.)

It was cold, but the Emperor tried to walk tall and proud so as to look worthy of his internationally acclaimed clothes. The Lord of CUD asked His little boy, 'So?' Bursting a gum bubble as usual the little boy said, 'The Emperor's still naked. And the cold is going to kill him.' But down below The Lord could only see hordes of fashionable and wannabe fashionable people cheering the Emperor's fashionable clothes. Indulgently dismissing His gum bubble-bursting baby's remark, The Lord joined in cheering the Emperor's New Clothes—and the greatness of CUD.

Faking Success[1]

Most citizens of Indore came to know of the British Overseas Development Administration (ODA)—now called the Department for International Development (DfID)—in October 1987 through local newspaper reports about a six-member team that was in the city to discuss a slum project worth millions.[2] By then, ODA had been doing similar projects elsewhere in India for some years. Its typical slum project had physical infrastructure, and health and community development components and was implemented through urban local bodies with monitoring and steering committees at the state level. Capacity building through training and study visits to other cities and abroad was an integral part of its projects and, at times, it also funded some city infrastructure in support of its in-slum infrastructure.

The Indore slum project had all these features with one significant difference—it used 'slum networking' for infrastructure provision. Slum networking is supposed to be a holistic approach to not just slum improvement but urban improvement.[3] For slums it promises much-improved quality of life through engineering innovations, notably creation of individual infrastructure. For the city, it promises much-improved infrastructure and environment, notably cleaning up rivers by eliminating flow of untreated sewage into them.

In March 1988 British assistance worth Rs 390 million for the Indore Habitat Improvement Project for improving 183 slums (with 80,000 families) over five years was agreed.[4] But it was only after Indore Municipal Corporation (IMC) agreed to take maintenance responsibilities after Indore Development Authority (IDA) had completed project works that final approval was accorded in December 1989.[5] The project, originally meant to be implemented over five years between 1988 and 1993, finally started in 1990 and even then not quite in dead earnest.[6] Community development started in March 1990, the first community hall was inaugurated in August 1990 (but remained unused for months) and forty neighbourhood groups had been formed by December of that year.[7] Other works, however, started later and the state-level monitoring committee was constituted only in February 1991.[8]

In Indore the slow start attracted flak from various quarters—local media, slum dwellers and even the ODA.[9] But in Delhi, there was greater optimism. The chief of the Urban Poverty Office in the ODA gave a talk on the project at the Human Settlements Management Institute (HSMI), India's premier training organization for urban development, and research and training wing of the Housing and Urban Development Corporation (HUDCO). He told a story about puppets.[10]

Slum dwellers were trained to make puppets. Although they made puppets as good as any, they found it difficult to sell them. Then, with the help of project staff, they came up with an idea. After school, children from the slums would go to shops and ask for the brand of puppets made by the slum dwellers. The shopkeeper would try and sell them other brands, which they would refuse. A week or so later, someone from the slums would go to the shops with their puppets. The shopkeepers would exclaim, 'Ah, these are the puppets the children have been asking for!' Once in shops, the puppets sold well. The chief of the Urban Poverty Office said vocational training was a tricky component. In Calcutta they had done a lot of beautician training and women found jobs because Calcutta ladies spend on themselves. In Andhra Pradesh this did not work well. In one project, there was more damage than failure to provide jobs. Training was given in bidi making, but there was only so much demand. Much of the stock could not be sold and bidi-makers, including children, began to smoke. In Indore, he said, they had used all their experience and were sure that the Indore Habitat Improvement Project would be a very successful slum project.

■

In Indore, ODA, which had been critical of project progress till October 1991, came to appreciate IDA's efforts by January 1992 and was quite satisfied with it by May.[11] The camaraderie between IDA and ODA was fortuitous in the run up to the British Prime Minister John Major's visit in January 1993. ODA had many projects in India, but its slum projects were the flagship of British development aid, inasmuch as other bilateral agencies had not yet made noteworthy forays into this investment arena. And Indore was where a 'new, improved' ODA slum project was in place. It came to be that John Major's itinerary included Indore, where he would spend twenty-eight and thirty-two minutes in two slums improved with British taxpayers' money. For residents in these slums conditions improved virtually overnight. Dustbins, toilets, bathrooms and even a statue of Buddha were frantically installed.[12] Residents blessed the British prime minister for this windfall.[13] Cynical journalists wrote against this charade.[14] A cartoonist captured the spirit of the situation in his drawing of two IDA engineers in conversation, saying: 'If we had information of "his" arrival earlier we could have changed huts into bungalows!"'[15]

The stage management worked. The prime minister left 'very pleased with the improvements'.[16] The duration of the project was extended to 1995 and the amount of aid to Rs 424.5 million.[17] One of the slums John Major visited was declared a 'model slum', though it was not renamed in his honour.[18] The cover of the project annual report for 1993 had a picture of him in one of the slums under the project. After a few copies had moved on, it was noticed that the Indian flag in the picture was upside down. The copies were withdrawn and the picture substituted by another one of the visit.

In Delhi the mood was jubilant and preparations under way to get greater mileage out of Indore. The unedited videotape on ODA's award submission for the 1993 World Habitat Award had a woman describing the operations of the saving and credit group in her slum. Without faltering even once she gave details of group size, saving amounts, periodicity of collections and meetings, loan amounts, loan conditions, default management and whatnot. The camera stayed on her face even after she had finished. 'OK?' asked someone outside the view of the camera. 'Uh uh. But she forgot to mention ODA,' replied someone else, also outside the shot. 'Please start with "In the ODA project..." and say that again,' asked someone of the lady. The lady obliged.[19]

In Indore in 1993 things were not so rosy. The local press reported cases of mismanagement.[20] An erstwhile member of the high-level monitoring committee alleged misuse of funds.[21] There were complaints of water-borne diseases from various ODA slums, which were attributed to contamination of water due to choking of underground drains installed under the project.[22] At the end of May that year, a death from jaundice was reported. A local newspaper carried a highly critical article on the ODA project, which said, 'After four years and more than Rs 210 million there isn't a single slum that IDA can show and say this is the ODA project. In some places more work has been done. These are the slums that ODA teams visit.' The article also reported that of fifty slums in which underground sewage lines had been laid, drainage was choked in most on account of engineering defects and also because there was not enough water to drink, leave alone flush toilets. It also highlighted the risk of water contamination on account of water and sewage lines running close to one another in narrow slum streets and said that an IMC engineer had written to IDA about this.[23]

Nevertheless, in July 1994 in Leicestershire, UK, the Building and Social Housing Foundation (BSHF) presented the World Habitat Award ('a cash award of £10,000 and an individually designed and crafted silver trophy') to Indore's slum project for its 'pioneering work in developing an innovative and successful approach to slum improvement... Slum Networking'.[24] BSHF 'carries out research into all aspects of housing, concerning itself with the immediate and practical problems of housing today as well as attempting to look to the future in a progressive and imaginative way'. The World Habitat Award competition, a major area of BSHF activity, was initiated in 1985 'in order to identify innovative and successful human settlement projects throughout the world which could be replicated elsewhere'.[25] There were 121 entries the year Indore's slum project won the award.

In Indore in 1994 slum dwellers continued to allege poor quality of work and even complete wastage of funds, e.g., installation of underground drains in settlements where surface drains existed, even though underground drains had gotten choked almost everywhere they had been installed.[26] Problems became acute once the rains started.[27] Even politicians joined in criticizing IDA and the drainage works.[28] The Habitat Award may have impressed the international development set, but local newspapers saw little to celebrate. One report cynically said the project had won the award 'in spite of slush, filth, inadequate water, roads full of pot holes'.[29] IDA and ODA, however, were thrilled. A picture of the trophy sat proudly on the cover of the project's 1994 annual report. Project duration was further extended to 1997 and funding to Rs 605 million.

In November 1995, an air-conditioned bus stopped outside an

improved slum instead of the city palace, because the people inside were habitat professionals, not tourists (though many sported sunglasses and caps). They were from developing countries from around the world—Cameroon, Guyana, Uganda, Malawi, Mexico, Bolivia, Chile, Colombia, Uruguay, Ukraine, Sri Lanka and Pakistan. And, of course, from London and New Delhi.[30] 'Bursary funding was made available to meet the costs of participants from developing countries.'[31] The bus, presumably, was arranged out of project funds and key project staff was hospitably assigned to take the delegates on their guided tour. When the delegates disembarked, their 'guide' told them all about the improvements.[32] The visitors nodded in understanding and appreciation.[33] Participants of the 'international study visit' that BSHF organizes 'each year in collaboration with the United Nations and national governments in order that the winning World Habitat Award housing solutions can be made better known and their replication encouraged throughout the world' left Indore very impressed.[34]

Although they missed it, at the time the BSHF delegates were in Indore, there was a veritable malaria epidemic in the slums, attributed to the squalor resulting from choked drainage.[35] Other problems had also been noted by then. A newspaper reported from a survey of thirty-one neighbourhood groups: 'Revolving Fund accounts were not in order. Maintenance of Community Halls was poor. Colour TVs were often found in private homes rather than in the Community Hall. There was enough evidence of political hijacking.'[36] Post-project sustenance problems were also emerging with the prevarication on signing of tripartite maintenance agreements between neighbourhood groups, IDA and IMC.[37]

∎

On a cold day in January 1996 a Cambridge-educated middle-aged engineering consultant from Ahmedabad warmly described his Indore slum project at a resort on the Delhi–Jaipur highway. He was speaking at the Second Expert Group Meeting on India's Best Practices for the UN Habitat II Conference later that year. 'Best Practices' are supposed to 'have resulted in tangible improvements in the quality of life and in the living environments of people in a sustainable way'.[38] India's National Report for Habitat II (including Best Practices) was being prepared on behalf of the Union Urban Development Ministry by HSMI/HUDCO under the supervision of a National Steering Committee and the guidance of an Advisory Committee. HSMI's international partner, IHS-Rotterdam, was also wholeheartedly involved.

The engineering consultant from Ahmedabad had slides from Indore to show the clean streets, the engineering details of the innovative sewage provision, the plantation. There were slides of tree-guards that he said the 'community' had creatively improvised. There were slides of the uses to which community halls were being put. There were slides of slum children smiling. He was earnestly pleading for wider consideration of cost-effective and participatory approaches such as the one he had designed for Indore. His eyes shone as he spoke of the possibility of a slum-free India.

Among those present were several engineers, some of whom were highly critical of the engineering approach. Most others, especially non-engineer and non-government participants, however, dismissed this criticism. This was partly because they did not understand engineering details, partly because they considered themselves more progressive than the 'government engineer types' and had no patience with their conservative views, and partly because the earnest middle-aged man was so earnest and had been to Cambridge. As everyone moved towards lunch served on the lush lawns, the support for Indore's slum project and its earnest creator was as tangible as the lavish luncheon spread. Indore's slum networking was included in the national Best Practices and subsequently in Istanbul at the Habitat II Conference in June 1996 it was selected as a Global Best Practice.

■

In Indore the summer of 1996 brought project beneficiaries (or, perhaps, Project Affected Persons?) more water shortages, more choked drains, more diseases, more monsoon mess, and more cause to complain about the shoddy project infrastructure and poor quality of IDA's work.[39] In March 1997, when the project was to end, IDA held an emergency meeting and wrote to the chief minister and, persuaded by the state government, ODA extended the project by three months.[40] Also in March 1997 local press reported rampant water contamination in the slums and imminent danger of malaria and dengue due to contamination in the 'lake' created in part of a main storm water drain to demonstrate citywide benefits of slum networking and much talked about in various award citations.[41] In mid-1997 an impact assessment study, commissioned by none other than ODA, was carried out. This included a survey of nearly 600 families in ten systematically sampled slums. This professional survey found what laypersons in Indore already knew and award juries and study visits had failed to see.

Although individual toilet and water connections were the main features that set this 'successful' project apart, at the end of the project only a third of the households had private toilets and only a sixth had private water supply. There were many reasons why people had not made toilets, notably because they did not have any legal ownership rights of their homes (in spite of the existence—since 1984—of a unique state legislation granting tenure rights to hutment dwellers) and they did not have space. Three-fourths of those who had made toilets did not have private taps. In some cases no water mains had been installed even though sewage lines were in place and people had connected toilets to them.

Where water mains had been provided, inadequate water pressure was the main reason for not taking connections. Those who had made connections had lowered their taps to cope. During water supply hours heads and shoulders of men, women and children (ones that were at least 4 feet tall) could be seen above ground level as they stood in 'pits' that dotted the streets and filled water from lowered taps. There was significant ground water tapping, with local councillors 'providing' bore wells, usually with large tanks for community storage and occasionally with a piped network to shared taps. This appears to have had considerable political currency, though it did not augur well for ground water reserves, not to mention the absurd economics of having both an underground network of water pipes (provided under the project) and a network above the ground (provided through political intervention).

Meanwhile, since only a third of the families had connected to the underground sewage and most of these had no private taps and, presumably, were not according high priority to flushing toilets with the water they had to fetch from elsewhere, the underground drainage could not have attained self-cleansing velocity. The soft landscaping that was to have helped hold the soil back from flowing into the sewers had also not materialized, partly on account of inadequate water and partly because residents found it more useful to extend their tiny dwellings into the areas reserved for soft landscaping. Understandably, choked drainage had become the most visible outcome of the celebrated slum project.

Sewers were often overflowing on to the streets. In any case, the two-thirds of the houses that had not connected to the sewage line were discharging sullage on to the streets. In the absence of open drains (omitted on the assumption that all sewage and sullage would get piped and the rainwater would simply run off the innovatively designed street surfaces) the streets were, literally, a mess. The 'river' that the project had promised remained what it was—a polluted and stinking drain. The 'lake' that had been created in its midst at considerable expense after removing four settlements in public interest was no more than a cesspool.

All this was duly reported to ODA and others.[42]

■

In May 1997 IDA's attention was drawn to the findings of the impact survey, but it denied the scale of the problem and attributed the alarming findings to a poor sample. It claimed there were no technical flaws and cited the international honours in support of this claim. However, at the end of the project IMC refused to take over. In June the mayor, municipal commissioner and IMC officers went on an inspection following complaints of sullage accumulation in homes. Angry residents confronted them and said that the ODA project infrastructure was a nuisance they did not want. The mayor directed his staff to pump the water out and bill the expenses to IDA.[43] Four months later, following a similar problem in another slum, the municipal commissioner wrote to IDA to say this was not a maintenance issue and IDA should rectify technical defects and, pending that, make necessary arrangements for removal of sullage.[44] Three weeks later, the mayor once again wrote to IDA, demanding rectification of drainage defects before handing slums over to IMC.[45]

On 12 November 1997 the municipal council did not admit an adjournment motion on outbreak of cholera in four slums under the project on the ground that these slums came under IDA. At an IDA meeting thereafter, officials said the slums were under IMC and there was no way in which open surface drains could now be provided in place of underground drainage, as had been suggested by IMC.[46] On 13 November the divisional commissioner, along with the mayor and officers from IDA and IMC, visited a number of slums where sewage was backflowing from sewer lines into homes and directed both agencies to prepare slum-level action plans for solving the drainage problem through joint effort.[47]

In March 1998, a local newspaper reported in detail the findings of a survey it had conducted in twenty-two project slums. The feature was titled 'Conditions have not improved even after spending 600 million'.[48] In April, another newspaper carried on its front page a report on the stink emanating from the 'lake' developed under the project. It said the stink was unbearable, the lakefront shopping complex had not been sold because of the stink and boating had to be stopped for the same reason. The CEO of IDA, however, denied that there was any bad odour and said, 'what happens sometimes is that with a gust of wind bad odour is sensed'. The divisional commissioner also proclaimed there was no bad smell but, in view of the complaints, the administration was planning to install plants, drop some fish and open one of the sluice gates to allow some water to flow.[49]

In June 1998 malaria and water-borne diseases took lives in the improved slums. Over half the drinking water samples gathered were found to be unsafe.[50] The city authorities responded by distributing chlorine tablets, sachets of ORS and packets of bleaching powder. But people said this was no solution. The growing resentment manifested itself in an incident in one of the project slums where people hung effigies of health officers as a mark of protest.[51] The Indian Medical Association in Indore warned that diseases like hepatitis, typhoid and cholera could take on epidemic proportions if nothing was urgently done. The project works were roundly criticized.[52]

On 9 October 1998, a year after the official impact study had confirmed the alarming and tragic impacts that local newspapers had been reporting for over five years, in a glittering ceremony at the Alhambra Palace in Granada, Spain, Indore's slum project bagged the Aga Khan Award for Architecture. This was the seventh time the triennial award had been presented and the $500,000 prize fund marking the twentieth anniversary of the award made it the world's largest and most prestigious. One of seven winning projects from over 420, the

Slum Networking of Indore City won the award for 'transforming the environment and improving the quality of life by providing a clean and liveable habitat for its citizens'.[53] A literary award for the most creative adaptation of the Emperor's New Clothes might have been equally much in order.

Making Policy

In 1997 the urban development ministry (which had been responsible for including Indore's slum project as national Best Practice for Habitat II) asked HUDCO/HSMI (which had suggested this inclusion) to prepare a slum policy along with ODA (which had funded the Indore project) and Birmingham University (which had coordinated the project impact study). India's Draft National Slum Policy (DNSP)—duly endorsed by NGOs at regional consultations—was circulated at the end of 1999. It suggested listing of slums and issuing identity cards to slum dwellers to make them eligible for slum improvement on tenable sites and resettlement from untenable ones. It defined 'tenability' in terms of 'untenability', which it defined in terms of 'hazard to user' or 'public interest'. It spelled out strict conditions for resettlement and strongly advocated in-situ improvement. Besides a range of social services, it emphasized provision of individual infrastructure. It did have provisions for granting land tenure rights to slum dwellers, predicated upon streamlining acquisition in the case of private land and conflict resolution in the case of public land. Perhaps acknowledging the difficulties in this, it recommended improvement even without tenure. A substantial part of it dwelled on implementation in the spirit of the 74th Constitutional Amendment, which is about decentralization. All in all, what DNSP seemed to be leading to was large-scale slum upgrading, with individual infrastructure, with or without tenure through convergence, participation and suchlike—much like what had happened in Indore.

Although slum upgradation is a global paradigm with considerable currency, it is noteworthy that there is no conceptual or empirical basis to justify it as a permanent solution. Indeed this is no more than a paradigm on the rebound, so to speak. Slum upgradation became popular following problems with insensitive resettlement. Individual infrastructure in slums became popular following problems with community infrastructure. Interventions without clear tenure became popular following problems with granting tenure. After years of experimentation, there is no evidence to show these alternatives really work better than the ones they sought to improve upon. On the contrary, it is becoming clear that many times they don't. Most slums 'improved' several years ago are still slums—albeit pucca instead of kutcha slums. In individual infrastructure provision different problems have surfaced due to wider capacity constraints and inherent complexity of operation and maintenance in high-density situations. Improvements carried out without tenure have brought an implicit promise of security (leading to investments by people)—a promise that has often not been kept (at great cost to the people). While provision of basic services in slums is essential from a basic rights perspective, in most cases it can only be seen as an interim solution pending interventions that are not just humane but also sensible and equitable.

The DNSP, however, is less of a slum policy and more of unstinted slum improvement advocacy. Throughout, the emphasis is on upgrading on an as-is-where-is basis, starting with the objectives, which are all about creating awareness and strengthening the legal and policy framework for ensuring universalization of this 'model'.[54] Even the section on resettlement begins with the statement that 'this document primarily endorses and promotes an upgrading and improvement approach'.[55] This emphasis subsumes all housing interventions for the poor as the DNSP says housing schemes for them 'should be targeted at registered slum dwellers. In-situ upgradation should be given priority within such schemes.'[56] Even as it admits that 'slum development is still "trial and error"', the DNSP does not dwell too much on lessons from the past. Instead it merely extrapolates the Indore model to a national strategy.[57]

The unsung tragedy of Indore is evidence enough that the DNSP is unlikely to serve the purpose for which it was needed. But poor policies do more harm than fail to deliver and it would be worthwhile to dwell a bit on the likely—and very worrying—consequences of this policy.

■

The most worrying likely consequence of the DNSP is slummification. Planning exclusively for the past, the DNSP says nothing about preventing slums. So they will keep growing. Then it wants to list 'all under-serviced settlements' as slums.[58] So most built-up parts of Indian cities will become 'listed slums'. Next it wants to facilitate 'shelter upgradation' in them. Now, this is an outcome of regularization or service provision or any other form of perceived tenure security and it is well known that unregulated shelter consolidation in puny plots in dense settlements results in detrimental impacts on quality of life. Yet, instead of as an outcome to be regulated, the DNSP wants to view this as a process to be facilitated. So all kutcha slums will become pucca slums. At the same time, the DNSP wants to declare slums 'high-density, mixed land use' areas, i.e., they can have more dwelling units in a given area than are normally permitted under housing norms as well as shops, industries, etc. So areas that are under-serviced will become over-stressed.[59] Well-serviced housing areas, on the other hand, will continue to be spared the problems attendant to coexistence of homes and commercial establishments. So we will see an exacerbation of citywide unbalanced mixed land use trends—aptly called 'garbage dump syndrome'—of concentration in 'slums' of non-residential uses owned by people from all over the city, who can not or will not set these up in their own residential areas. Then the DNSP wants to install failure-prone infrastructure options. So we will have more expensive disasters like the 'successful' slum project in Indore.

The second likely and worrying consequence of the DNSP relates to distribution of urban land. Several legal and policy measures exist to improve land supply for the urban poor, such as reserving land for low-income housing through master plans or under development funding and licensing conditions, and through laws like the Land Ceiling Act to make available to the poor surplus or idle land. However, tardy implementation of such measures in particular and inefficient design paradigms and vested interests in the use of urban land in general have combined to maintain and diminish the marginal shareholding of the urban poor in urban land. In many places it is estimated that a third to two-thirds of the urban population live in a tenth or less of the urban land—and that too in pockets that are the most marginal. From the perspective of land supply, slums are not so much the problem as the manifestation of the larger problem of inequitable land distribution. The DNSP also makes the right noises about equity. It speaks of 'greater emphasis on equity and distributive justice' and improved 'resource allocation and use'.[60] But having said this, it goes on to wholeheartedly advocate an option that directly endorses the notion that a majority section of the urban population must live in a very small share of urban land. It further recommends mixed land use in slums and use of community halls in them even for primary schools—meaning that workplaces of the poor and schools for their children will also remain confined to this meagre land. It does not even mind if some of this land, if of high value, is taken over by the private sector.[61] It speaks of 'supply/recycling' of land for the poor—thereby offering governments an alternative to fresh land supply for them.[62] Sure, it speaks of the need for 'ensuring continuous supply' and for new schemes to 'make sufficient provision for land to house low income workers'.[63] But it makes no reference to similar promises made (but not kept) in earlier policies, plans and laws and seems to condone past errors of omission and commission that have led to inequitable urban land distribution and, thereby, to legitimize the resultant appalling inequity and its perpetuation.

The third likely consequence relates to 'integration'. Expectedly, the DNSP pays a lot of lip service to this. The very first objective mentions 'integration'. In-situ physical improvements are justified on the basis of the 'fact' that 'evidence from existing slum improvement projects clearly shows that an improved physical environment greatly facilitates the integration of the settlement in the wider urban area'.[64] In-situ social services are justified on the basis of the 'fact' that 'effective delivery of these services would also reduce social inequities and promote integration of people residing in slums into the social and economic networks of the city as a whole'.[65] There is even a separate section on 'planning for integration', which reiterates the need to 'modify existing planning framework' to ensure slums 'can be properly integrated'.[66] Even as it says all this, the DNSP wants slums (which are ultimately to be integrated) first to be 'demarcated from regular planned neighbourhoods inhabited by better-off residents' and the slum residents to be registered.[67] (This, it says, is 'to prevent ineligible beneficiaries being included in development programmes', though nowhere does it specify who is 'ineligible' and why.)[68] Registered residents of slums are to be issued a 'suitable identity card'.[69] This ID (and not, say, the election ID card or for that matter other constitutional rights as a citizen) will make the (integrated) cardholder 'automatically eligible to receive basic minimum services'.[70] In the process of creating this distinctive ID for slum dwellers, the DNSP also envisages their wholehearted participation in every stage of 'improvement', besides community contributions, user charges and even a consolidated service tax. In fact all that the poor are not expected to do is to refuse these priced 'benefits' or to opt to pay the same price for sensible settlement in reasonable sized plots in some decent location.

Finally, there is a matter that relates not just to the DNSP but to most social sector collaborative efforts of government, donors and NGOs. These efforts usually impose top-down global paradigms agreed to by 'experts' (read regular attendees of workshops, seminars, conventions and conferences). They then piously plead for 'participation' by communities and local bodies in implementation of these predetermined paradigms. 'Empowered' with long lists of responsibilities, local bodies and people are then offered 'partnership' of the wider 'civil society', which—irrespective of whether it is driven by charity or enlightened self-interest or donor funding—is basically not accountable to the people or local bodies. The DNSP also envisages a substantive role for civil society (with tax concessions and other incentives) in areas that could, and should, be handled by government in a welfare state. And it does so without suggesting even the need for, leave alone details of, a system of checks and balances to ensure quality, competence or accountability. The fact that slums have been reduced to a vote bank of politicians was bad enough. To make them the constituencies of do-gooders driven to do good only when and for as long as it pleases them—through no less than a national policy in a welfare state—is, surely, a bit too much.

Unmaking Policy

Perhaps the only section of the DNSP that absolutely everyone would have appreciated is the one on resettlement—not because it has anything brilliant to say about resettlement but because it spells out guidelines to stop wilful and painful summary evictions.

> Alternatives to resettlement should be fully explored before any decision is taken to move people. Relocation distances should be minimized to reduce the impact on livelihoods.

Resident dwellers must be provided with some choice of alternative sites and where feasible, an alternative rehabilitation package. All resettlement sites should be adequately serviced and provision should be made for public transportation prior to settlement. The livelihoods of affected people must be sufficiently compensated within a fixed period. Participation of primary stakeholders, particularly women, in planning and decision making is a pre-requisite for any resettlement process. Women's particular needs and constraints must be specifically addressed. Any urban development project that leads to the involuntary resettlement of communities must make provision to cover the costs of R&R. All stages of the resettlement process including the transition and follow-up periods should be closely monitored and supervised by the ULB with community representatives.[71]

This is more than what the most vocal anti-eviction agitators have ever asked, more than what the most generous courts have ever ruled, and more than what the most caring projects have ever designed. And this wish list was available in no less than the draft of the national slum policy of India. Surely that meant there would be no more summary evictions—at least not by those who wrote the policy or without strong protests by those who had endorsed it.

■

The last date for sending comments on the DNSP to the urban development ministry was mid- January 2000. The unmaking of the policy began a month after that, when the Supreme Court of India, in a public interest litigation (PIL) on garbage management in Indian cities, ordered slums and litter to be removed from the capital.[72]

The apex court noted that Delhiites were increasingly suffering from 'respiratory and other diseases, the river Yamuna is highly polluted, and garbage and untreated domestic and industrial waste is being either freely dumped into the said river or is left on open land'. It further noted that 'when a large number of inhabitants live in unauthorized colonies, with no proper means of dealing with the domestic effluents, or in slums with no care for hygiene, the problem becomes more complex'. It felt that 'creation of slums resulting in increase in density has to be prevented'. It observed that 'creating of slums appears to be good business and that promise of free land in place of a jhuggi attracts land grabbers'. It remarked, 'rewarding an encroacher on public land with [a] free alternate site is like giving a reward to a pickpocket'. It ordered appropriate steps to improve sanitation in existing slums 'till they are removed'.

The history of this order goes back perhaps a decade. In 1994, in Bangalore, the municipality was dumping garbage on the outskirts of the city because it had run out of dumping sites. One Almitra Patel set about trying to solve the problem around her farm and soon found it was not possible without solving it for the city. Around the same time, in Chennai, Exnora (an organization known for its garbage management initiatives) was born with Captain Velu as a member. In October 1994, Velu, Almitra and one of her neighbours in slogan-emblazoned jumpsuits drove a banner-covered red van into the municipal offices of twenty-nine cities collecting data on garbage management. In 1995 Velu and Almitra went on a second trip, eventually covering sixty-three municipalities. In December 1996 Almitra filed a PIL in the supreme court. In January 1998, the court appointed a committee and, based on its report, the Ministry of Environment and Forests issued draft rules for Municipal Solid Waste Management and Handling in September 1999.[73] It was while monitoring the progress made by various cities in relation to this PIL that the apex court gave orders (in February 2000) that were quite contrary to what the DNSP (circulated at the end of 1999) had suggested.

In the same order, the court directed authorities in Delhi, 'the capital of the biggest democracy in the world', to keep the city 'at least reasonably clean' by, among other things, levying fines on those who littered. Let us digress a bit to dwell on what followed this direction.

For Delhi, where the court had in recent times ordered authorities to do their job regarding vehicular pollution, river pollution, industrial relocation, etc., this was another reminder of 'repeated failures of the government on the one hand, and the continuous march of the judiciary in areas of governance, on the other'.[74] A city editor wrote, 'Delhi needs a Thanksgiving Day. To thank the Supreme Court...'[75] From the authorities there was 'correct' optimism. The chief of New Delhi Municipal Committee (NDMC) was optimistic because 'Indians who go abroad are quick to adapt to anti-littering laws' and Delhi's chief minister, Sheila Dikshit, was optimistic because her government was 'serious about cleaning up the city' and the court 'had strengthened its hands'.[76] Then there was a prevaricating discussion on whether fining was practical and possible under the Municipal Act (whereby sanitary inspectors only issue challans and offenders appear before a magistrate to pay).[77] Then Sheila Dikshit said her government would launch a three-month campaign. Her emphasis, as always, was on citizens' participation—'youth and student community, residents' welfare associations, industry bodies and schoolchildren', besides some 'celebrities like (singer) Daler Mehndi and (designer) Ritu Beri'.[78] There was also an acrimonious debate on who would implement what the court had ordered. The mayor said that this was the job of the Municipal Corporation of Delhi (MCD), not the Delhi government, and that the municipal commissioner would prepare a comprehensive report.[79] In his report, the commissioner said sanitation staff would also sweep on Sundays and holidays and advertisements would be put in newspapers to warn people.[80]

The MCD figured out that sanitary superintendents could collect Rs 50 from those who littered, not as a fine but as cost for disposing of dumped garbage, and NDMC was planning special uniforms for its superintendents. MCD's drive got off in first gear in March 2000. Twelve superintendents were deputed—without vehicles and in addition to their normal duties—to penalize litterbugs in 1400 sq. kilometres of municipal area.[81] Three thousand new yellow and green bins were to be installed and two days spent on educating shopkeepers.[82] It was soon clear that shopkeepers were manageable, but superintendents could do nothing if 'mobile' litterbugs refused to pay.[83] They kept fining mainly petty shopkeepers with, naturally, no significant impact on either litter or attitude towards litter.[84] They did collect Rs 24,000 in fines by the end of June, but this was, perhaps, a pittance compared with the costs incurred on collecting it and, in any case, not the intention behind the court order.[85] In August, the court castigated MCD for its lethargic efforts and directed it to start door-to-door garbage collection as was being done in Bangalore.[86] When MCD submitted that such a scheme tried out in 1996 in some localities had failed, the court commented that it was because it was not with enthusiastic public participation as in Bangalore.[87] MCD promptly shifted gears to comply with the latest court orders. Leaving litterbugs to litter, door-to-door collection was started in some areas after deploying seventy trucks mounted with loudspeakers (presumably for enthusiastically soliciting participation).[88]

In September 1999, in a different PIL, the Delhi High Court restricted the use of slow-moving tractor trolleys, resulting in a crisis for MCD, which was using these for removal of debris and silt.[89] The major problems with solid waste management in Delhi, in fact, relate not to collection but to transportation and disposal. A study carried out in 1997 had found transportation capacity constrained because many vehicles needed replacement or were not designed for refuse transportation or were being sub-optimally deployed.[90] It had also found that the incinerator-cum-power generation plant set up in 1989 was not functional and one of two composting plants had closed down in 1992 and the second was functioning at a fifth of its capacity.[91] Solid waste disposal was mainly by way of sanitary landfill on four MCD sites, none of which was operating according to a long-term plan and the capacity of all would soon be exhausted.[92] In February 2000, the Delhi government 'announced' it would set up ten composting plants, but did not have the land yet.[93] Uptil then MCD had only 'sought five new sites' for landfill, though it was proudly greening used-up sites.[94] By mid-2000 the Delhi government was still 'zeroing on sites' and planning composting plants, though Sheila Dikshit did distribute some 'environment-friendly scientific garbage collection rickshaws' with green and yellow bins to some housing societies on World Environment Day.[95]

Obviously, fining litterbugs or collecting garbage door-to-door would not go very far. At best, MCD would end up dumping garbage collected from public bins (after litterbugs were disciplined) and private doorsteps (with full participation and with or without scientific rickshaws) around another Almitra's farm.

It was unfortunate that slums got painted culprits in this scenario. It is true that piles of garbage are visibly higher in slum areas. This is not because slum dwellers are worse offenders but because they tend to be left out of the purview of municipal sanitation services. Further, slum dwellers score higher than non-slum dwellers in terms of the 'reduce, reuse and recycle' mantra of waste management. The amount of solid waste they generate is far less, if only because they can afford lower consumption levels. And reuse and recycle are the norm rather than the exception, common practice rooted in necessity rather than contrived occasional 'best practices' rooted in fashion. Also, it is the reuse and recycling efforts of armies of ragpickers—incidentally also slum dwellers—that contribute significantly not only to material savings but also to reduction in transport and disposal loads on overburdened solid waste management systems in our cities. Remove the ragpickers from the garbage handling system and each one of our cities will be buried that much deeper in filth because most of the rest of the citizenry simply does not seem to know how to deal with its garbage, except in sanitized seminar talk environs. But be all this as it may, in February 2000 the Supreme Court of India ordered both slums and litter to go.

■

At least three other cases of court orders for slum clearance made national news around the same time.

In a PIL seeking removal of slums along railway lines in Delhi, the Delhi High Court issued directions to the Northern Railways in December 1999. In March 2000, the Railways issued eviction notices to residents in Wazirpur slum, just one of over a thousand slums in Delhi.[96] With the Congress in power in Delhi, any eviction initiative by the BJP-led coalition government at the Centre was material for vote-bank politics. Sheila Dikshit wrote to Railway Minister Mamata Banerjee asking her to first devise a rehabilitation plan in consultation with the Delhi government.[97] Mamata Banerjee being from a non-Left party in Bengal (a traditional Left stronghold) and Wazirpur being an industrial area (with some Left presence) made the matter meatier. But it was the arrival of former prime minister V.P. Singh on the scene—during whose tenure at the turn of the 1990s slum dwellers had been issued ID cards entitling them to resettlement benefits—that made it politically sensational.

In a most dramatic emergence from political hibernation, a couple of hours after a routine dialysis, V.P. Singh arrived in Wazirpur on demolition eve to declare jihad against evictions. He announced to a large gathering of slum dwellers, 'I will stay with you tonight in your time of need. Together we will brave any bulldozer, any bullet or lathi which tries to demolish a jhuggi'.[98] Taken by surprise, Mamata Banerjee issued instructions to defer the demolition.[99] V.P. Singh said this was a victory for the poor.[100] With other former PMs and others, he met the prime minister, who referred the matter to the Urban Development Minister, Jagmohan.[101] Jagmohan said that under Delhi's slum policy the landowning agency had to pay for rehabilitation, but since the Railways had no policy to compensate the slum dwellers removed from its land, he would take up the matter with Mamata Banerjee.[102] In May 2000, the high court was told that the urban development and railway ministries were coordinating at the ministerial level to identify an alternative site to shift the residents of Wazirpur.[103]

A similar story unfolded in Mumbai. In a PIL filed by Citizens for a Just Society (CFAJS), the Bombay High Court ordered the Central Railways to demolish encroachments in the safety zone of suburban tracks.[104] There were nearly 12,000 huts within 30 feet on the suburban lines.[105] These settlements hamper proper drainage along the tracks, leading to water logging, which loosens the soil beneath the tracks. And trains have to share tracks with children who have nowhere else to play and people who have nowhere else to ease themselves. The risk of accidents resulted in reduced train speeds.[106] A letter from the Railway Commissioner of Safety threatening to suspend services on the Harbour Line (connecting Mumbai and Navi Mumbai) if the safety zone was not cleared is indicative of the extent of risk.[107] Following this letter and the court's orders, a drive was started at the end of February 2000 to demolish huts that had come up after 1995 (the state's cut-off date for regularizing slums).[108]

Over a thousand huts were demolished by 4 March.[109] Some of those evicted claimed they had been around before 1995. Maharashtra's housing minister, Rohidas Patil, 'thundered that the Railways had "stabbed him in the back"'.[110] Congress leaders 'forced the government to stop providing police protection to the demolition squad'.[111] The Railways had to suspend the drive till SPARC (an NGO that had filed an intervention) demarcated post-1995 huts.[112] SPARC went about its survey and the Railways went about removing debris.[113]

CFAJS lambasted Rohidas Patil for derailing the drive and objected vehemently to SPARC's intervention. It said that the court in an earlier hearing had declined SPARC's offer to raise funds for house construction after the state provided land and infrastructure. The court had observed that SPARC was not a builder. CFAJS, on the basis of its scrutiny of SPARC's accounts, alleged 'reason to question the credentials of an organization with expenditure of this nature'.[114] It informed the court that the chief secretary had held a meeting on 3 March with the Railways, state officials and SPARC. In this meeting it had been decided that huts eligible for resettlement and rehabilitation (R&R) would be resettled under the Mumbai Urban Transport Project (MUTP), being negotiated with the World Bank, and pre-1995 huts not eligible for R&R would be reconstructed in-situ with building material assistance from the Railways. This, CFAJS submitted, showed 'the government is ignoring and neglecting the earlier HC order'. It said MUTP negotiations had been going on for a decade and linking MUTP to removal of railway land encroachers was unwise.[115] It said the state's cut-off date was not applicable to railway land, only declared slums were entitled to rehabilitation under the state Slum Act, and huts along tracks were encroachments, not slums.[116] It referred to the supreme court ruling that giving an encroacher a free alternate site 'is like giving a reward to a pickpocket'.[117] From the point of view of commuters also, it was hardly relevant if a hutment along the track was pre- or post-1995.[118]

On 7 June, the high court ruled that removal of encroachers from the safety zone need not be linked to rehabilitation policy.[119] The government filed an affidavit saying demolitions without rehabilitation would jeopardize MUTP.[120] All it wanted was some land from the Railways. The Railways said it would follow court orders and not World Bank diktat and was willing to throw out encroachers by the end of the year. SPARC said the Railways 'behaved differently in court, but were cooperative in meetings'. The court wondered if it would be right to give railway encroachers the status of Project Affected Persons.[121] The demolitions, suspended during monsoons, recommenced in September. The government was committed to rehabilitate only the 4300 pre-1995 hutments by end of January 2001 in phases.[122]

In 1997, also in Mumbai, in response to another PIL filed by the Bombay Environmental Action Group (BEAG), the Bombay High Court had given detailed directions for clearance of slums from Sanjay Gandhi National Park. By 31 December 1999, the deadline set by the court, less than 500 families had joined the rehabilitation scheme. In beginning March 2000, the court ordered clearance of all slums in the Park by 21 March. While allowing the slum dwellers some more time to pay Rs 7000 towards rehabilitation, the court said that slum dwellers were 'not entitled to anything' and should be glad they were getting an alternate place at such low cost.[123]

Slum dwellers 'vandalized the BJP and Congress offices' to protest against the failure of these parties to help them.[124] They 'created a ruckus in the court' and had to be ordered out. The BEAG told the court they had been brought there by Nivara Hakk Suraksha Samiti (NHSS), an NGO, which had sent the BEAG a letter after the last order, pointing out that demolishing 33,000 huts would displace 200,000 people and proposed their rehabilitation on the Park periphery. The court, taking serious note of this, directed the government to investigate the antecedents of P.K. Das, joint convener of NHSS.[125]

Two days after the courtroom drama, at the YMCA, a US-based community activist on a month-long visit to Mumbai to 'educate slum dwellers on their basic right' showed them a video on 'how their brethren in Boston rallied and fought with government authorities'. Commenting on their demonstration in the court, he said, 'They have taken a step in the right direction'. At the same forum, a retired high court judge released the Indian People's Tribunal (IPT) report on recent slum demolitions in Indore. Advocate Maharukh Adenwalla, a member of the IPT team, said the report was 'a reflection of the governmental attitude in all states'.[126]

At the end of March, P.K. Das said in a newspaper interview that huts 'facing demolition account for four lakh people' and reiterated NHSS's view that 'land on the Park periphery should be used for rehabilitating them'.[127] In April, film actress and Member of Parliament Shabana Azmi, also head of NHSS, met Chief Minister Vilasrao Deshmukh and urged him to pass a law to resolve the uncertain situation in which slum dwellers were living.[128] Politicians from various parties also approached the chief minister in the matter. Some suggested that 'government should ask the court to delete the area occupied by the dwellers from the forest map'.[129] V.P. Singh also wrote to the chief minister. At a public meeting organized by NHSS, he announced he would block bulldozers and urged slum dwellers to do the same. Shabana Azmi urged women to take the lead.[130]

At the end of April, hearing an intervention petition by residents in another portion of the Park challenging inclusion of their land as forest land even after it was de-reserved in 1965, the court granted them a stay.[131] But (despite protests and rallies and political and NGO interventions) demolitions in the rest of the sprawling Park continued for several days amidst tight police security.[132] Meanwhile (possibly because of protests and rallies and political and NGO interventions) only 6000 families had paid up to join the relocation scheme and the rest now faced homelessness.

In early April a group of affected residents had filed an appeal in the supreme court. Ram Naik, Union minister and MP from north Mumbai, told newspapers that ownership of a lot of forest land was disputed, the Forest Act was enacted only in 1980, the Park was declared a forest only in 1995, most huts existed before 1980 and the corporation had provided them civic amenities. He said the appeal filed in the apex court prayed for a stay to enable slum dwellers to represent their case properly.[133] On 8 May, the supreme court rejected the appeal.[134]

■

Through all this, not one reference was made to the DNSP's exhaustive provisions for resettlement. Instead, every slum saviour was making his or her own 'original' demand for policy, even as the DNSP not only existed but also offered more than what any of these good men and women were singly or as an assemblage demanding. At a press conference at the end of March 2000, V.P. Singh had demanded a national policy to ensure that 'alternate lands were allotted to slum dwellers whenever they were evicted'.[135] Again, in mid-April, he said, 'no proper policy had been developed by the Government for the procedure to be adopted in relocating jhuggi dwellers'.[136] In a newspaper article he wrote later in April he said, 'An all India policy should be announced'.[137] The rally organized by his Jan Chetna Manch in Delhi in May was also meant to be 'an endeavour to pressure the Government to re-work the housing policy incorporating the duties of the State towards slum dwellers'.[138] The former PM not only stressed the need for a national slum policy, he said he had conveyed the need for a slum policy to the present PM who had also admitted the need for a slum policy.[139] Addressing his well-attended rally, V.P. Singh 'gave a year's notice to the Government to develop a national policy on slums'.[140] Ironically, at exactly the same time, the convener of a federation of Delhi NGOs, working closely enough with V.P. Singh to have co-authored Jan Chetna Manch's 'discussion paper', had called a national meeting to discuss the DNSP.[141]

Likewise, in April, in Mumbai, Shabana Azmi asked the state

government to come out with a slum policy even as the DNSP (which already incorporated NHSS's 'demand' for proximous relocation) was being discussed at a seminar in the same city in the same week.[142] What SPARC was doing (demarcating post- and pre-1995 slums), on the other hand, was not in the spirit of the DNSP, which suggests continuing registration rather than approaches based on cut-off dates.[143]

The matter of slums on railway land in both Delhi and Mumbai, for instance, might have been settled to the greater advantage of slum dwellers if anyone had taken the DNSP seriously. For slums on central government land (including railway land), the DNSP suggests a process for 'conflict resolution' in which the urban development ministry is to 'play a pro-active role in resolving disputes' so that, among other things, 'R&R activities can be negotiated more effectively'.[144] Under the slum policy that the Urban Development Ministry itself had drafted, it should have led the process of 'conflict resolution' in both these cases to ensure adequate R&R in line with its policy. Instead, Urban Development Minister Jagmohan merely restated the conflict when he said referring to Wazirpur that Delhi's slum policy requiring landowning agencies to contribute towards R&R did not match the Railways' policy in respect of encroachments. Even after the DNSP, 'concern' for Wazirpur's slum dwellers did not arise out of the slum policy but because of the personal intervention of a former PM. Likewise, the contention in Mumbai that the state R&R policy did not apply to central land was a re-statement of the conflict the DNSP sought to resolve. Once again, 'concern' for slum dwellers did not arise out of the slum policy, but because of the insistence for R&R by the World Bank.

The Indian Railways owns 4.2 lakh hectares of land, mostly in narrow strips along tracks, which is home to a sizeable section of the slum population.[145] Indeed, the Railways is a singularly appropriate central agency for the urban development ministry to start with the 'proactive role' in 'conflict resolution' under DNSP. Moreover, an opportunity arose when the Railways, having decided on a populist budget envisaging revenue generation through non-tariff measures, signed an MoU for joint property development with HUDCO in January 2000, days after the DNSP was circulated.[146] HUDCO Chairman V. Suresh, who had been personally involved in drafting the DNSP, signed the MoU in the presence of Jagmohan as well as the then Minister of State for Urban Employment and Poverty Alleviation S.S.

Dhindsa, whose officers had just circulated the DNSP. But none of the policy makers saw fit to build into this MoU measures to ensure the 'conflict resolution' the DNSP envisaged. Nor did any NGOs (involved in drafting it) draw attention to these possibilities. Just as they said nothing when an elderly and ailing former PM took to sitting in front of bulldozers in the capital to ask the government to stop doing what the DNSP already forbade and demand a policy when the DNSP already existed. But V.P. Singh was doing more than being ill-informed. He was making out a case not only against demolitions, but also for special ration cards for the poor so that they could get rations at half price. Both these were issues that concerned the poor the most. A columnist noted V.P. Singh had 'usurped the poor's agenda from the Congress, which has the government in Delhi and the NDA, which has the government at the Centre'.[147]

In the capital's politics (euphemistically called governance) it was not the ill-informed nature of V.P. Singh's demands but the political threat they posed that evoked an even more absurd 'policy' response. In May 2000, Congress President Sonia Gandhi, while laying the foundation for a state-of-the-art flyover, expressed anguish over the unfairness of the fact that the rich were building huge structures while the poor did not have shelter. She said, 'every time poor slum dwellers are uprooted they should be provided with alternative dwelling place', adding, 'I hope the Delhi Government will work towards this'.[148] On cue, the Delhi government announced a 'new' slum policy the following day.[149]

Delhi already had an 'old' slum policy with a 'three-pronged' approach. Where the landowning agency does not need the land under slums, plots are reconstituted to generate a planned layout with tiny plots as a 'permanent' solution. Where the landowning agency does not need the land immediately but wants to keep its options open, the Slum Department provides minimum services (brick paving, community taps or pumps and community toilets). Where the landowning agency wants the land immediately, it has to contribute towards resettlement and the Slum Department, after collecting contributions from slum dwellers as well, puts in its share and develops alternative tiny plots wherever it is given land.

The 'new' policy only spoke of resettlement, extending the cut-off date from 1990 to 1998 and increasing the plot size from 18 to 20 sq.

metres. To get an idea of what this is worth, consider, one, that there are about 600,000 slum families in Delhi and, two, relocation of about 6000 in the previous year was 'a record of sorts'.[150] Under the 'old' policy it would take a hundred years to resettle existing slum families. The 'new' policy, with marginally larger plot sizes and a later 'cut-off date', would stretch this a little longer.

Meanwhile, this 'new' policy was different from the DNSP to the extent that it said nothing about the R&R process and nothing about slum upgradation. Any doubts that it was anything but a reaction to V.P. Singh's intervention in the Congress vote bank were put to rest with Sheila Dikshit announcing a *sammelan* (meeting) of jhuggi residents. She said the idea was to tell slum dwellers what the policy had to offer.[151] To most, it was obvious the idea was to match V.P. Singh's rally tally.

There was also a cheeky report on the 'encroachment policy' that the Delhi government had promised a year ago. The chief minister's office said the policy just announced was 'a slum policy and encroachment policy combined'. Principal Secretary Suman Swaroop said the slum policy deals only with jhuggis and the Land Department must be drafting the encroachment policy. Minister of Land and Building Parvez Hashmi said, 'Yes, yes… It will be ready in 15 to 20 days.' Additional Secretary Asha Nayar in the Land Department said, 'A policy on encroachment? No we are not drafting it.'[152]

And, no one pointed out that the DNSP had been disregarded in what was the first slum policy-making exercise after the DNSP—not the union ministry or HUDCO in Delhi, nor the Delhi NGOs 'involved' in drafting it, nor the British High Commissioner who called on Sheila Dikshit days after she announced a slum policy that completely ignored the national policy drafted with the wholehearted cooperation of the British government's aid agency.[153]

Jagmohan, meanwhile, had turned his attention to unauthorized additions and alterations in DDA flats which are home to a sizeable proportion of the middle-income population—and BJP's vote bank—in Delhi. MPs from Delhi (all of them at that time, including Jagmohan, were of the BJP) were extremely agitated. Two days after the Delhi government announced its 'new' slum policy, they issued statements urging BJP Prime Minister Atal Bihari Vajpayee and BJP Home Minister L.K. Advani to stop Jagmohan's 'senseless' demolitions of 'small deviations' in DDA flats. They also sought from the PM a housing policy for Delhi 'specially in respect to dwelling units in jhuggi clusters'.[154] Three days later they met the PM about the demolitions and after the meeting came out and told the press 'those living in jhuggi clusters should be relocated' and 'each family so dislocated would be given around 25 sq. metres'.[155] This was all of 5 sq. metres more than what the Delhi government had just announced. In effect, the BJP MPs were airing their personal views, with no reference to their government's national policy or the policy announced by the duly elected Delhi government.

Of course, the DNSP was just a 'draft'. It was not binding on state governments. Nor was it fair to expect all politicians and ministries in the central government to know of it. But surely even a 'draft' policy drawn up by the urban development ministry through its own public sector undertaking HUDCO could be considered binding on them. Yet, in mid-2000 after circulating the DNSP, these two arms of the government came together to disregard it in the largest post-DNSP slum intervention—relocation of 60,000 slum dwellers from various places in Delhi to Narela, planned since 1962 to be a self-contained sub-city but yet to be developed as such. The resettlement was the brainchild of Jagmohan and HUDCO was helping with designing it, giving construction loans and forming women's groups for recovering them.[156]

The provisions of the DNSP were all contravened in the Narela resettlement project. The DNSP recommends that alternatives to resettlement should be fully explored before any decision is taken to shift people, but people were moved even from sites meant for residential use. They were evicted to a site miles away from their current locations, during the monsoon, under a nothing-but-Narela option even though the DNSP states that relocation distances should be minimized and a choice of alternative sites must be provided. The DNSP also requires that all resettlement sites be adequately serviced and provision for public transportation be made prior to settlement. But, even after relocation, Narela was still 'being developed' and there were serious water and power problems. Long after people had been shifted, the minister said the 'police commissioner has been requested to set up a police chowki', the first 'secondary school with an elegant design is coming up' and that the transport minister had 'assured (him) that bus service would be augmented'. The DNSP speaks of sufficient compensation for livelihoods; the only options on offer were jobs in non-conforming industries yet to come up in the industrial area yet to be developed. The DNSP requires participation of primary stakeholders, particularly women, in planning and decision making and the resettlement process to be closely monitored and supervised with community representatives. But community organization by way of forming mahila mandals started only after relocation.

The Delhi Urban Development Minister A.K. Walia visited Narela with senior officials a couple of days after the relocation started. After his 'survey', he said the relocation had been done haphazardly and basic amenities were not available. He said, 'It is not practical to relocate the slums on the outskirts' as this 'only encourages the slum dwellers to sell the plots and return'. Two months after the Delhi government had announced its 'new' slum relocation policy, the minister demanded that the union government grant immediate permission for in-situ upgradation of all slum clusters.[157] In October, another two months after its minister's had demanded in-situ upgradation, the Delhi government reiterated its slum relocation policy and sent it to the union government for approval.[158]

In November 2000, while inaugurating an international conference on Housing for the Poor in Mumbai, Jagmohan announced that the union government would soon come out with a policy to tackle the proliferation of slums. V. Suresh was also present at the conference.[159] In January 2001 the union Urban Development Ministry (again with HUDCO) prepared the national report for the Istanbul+5 UNCHS (Habitat) Conference. The report made no mention of the DNSP (despite the consultative process by which it was made) nor the Indore slum project (which had promised to put us on the fast lane to slum-free cities). It did however mention the Narela resettlement scheme as a 'happy example of relocation and rehabilitation'.[160]

In the midst of all this, on 24 August 2000, Almitra Patel, on the basis of whose PIL on garbage the supreme court had ruled cleaning and clearing of slums, 'submitted to the Court a brief note and table of Myth vs Reality on slum issues'. On the basis of this brief note and table the apex court granted Almitra Patel, who had come to it with a petition on garbage management, permission to prepare and submit 1 Action Plan for Slum-Free Cities.[161] It did seem like national policy making had been reduced to just a routine exercise in word-processing, photocopying, spiral-binding, distributing and discussing at 'consultations'—fashionable but illusory fabrication that made tailors look busy but left the Emperor naked.

Start New Game

The urban development ministry, based on reports prepared by HUDCO, had nominated Indore's slum project for the UN Global Best Practice Award in 1996. HUDCO, on behalf of the urban development ministry, had veritably extrapolated it into a draft national policy by 1999. In November 2000, by which time policy makers had reduced national (slum) policy making to a forgettable farce, the Urban Development Minister Jagmohan and HUDCO Chairman V. Suresh visited Indore.

For Indore Municipal Corporation, which was defaulting on World Bank loans, the efforts of BJP Mayor Kailash Vijaywargiya and BJP MP Sumitra Mahajan to bring the go-getter urban development minister along with the premier funding agency's chairperson to Indore were full of promise.[162] Around the same time, Indore also received the attention of the World Bank (through its Urban Management Programme) and USAID (directly and through its FIRE project) along with several NGOs to start new 'games of development'. IMC was keen to show Jagmohan and Suresh major problem areas, including lack of amenities in slums and pollution in the 'river'.[163] This was even as Indore was slum free, with a clean river flowing through it according to the claims of the urban development ministry and its premier public sector undertaking. The truth, of course, was different and did not escape the notice of the visiting dignitaries, if only because Jagmohan, in his inimitable style, chose to take stock of the city's problems not at meetings but through first-hand visits to various places on both the days he spent in Indore. In the very first slum he visited, Jagmohan was told that despite the ODA project people were living in hellish conditions and was shown knee-deep slush on the streets (where there should have been 'innovative roads-as-storm-water-drains').[164] In the next slum, a woman insisted he see the muck in the drains (where there should have been only duly piped sewage and sullage) and Sumitra Mahajan had to intervene. A little further, people insisted that he walk on the filthy street (where there should have been landscaping and pretty tree-guards) and Kailash Vijaywargiya had to intervene.[165] The next morning Jagmohan heard women's water woes as they filled water from a tank (when they should have had private taps at home).[166] Jagmohan was 'most pained' by the sight of the nalla (which should have been a clean river).[167]

Jagmohan made several promises.[168] The urban development ministry would coordinate with other ministries to secure approvals and funds for the multi-faceted development of Indore. HUDCO would provide cheap loans for housing and infrastructure. It would also provide Rs 25 lakh for setting up a building centre to develop low-cost technology and provide designs and financial assistance to IMC to develop a millennium park in 30 acres and a scheme for water and waste management. Financial assistance would be provided to strengthen Pitri Parvat—a commemorative tree plantation scheme—in which Jagmohan planted saplings in the memory of his parents. In an unauthorized colony that Jagmohan had visited, there would be a 'pilot project' with a grant of Rs 35 lakh from HUDCO's Ideal Slum Scheme and soft loan assistance of Rs 2 crore from central schemes. In one of the ODA slums Jagmohan visited, he was very impressed—not by the ODA project, but by the work of a charitable organization, Sewa Bharti—and not for slum improvement 'hardware', but by the absence of alcoholism and child labour, etc.[169] The minister said several more such endeavours were needed to make Indore an ideal city.[170] V. Suresh also praised the slum the minister praised.[171] HUDCO assistance for more such efforts was announced; HUDCO was even going to open an office in Indore.[172]

Jagmohan said he was 'pained' to see the city's slums, but he did not take HUDCO to task for its ostrich-like denial of the reality of Indore's slum project. Instead he spoke of relocation of huts that were along the nalla and of creating a green belt along it.[173] Ironical, since it was precisely the location of slums along natural drainage channels which formed the basis of the slum networking concept applied in Indore and which had been put on a pedestal by his ministry and HUDCO. And unfair, for doubly damning the slum dwellers with the implicit threat of evictions even after they had made investments in the wake of the celebrated slum project.

Jagmohan said, 'in view of limited resources, slum development is possible through willpower and community participation'.[174] V. Suresh said slums 'can be developed with the help of communities'.[175] For the urban development ministry and HUDCO these must have been routine announcements during a routine 'successful' visit. For the 'community', whose participation they had been claiming and misery they had been celebrating for nearly five years, these statements could only have brought utter despair and loss of a last hope. Undoubtedly, the Emperor in Indore not only knew that he was naked, but also that the shifting games of governance had left him thus.

■

The tale of Indore's celebrated slum project and the Draft National Slum Policy that resulted from it after wide consultations is a terrible tale. Faking success out of a civic disaster and making and unmaking national policy on a day-by-day political expediency basis is pathetic. But the greater pathos is that this terrible tale is by no means unique; so many slum saviours coming and going with note banks and vote banks larger than what they came with while slums remain is evidence of this. For those who watch from the sidelines the ludic histrionics of civil society and governments as they 'play' with the 'slum problem', the patterns of these games can be very absorbing. The players and alliances keep changing as do rules and strategies. But after each game, sooner or later and quite irrespective of the players' tall claims of its impact, the board is restored pretty much to status quo ante for a new game. And the 'slum problem' seems to have become the goose that lays the golden egg in the game—no one wants to kill. There may be some doubt about which player/alliance gets to keep the egg, but there is no doubt at all that, in the scheme of things that is current, the goose will thrive.

2

The Great Terrain Robbery

Sickly Cow was feeding at the Municipal Garbage Dump, its posterior blocking the road. The Lord of Contemporary Urban Development happened to pass by. Surprised, the Lord asked, 'Why are you not in your Meadow?' Surprised, Sickly Cow asked, 'My Meadow?' and looked in the direction of Fence. Following its gaze, the Lord said, 'Ah! Fence minds your Meadow. It has settled milch cows, quality excreta is used to grow grass and milk sales will bring revenue. It has also let in some imported pigs to help mind your Meadow.'

Just then a car screeched to a halt and, what with all the nervousness on account of the Lord and the Car, Sickly Cow eased itself on the road. Exasperated, the Lord asked, 'Why are you not in the Meadow? Why are you obstructing traffic and messing up the place?' Confused, Sickly Cow stammered, 'My Lord, but Fence…' The Lord cut Sickly Cow short and said, 'Don't whine about Fence. If you don't like Fence, change Fence. But leave the Dump and go live in the Meadow or… die.' So saying, the Lord left.

Sickly Cow went to Fence and said, 'My Lord has said I must be in the Meadow'. Fence rolled its eyes heavenwards and said, 'My Lord wants the moon! The Meadow is full. Chaps here want larger plots and lots for calves and piglets. Even the expansion scheme is full.' Sickly Cow was persistent. 'My Lord said otherwise I will die.' Fence was dismissive. 'Pah! You are managing fine at the Dump.' Sickly Cow was insistent, 'My Lord said you, Fence, are for me and I can change you'. Fence sized up Sickly Cow and said, 'Do you have a leader or celebrity to speak for you? Send her over and I will see what I have to do.'

Sickly Cow came away and told all other Sickly Cows what the Lord had said and what Fence had said. Next morning they arrived in hundreds. Fence was alarmed at their numbers. Friends of Fence said not to worry. 'They are just a mob without a leader'. On cue Old Fence, hanging around the Meadow ever since the last fence changing, looked up, drooled over the sea of Sickly Cows, amiably ambled to the head of the mob and announced, 'This New Fence here has eaten up all your grass and driven you to the Dump'. New Fence saw thousands of pairs of accusing cow eyes turn upon it and stammered, 'No, dear cows, it was Old Fence that ate up your grass. If it weren't for the pigs I myself would starve…' New Fence and Old Fence began trading charges. Sickly Cows became righteously riotous. Milch cows and imported pigs looked on from the Meadow. Other Sickly Cows looked on from farther afar. The Lord of CUD looked down from above.

As the pandemonium grew, the Lord switched on his computer, input Scenario and pressed Enter. The screen flashed the default Old-fashioned Urban Development Option. 'Evict imported pigs. Downsize lots of milch cows. Get the right numbers. Equitably divide the Meadow amongst all cows. Introduce measures to stop fences from eating grass.' The Lord shook his head and clicked Next. The screen flashed the CUD Option. 'Leave the Meadow to milch cows and pigs (they keep it green whereas Sickly Cows will mess it up). Let as many Sickly Cows as needed to cool tempers remain in the Dump and pack the others off to some wilderness. Use space that becomes surplus after throwing out Sickly Cows to expand the Meadow. Change the laws that say Dumps are only for garbage, Meadows are for all cows and Fences should not eat the grass.'

The Lord issued the necessary directions for the CUD Option to be executed. Some Sickly Cows were packed off to the wilderness, where they starved to death. Milch cows and imported pigs got more Meadow and were happy. Fence grew plump and was happy. Old Fence made plans for next fence changing and was happy. Sickly Cows ate at the same Dump and were, well, not happy, but glad to be left alone and alive. The Lord saw almost everyone happy and was happy. And CUD went on…happily.

Industrious Hooligans

In mid-November 2000, most of Delhi's factory owners and workers closed their factories and took to the streets. On 17 November, 4000 of them held a government engineer captive for hours in Northwest Delhi.[1] On 18 November, 1500 of them prevented government officials from coming near their factories in East Delhi and West Delhi was caught in traffic jams as thousands came out to demonstrate.[2] On 19 November they were all over the capital. They marched in protest, jamming major arterial roads and throwing traffic out of gear. They roughed up government officials and deflated tyres, forcing the officials to retreat. In places they stoned buses, getting *lathi*-charged and tear-gassed.[3]

Politicians of all hues rallied around.[4] The Delhi unit of the Congress urged Sheila Dikshit's Congress government in Delhi to safeguard the interests of the factory owners and workers.[5] Madan Lal Khurana, former chief minister of Delhi and senior leader of the Bharatiya Janata Party (the leading party in the ruling coalition at the Centre and the party in power in Delhi before), announced he would spearhead their agitation.[6] Opposition politicians supported them. Politicians in power instructed the police to 'go slow'.[7]

And on 20 November all hell broke loose. Factory owners and workers became a 'mob' that made front-page news with screaming headlines about Delhi being held to ransom, ravaged.[8] City page headlines detailed what the 'mob' had done.[9]

On 21 November, although the police hinted at possible escalation of violence and warned residents of disturbed areas that they would have to bear the cost of additional forces, its 'toughest' call, it seems, was handling a 500-strong 'mob' that stoned buses and was dispersed by teargas.[10] Indeed, with local politicians moving on from the 'mob game' on the streets to the 'blame game' in the Assembly, the 'mob' all but disappeared.[11] Factory owners and workers continued to protest and snarl up traffic, but the previous day's arson and looting did not recur.[12]

Also on 21 November seventeen-year-old Irfan, 'a worker in a Walled city-based garment unit' or, perhaps, 'a shop worker, who was headed for work' succumbed to the police bullet injury he had received the previous day.[13] (Seventeen-year-old Ajab Singh, 'apparently just a passerby' who got in the way of another police bullet, and fifty-three-year-old Bhiku Ram, another passerby who got in the way of a postal van reversing in panic, had already become casualties of the previous day's violence.)[14] And it was on 21 November as well that the Supreme Court of India said to the Delhi government, 'You have hooligans holding the city to ransom'.[15]

■

The story of how the industrious of Delhi came to be hooligans has its beginning in March 1995 when the supreme court, hearing a public interest litigation (PIL) filed in 1985, ordered H-category industries to be closed in Delhi. H-category is a list in Delhi's statutory Master Plan that names various types of hazardous and noxious and/or heavy and large industries that are not permitted in Delhi.

The first thing that resulted from the court's order was the realization that 'none of the various departments involved seem to have up-to-date comprehensive lists of industries'.[16] From then to the end of this story there was never any clarity on the numbers involved. (The numbers in the following paragraphs are very confusing and have been included to make precisely this point. They are purely incidental to the story being told here.)

In 1995 some lists were placed before the court. The largest comprised 8500 hazardous and noxious industries found in non-industrial areas in a random check of about a fifth of the total units in the city. A second list named 256 hazardous units identified in industrial areas in the mid-1980s. Two more lists (meant to be illustrative) noted seventy-seven big industries and 327 units that had been told to install pollution control devices. Obviously, there were more H-category units, but the total of these numbers placed before the court became the working figure. Delhi Environment Minister Sahib Singh Verma told the Assembly that closure notices would be sent to 9000 units.[17] Subsequently, notices were issued to 1226, nearly half of which objected to being included in H-category.[18] On 8 July 1996, the court ordered closure of the first batch of 168 H-category units by 30 November, a deadline that was met.[19]

As the court monitored closure of more H-category industries, some contested the criteria for categorization and some sought a 'third option' other than shut or shift—of switching to permissible activity.[20] The matter of land that became available after closing and shifting became a contentious one (we shall return to that later). The matter of workers' compensation became the most telling tragedy. In December 1996, the court ordered six years' wages as compensation if a unit opted to shut rather than shift. This was a significant order since many units had been planning to close, leaving workers in the lurch.[21] But non-compliance with the order forced thousands of workers into penury.[22] In May 1997, Delhi Minister for Industries H.S. Balli said, 'the labour department will be coordinating with the management of some industries for payment of compensation within a week'.[23] But, over a year later, the deputy commissioner of labour said, 'We don't know anything about how many people were unemployed or whether they received compensation or not. We are not a party to the problem.'[24] Later there was the case—presumably just one of many—of 2300 workers affected by the shifting of Birla Textile Mill. Workers alleged there was no factory at the new site—only a structure housing twenty-four machines which had been shifted on which only thirty persons could work. After a favourable court verdict in December 1998, the workers arrived there to report for work and claim wages and shifting allowances. On its part, the management filed a petition asking for a review of all court orders in the matter since 8 July 1996.[25]

Meanwhile, in 1996, the Delhi government had done a survey that put the total number of industries in the city at over 126,000, including over 97,000 (H- and other category) units in areas not meant for them.[26] In April, the court had directed shifting of these 'non-conforming' units by 31 December 1996.[27] By October, the government was talking of relocating only 40,000 units.[28] Subsequently, having begun to acquire land and invited (and received over 52,000) applications for relocation, it persuaded the court to remove the deadline.[29] Chief Minister Sahib Singh Verma (the BJP was still in power, but the chief minister had changed) said, '25,000 units opting for plots up to 100 square metres will be allotted plots before April 1997'.[30] But in June 1997 H.S. Balli, the industry minister, was still saying, 'The process of land acquisition and scrutiny of applications are on'. Meanwhile the Delhi government was paying interest on the Rs 100 crore it had borrowed from the central government for land acquisition, as well as on earnest money (aggregating Rs 270 crore) deposited by those who had applied for relocation.[31] In September, Delhi finance minister, parroting what the chief minister had said a year ago, said changes in Delhi Finance Corporation (DFC) were being considered to allow government aid for relocation.[32] The total cost was estimated at Rs 5000 crore—DFC had only Rs 150 crore—and the possibility of a World Bank loan was being explored.[33]

In 1998 prices of onions skyrocketed and the BJP government had to pay in the Assembly elections. Sheila Dikshit's Congress government that replaced it also made little headway in relocating industries. In June 1999 it moved to acquire 800 acres, but ran into problems.[34] On land already acquired, no development had started. Subsequently an undertaking of the Railways was appointed to prepare plans for industrial estates, but took a year to submit its report. Delhi Industry Minister Narender Nath said that in any case only 15,000 units could be accommodated on the land acquired so far.[35] Total land required to accommodate all the units that had to be shifted was now estimated at 5000 acres.[36] In view of 'shortage of land', the government began 'rethinking its decision to shift all industries'.[37] This 'rethinking' crystallized into the idea of declaring residential localities where 'industries comprised more than 70 per cent of the plots' as industrial areas through an amendment in Delhi's Master Plan.[38] The government decided to seek a two-year extension of the 31 December 1999 deadline that the court had set in September 1999.[39] Its affidavit spoke of the new 'rethinking' and of 23,000 'eligible' applicants (the 'eligibility' criteria were not made clear and nearly 9500 others filed appeals) and did not mention units that had not applied for relocation (whose number was now put at 25,000).[40]

■

Let us pause in this saga of misplaced industries and misguided governance to reflect on how this matter came to engage the city's attention. The matter of industries in areas not meant for them was a land use planning issue. The matter of workers affected by closure of industries was a labour issue. Never in recent history had such matters agitated so greatly the minds of so many urbanites. But this time they did. The credit for this goes to a coincident court case that firmly connected the word 'polluting' (the most convenient boogey man of middle- and upper-class urbanites) with the word 'industry'.

This was the *maili* Yamuna case in which the supreme court, taking *suo moto* cognisance of a newspaper report on the state of

Delhi's very own and very *maili* (polluted) Yamuna river, ordered stoppage of discharge of untreated sewage and industrial effluent into the river in February 1996. It ordered the government to build sixteen sewage treatment plants and fifteen common effluent treatment plants (ETPs).[41] What followed must surely place the case amongst the most *public* ones in its genre. Yamuna's pollution became the talk of Delhi's cocktail circuit. Delhi's children got to know that what they had been calling a river was actually a shit stream. An expert even said, 'At present, we can only assess pollution of the sewage in (the) Yamuna as hardly any water is left (in it)'.[42] The city gleefully watched the government get a dressing down by the court in hearing after hearing. Many a bureaucratic head rolled.[43]

The government was moving at its usual pace for the usual reasons and, in the case of the Congress government, one unusual reason—of having thought of an 'alternative'.[44] The alternative was to lay a deeper (covered) sewer channel along the Yamuna into which the sewage currently flowing into the river would be diverted, treated at one point and released for agricultural use in neighbouring states in return for raw water to fill the river. In mid-1999 it was reportedly talking of asking the World Bank to fund this scheme, estimated to cost Rs 20,000 crore.[45] The media did not report the World Bank's reaction.

In September 2000 the union environment ministry told the court that sewage treatment plants—which were expected to take care of 85 per cent of the pollution in the Yamuna—would take at least five years to construct.[46] It was also not clear if they would really manage to stop sewage pollution in the river altogether, considering that even existing plants were mostly dysfunctional because of power cuts or connecting sewer lines not having been laid, besides which the dilapidated trunk sewage system needed refurbishing at an estimated cost of Rs 435 crore.[47] Even common ETPs in planned industrial estates which were expected to take care of most of the rest of the pollution would take time. Till the end of 2000 not one was operational.[48] It was also not clear if and how far these would help in the present circumstances. They would, at best, make waste water clean, though the water would very likely still need to go through sewage treatment plants, which were yet to be made. In any case, industrial solid waste also had to go somewhere. Since no special sites for industrial waste existed, it would end up either in sewers or in garbage and from there, into the Yamuna or, worse, ordinary landfill sites from where it could contaminate soil and ground water.[49]

Obviously, cleaning the Yamuna needed more creative management of the city's sewage and industrial waste than installing ETPs. Yet, when the court in September 1999 had ordered the government to stop discharge of industrial effluent into the Yamuna by 1 November, all the government had done was to direct polluting industries to install ETPs![50] This act of government was made all the more arbitrary by its timing. So far industries in areas meant for industries had been asked to contribute towards installation of common ETPs and industries in areas not meant for industries were awaiting relocation by a deadline just days away. Now all were asked to invest in individual ETPs, for which the government also forgot to lay down any norms.[51]

Expectedly, the court deadline came and went. This was followed by strictures against the government, followed by a hasty closure drive in which notices were issued to 1384 industrial units and 983 were sealed.[52] These, it turned out, included non-polluting units and units that had already installed ETPs, and there were protests, followed by a Cabinet meeting, followed by a statement by the industry minister, who said industry owners were being given another chance to prove that they had installed ETPs.[53] Within a week 900 applications for review were filed.[54] Ten days after they had been sealed, 372 units were de-sealed.[55] On 24 January, the court ordered they be re-sealed.[56]

In March 2000 the court set a new deadline of 28 April, making the chief secretary responsible for meeting it.[57] Chief Secretary Omesh Saigal chalked out a plan, but was transferred.[58] On 28 April (by when the Delhi government had chaotically closed 2855 polluting units with no improvement in the Yamuna), the court issued notice to the new chief secretary, P.S. Bhatnagar, to explain why a fine should not be levied for non-compliance.[59] More units were chaotically closed with no consequent improvement in the *maili* river. In May the court slapped a fine of Rs 10,000 on the Delhi government for failing to clean the Yamuna.[60] Once again, more units were chaotically closed but did not result in any improvement. In July, the court warned the administration of a stringent penalty if the quality of river water was not improved in three months. [61] And yet again, more units were chaotically closed with no consequent improvement...

∎

The turn-of-the-millennium court orders in the *maili* Yamuna case had two very serious impacts on the matter of relocation of industries from areas not meant for industries (and, indeed, on the practice and theory of urban governance itself).

The first impact was on the industries themselves. So far the industrial units had been watching the court repeatedly pull up the government for its failures to control pollution in the river and ensure that industries in Delhi were located in accordance with the Master Plan. Now they found themselves paying a preposterously disproportionate price for these failures. It became inevitable that they would, sooner or later, protest against the arbitrary and high-handed sealing, de-sealing, re-sealing and the obnoxious 'polluter-*hatao* instead of pollution-*hatao*' style of governance. Indeed, the lieutenant-governor of Delhi implicitly acknowledged this possibility in a noting in May 2000 saying that the government's failure to actually establish that an offence had been committed before sealing the units could throw them open to prosecution as such closure threatened the employees' right to livelihood.[62]

The second, and perhaps more far-reaching, impact was on the public perception of industries. As mentioned earlier, this case inseparably linked the words 'polluting' and 'industry'. After September 2000, when the court, fed up with the Delhi government's inaction in the matter of relocating industries, ordered the union urban development ministry to take charge, this association was further reinforced.[63] The ministry, instead of outlining a comprehensive approach to solve the problem of a hundred thousand industries in areas not meant for them, only announced immediate plans to shift or shut 'polluting industries' without clarifying that these were not the only industries that were in areas not meant for industries.

In the matter of the sewage-filled Yamuna, with the government in spite of strict monitoring by the supreme court having done no more than close polluting industries, the public at large had already been led (very mistakenly) to believe that all river pollution was caused by industries. Now, in the matter of a hundred thousand industries located in areas not meant for them, with the government(s) under strict monitoring by the supreme court still speaking only of shunting 'polluting units' out of Delhi, the public at large was led (very mistakenly) to believe that all industries were polluting. In the media-managed minds of Delhi's urbanites, otherwise caught between splurging surplus incomes on *phoren* branded goods and haggling over prices of *desi* items cheaply produced in the city's service industries, the industrious of Delhi had been painted as hooligans long before the Supreme Court of India described them thus.

Villainous Planners

At the centre of the entire controversy surrounding industries that were currently located in areas not meant for industries was the Master Plan. When the court set the ball rolling and said these industries had to be shifted because they were 'non-conforming', it said so with reference not to pollution laws but to the Master Plan for Delhi, which spells out where industries may or may not be. The Master Plan does the same for houses, offices, shops, green areas, etc. It spells all this out in the form of a broad land use drawing—a map of the city (including proposed expansions) in which land for different uses is marked in different colours. This drawing is based on ground realities at the time of making the plan and a set of principles that form the vision for the future. It is supported by an explanatory text that outlines this basis and provides detailed guidelines for the colours in the drawing.

One could think of the role of the master plan in relation to urban land as one would think of the role of an expenditure budget for family income. Both can help—but not guarantee—efficient and equitable distribution of resources for everyone's needs and wants. Mere existence of a budget does not necessarily ensure that those in charge of expenditure will not flout it to buy laptops for themselves while children go without uniforms. Mere existence of a master plan similarly will not stop the powerful from squandering precious urban land to build unnecessary unplanned cyber parks or world-class shopping complexes as monuments to themselves while letting the poor live and work in locations marked in the land use drawing for other city needs. Also, both are not carved in stone and allow for mid-course corrections to meet unanticipated needs. However, mindless or wilful changes to either would very likely mean that some gain at the cost of others.

It was a demand for one such change that gave a curious twist to this tale, perhaps the only tale of worker unrest in which slogans were raised not against any management but against a city's master plan.

■

When H-category industries were ordered to be closed in 1996 in Delhi, a common forum of thirty non-governmental organizations brought out a report that came down heavily on Delhi's Master Plan and branded it anti-people.[64] Four years and two city governments after the court had pressed the 'Start' button, the ranks of Plan-bashers had swelled, with the government of the day and the former government leading the anti-Plan tirade.

The groundwork for the big Plan-bashing party was laid with the Congress government's brainwave (in the middle of 1999) to get 'non-conforming' industries to 'conform' to the Plan by amending the Plan.[65] Till then, in its efforts to solve the problem, it had managed to allot 300 units in a yet-to-be-completed flatted factory complex and 500 plots in a partially developed industrial area just outside the city.[66] It had been routinely announcing its plans to develop the land acquired in 1995 by the previous government, but so far, a 'massive sign board announcing that the site was for "Shyama Prasad Mukherjee Udyog Nagar" was the only indication of impending industrialisation' there.[67] At this rate, it would take the government many many years to solve the problem. A Master Plan amendment, on the other hand, could in one elegant and quick stroke change much of the problem into the solution, while earning precious brownie points to boot.

This style of 'urban development management' was quite typical of the Congress government of the time, which had already mooted similar proposals in respect of slum clusters and unauthorized colonies, and this suggestion may have been made almost routinely by it. The Plan-bashing was precipitated a year later when Urban Development Minister Jagmohan (whose ministry was the one that had to ultimately authorize any Plan amendment) turned the proposal down. This reaction was also typical of the union minister, known for his authoritarian clean-up act. As the head of the Delhi Development Authority (DDA) in the 1970s he had masterminded for the then Congress government the massive relocation of 80,000 slum families to city outskirts. As the union minister for urban development in the BJP-led government he was now mounting massive bulldozing interventions, including packing off slums and polluting industries to live together happily ever after in a place meant to be a self-contained sub-city of Delhi. Many in government and among NGOs were unhappy with Jagmohan's interventions and for them his categorical rejection of the Delhi government's proposal to call some residential areas industrial seems to have become the proverbial last straw.

In September 2000, Jagmohan's ministry in its affidavit said, 'no amendment in the master plan of Delhi may be done to cover inaction or failure on the part of the local government'.[68] BJP leader and former Delhi industry minister H.S. Balli and city Congress chief Subhash Chopra threatened agitation.[69] Former BJP chief minister Madan Lal Khurana and Congress Chief Minister Sheila Dikshit both said the problem could not be solved unless the Master Plan was amended.[70] Former chief executive councillor, Jag Pravesh Chandra, in an edit-page article, said the Master Plan was not sacrosanct and Lieutenant-Governor Vijai Kapur at a seminar said DDA should lay down flexible guidelines for infrastructure.[71]

To-amend-or-not-to-amend remained a simmering question till November 2000. When the industrious turned hooligans, it became a burning question. Sheila Dikshit appealed to the Centre to change the Master Plan.[72] Madan Lal Khurana announced he was forming the Master Plan Badlo Action Committee to begin an agitation to change the Master Plan.[73] (A month later, the Delhi Congress launched a 'Nyay Yudh' for the same.)[74] BJP Mayor Shanti Desai called an emergency meeting to talk about amending the Master Plan.[75] A delegation of BJP MPs from Delhi (other than Jagmohan) met the prime minister to seek his intervention for amending the Master Plan.[76] The Congress Legislative Party passed a resolution to adjourn the Assembly the next day and march to the prime minister's residence to seek his intervention for amending the Master Plan.[77]

In parliament, Jagmohan 'bent a little, but did not break' and 'yielded an inch but refused a mile'. He said the Master Plan could be amended, if necessary, but only to acquire more land to relocate industries and to review the definition of household industries in terms of allowing greater power consumption and number of employees. The opposition walked out in protest.[78] Even ruling party members said the Congress government in Delhi was responsible for 'messing up', mainly because it did not request the supreme court to allow it to amend the Master Plan and, instead, repeatedly assured it that it could solve the problem otherwise.[79] In an unprecedented move, the Delhi Assembly passed, after the four BJP MLAs present had staged a walk-out, a censure motion against Jagmohan, expressing 'strong disapproval' over the statement made by him in parliament.[80]

■

Through all this no one had the exact numbers. How many of Delhi's industries were in areas planned for them? How many were in areas not meant for them? How many were licensed and by whom? How many were polluting and by what standards? How much did they contribute to polluting the Yamuna? How many were otherwise problematic—either for themselves or for their neighbours or the city?

It was a shocking comment on the state of governance that, despite five years of involvement of the supreme court, these basic statistics were missing from the debate. It was especially appalling coming from a government headed by Sheila Dikshit, who claimed to be green 'by choice, not by chance', wholeheartedly involved in a Rs 40 crore World Bank project for studies on infrastructure and environmental imperatives as well as in a hi-tech digital mapping project for Delhi to provide relevant planning data at the click of a mouse.[81] Surely, with her heart in the right place and so much public investment already made on understanding the state of affairs, basic figures were not too much to ask for. But they remained elusive—at the click of a mouse or otherwise.

With the factory owners and workers on the streets and with both parliament and the Delhi Assembly in session, several figures were thrown up that, howsoever dubious, must be considered because the legislators were considering them and politicians had taken over planning. Madan Lal Khurana said in the Lok Sabha that the total units involved in the current impasse numbered 126, 000.[82] Kapil Sibal (a Congress MP) said in the Rajya Sabha that only 4000 of these were polluting.[83] Jagmohan said in the Rajya Sabha, referring to the report of the high-powered committee set up by the court, that out of 43,045 applications scrutinized by October 1996, 39,166 did not qualify for grant of licence under the Master Plan (meaning that at least 3879 did.)[84] Delhi Minister for Industries Narender Nath said in the Delhi Assembly that redefining household industries would benefit only a small number of units, variously reported by the media as 3306, 6000-odd, and not-even-10,000.[85]

It did seem that polluting units (which all agreed must go), units that could be licensed (which all agreed must stay) and units that would become permissible after redefining household industries (which all agreed also must stay) did not add up to very much. The large majority of industries operating in areas not meant for industries faced a choice between two options. The Congress or Sheila Option (which might have been the BJP or Madan Lal Khurana Option as well, except that the former chief minister had not announced it during his tenure) was to let them be. The Jagmohan Option was to relocate them some 30 km away or even farther.

The justifications that the section of politicians and civil society espousing the Sheila Option put forth hinged on words like 'humaneness' and 'pragmatism' and were wide-ranging. The livelihoods of hundreds of thousands of workers would be affected.[86] The economic base amounting to thousands of crores would be wiped out.[87] Such massive relocation would require lots of money and time.[88] Development of new industrial estates would also require the Master Plan to be amended.[89] The Master Plan was for the people and not vice versa.[90] The Master Plan was not sacrosanct and if the constitution could be amended so could the Master Plan.[91] The Master Plan had been amended before such as when unauthorized colonies were regularized.[92] The Master Plan had to be amended if problems of polluting industries, unauthorized colonies and shops in residential areas were to be solved.[93]

The justifications for the Jagmohan Option (largely articulated by Jagmohan himself) hinged on phrases like 'urban discipline'.[94] Relocating industries in proper industrial areas, where environmental and health guidelines were followed, would give better working conditions and housing facilities to the workers. The Master Plan was made for planned growth. Delhi was turning into a slum. This 'urban indiscipline' caused 40,000 deaths every year and nearly 1.2 billion activity days were lost due to ill-health (according to WHO). Should the government condone wrongdoing if it is done on a large scale? How would those clamouring for Master Plan amendments react if the posh residential areas in which they lived were to become full of industrial units?

For the industrial units, the Sheila Option promised status quo ante. They could continue to work in the conditions that the other half of the city could not even bear to read about, conditions that had engaged the attention of the apex court for five years and preoccupied the city executive and its politicians for at least two of those. The Jagmohan Option offered the promise of better conditions, but at least 30 km away, in yet-to-be-developed sites, in smaller plots and at prices that did not provide value for money. Not much of a choice in a free country! The Sheila Option required the Master Plan to be amended to let the industries be where they were. The Jagmohan Option required the Master Plan to be amended to let them be relocated elsewhere (where rural areas would get messed up so that industrial areas could be hastily developed).

The villain of the piece was obvious. 'Down with the Master Plan' became the battle cry in the capital at the end of 2000 when master plans in several cities in the country were being revised or becoming due for revision.

Grass-eating Fences

The Master Plan for Delhi came into force in 1962 to provide a blueprint for the planned development of the city. The DDA had already been constituted by an Act of Parliament in 1957 with the express mandate to promote and secure development of Delhi according to the Plan. To facilitate implementation, the government also came out with a progressive policy for socialization of urban land through public acquisition of the entire area proposed to be urbanized by 1981. This policy was meant to ensure availability of adequate land at the right time and at a reasonable price, control land values and prevent concentration of land in the hands of a few, thereby safeguarding the interests of the poor. A revolving fund was created for development and disposal of land acquired under this policy. The Delhi Development Act, the policy for large-scale acquisition, development and disposal of land, and the revolving fund to help operationalize it provided a uniquely facilitating framework for DDA to 'promote and secure' development according to the Master Plan.

Like any good plan, Delhi's Master Plan did not provide an either or choice between environmental and economic imperatives. It supported industrial development in the interest of balanced economic development, especially as it would be 'undesirable to increase the proportion of Government employment in the occupational structure of the city'.[95] It did say it would be unwise to locate large and heavy industries in Delhi. This was not because it considered them 'polluting' and wanted to export them to some place else, but because they would create an undesirable industrial bias in the economy of the capital and because Delhi did not have enough water and power to sustain them.[96] It included, accordingly, lists of undesirable industries and prohibited industries. Together, these lists are substantively the same as the H-category list that replaced them in the comprehensively amended Plan approved in 1990 and which was the basis of the court order of March 1995.

For other types of industries (including ones at the centre of the impasse in Delhi in 2000), the Master Plan used techniques like industrial zoning (the basis of the concept of 'non-conforming' units greatly touted later on) to obviate detrimental environmental impacts of economically essential industrial functions. The logic of industrial zoning is that it is easier to service industries—in terms of effluent treatment and waste sites as well as ordinary water, power and transport—when they are together rather than when they are mixed up with other uses needing less or different infrastructure.

When the 1962 Plan was prepared, there were 8000 industrial units in Delhi occupying an area of 1000 acres. There were only two planned industrial districts and most industries were scattered all over the city and required relocation.[97] The Plan set aside 5761 acres of land for industries within the urbanizable limits proposed for 1981. This land (unlike in the Jagmohan Option) was appropriately distributed with a view to ensuring that 'industrial districts are located in right relationship with residential areas'.[98]

The bulk of the land reserved for industrial use was in the form of industrial estates.[99] Besides these, the Plan proposed flatted factories— multi-storeyed structures near residential areas for small-scale, non-nuisance industries.[100] In (the then) central areas these were mainly for existing units that needed to be relocated from nearby. In (the then) outlying areas, they were for new units. For the former, 192 acres, and for the latter, 168 acres, were reserved.[101]

The Master Plan provided for combating industrial pollution

without making a big issue of it. Industrial estates were separated from residential areas by buffers.[102] While most existing industries were permitted to shift to any industrial area, noxious ones could only shift to extensive industrial zones (designed to handle higher levels of pollution) even if they were by definition not 'extensive'.[103]

The 1962 Master Plan (unlike the 'options' forty years later) did not envisage forced relocation. Enough choice of areas was provided and no one was expected to have to shift to some wilderness miles away from the city. It stated that the relocation process 'must be largely governed by the fact that there should be the minimum amount of dislocation of production and the workers should not be put to undue hardship'.[104] It laid down a time schedule that distinguished between noxious, nuisance and non-nuisance industries and allowed extensions to industries with higher capital value, more workers or more floor space per worker.[105] It said that industries to be relocated should be given priority in allotments in new industrial sites and incentives, such as more land than they occupied at present, loans, etc.[106] For relocation of small industries not suited to flatted factories, but unlikely to be able to afford industrial plots, it said government should develop industrial estates where space could be rented out to them and that, obviously, such 'estates should be built up in comparatively central areas'.[107]

A mid-term appraisal of the Master Plan implementation in 1974 found the number of industrial workers had been underestimated and space standards overestimated. After making the necessary adjustments, industrial land requirement for 1981 was modified marginally upwards to 6500 acres.[108] How much of this was developed is, like other numbers in this story, a mystery that even the Estimates Committee of Parliament, with all its privileges, could not unravel. According to a table in its report of May 1984, of a total industrial area of 2148 acres developed by all agencies, DDA had developed 2700 acres![109] In all of two decades since the Master Plan came into force in 1962, we had managed to relocate only 3300 units (and the Jagmohan Option in 2000 spoke of 'relocating' nearly 100,000). DDA had developed only 9000 industrial plots.[110] In 1981, there were 46,000 industrial units—majority of them, naturally, in areas not reserved for industries.[111]

In 1990, the revised Master Plan for Delhi was approved. In this, industries already 'prohibited' in Delhi as per the 1962 Plan were again prohibited and ones that had continued or come up in spite of being prohibited were given three years to shift.[112] The list of industries 'prohibited' in the 1962 Plan was expanded and included under the title 'Hazardous and Noxious Industries' as Section A in the H-category. (The objectionable 'characteristic' listed against each type, incidentally, is mainly fire hazard, not pollution.)[113] The types of industries already identified as 'undesirable' in 1962 were listed in Section B in the H-category under the title of 'Heavy and Large Industries'.[114] No new industries of these types or of the eighty-one types of 'Extensive Industries' included in the F-category were henceforth to be allowed in Delhi. Existing Heavy and Large Industries were to be shifted out according to the plan and policy for the National Capital Region.[115] Existing F-category industries in areas not meant for them were to be relocated in plots of at least 400 sq. metres in existing extensive industry zones and in new ones 'confined within about 265 hectares (or 650 acres) in two locations' in proposed urban extensions.[116] (The Jagmohan Option circa 2000 wanted to pack them *all* off elsewhere, including larger industrial areas in the urban extension, in plots of less than 250 sq. metres.)

In effect, only light and service industries were permitted in Delhi in the future, primarily because these service the city and are mostly small (77 per cent had less than ten and 91 per cent less than twenty workers in 1981).[117] Accordingly, besides being allowed in industrial estates, they were permitted in commercial areas and flatted factories all over the city. The Plan also defined small units (employing up to five persons and using up to 1 kW power) in seventy types of industries as household industries and permitted them in residential areas on the ground floor.[118] (It was this definition that all were agreeable to revise to allow consumption up to 5 kW of power and permission on other floors as well in 2000.)[119]

The revised Master Plan approved in 1990 also allowed for three industrial clusters to be surveyed, redeveloped and regularized after upgrading.[120] (In 2000 the Sheila Option was asking for many more to be regularized without being redeveloped and the three to which Jagmohan grudgingly consented were the ones already mentioned in the 1990 Master Plan document).[121]

On pollution (against which this holy war was being waged in the name of the Master Plan) the 1990 Plan only speaks of eighty-two water-polluting units, 30 per cent of which were in areas not meant for industries. For these it *only* says that they be shifted to industrial areas, where all polluting units must make individual or joint arrangements for effluent treatment.[122]

■

The most striking difference between the Master Plan land use drawings of 1962 and 1990 is that a large chunk of purple (the colour for industrial use) gives way to yellow (the colour for residential use). This was partly in view of most service industries being in the 'tiny sector' and because of policy decisions to restrict other industries and partly because of emergent priorities such as regularizing unauthorized colonies (in 1977) and allotting land to housing cooperatives. At least some of the industries that were being forced out of Delhi in 2000 were really paying the price for these older changes in the Master Plan (besides the related governmental failure to install sewage lines in regularized unauthorized colonies which contributed to polluting the Yamuna).

Incidentally, alongside the imbroglio about units that were never told about the land meant for them (either by government agencies for developing, licensing or policing them or by political entities and NGOs claiming to work in their interest), another 1071 unauthorized residential colonies were again waiting to be regularized. Which colour in the land use plan would change to yellow and who would become hooligans years later as a result of this are points to ponder. Meanwhile, the land use already changed from purple to yellow was not the only land that got stolen from the kitty of the industries.

Some of the extensive (F-category) industries at the centre of the controversy in 2000 had presumably come up after 1990 when they were forbidden. But who's to ask how many, how and why? In urban extensions, only 265 hectares had been earmarked for shifting some such (pre-1990) industries. At the minimum plot size of 400 sq. metres prescribed for them and allowing 25 per cent for streets and facilities, this land would have been enough for only about 5000 units. Yet, the Jagmohan Option was bent on stuffing many more 'extensive' industries of unspecified vintage in puny plots in urban extensions—all in the name of the Master Plan. The rest of the pre-1990 'non-conforming' (rather than unauthorized) F-category industries were to go to industrial areas already proposed in the 1962 Plan. The mid-term appraisal in 1974 had noted plot sizes in private cooperative estates were greater than in DDA's estates and recommended a review of requirements and utilization. Yet F-category industries were being axed before estates meant for them had been fully and efficiently (re)developed.

After discounting F-category units, (redefined) household units and H-category units that may have got left out in the court-ordered closure exercise because they were not polluting (but merely just otherwise hazardous), the number of light and service industries could have been about two-thirds of the total number of industries in places not meant for industries.[123] In industrial estates for such industries, the Master Plan proposes a wide range of plot sizes—from 30 to 1000 sq. metres. The average, based on suggested proportions of different sizes, comes to just over 200 sq. metres. In 1990, about 1533 hectares were set aside for new estates in urban extensions for such units.[124] After allowing for streets and community facilities, this quantum of land could easily accommodate 50,000 such units and if larger plots are disallowed it could accommodate more. This is what the Jagmohan Option seemed to be wanting. While it is possible to do such a 'fitting' exercise, it makes no sense because service industries, by definition, service the city and cannot be lumped altogether in some place miles from anywhere. This is precisely why the 1990 Master Plan proposes that these 1533 hectares be spread over sixteen industrial estates. But who's to ask why urban extensions yet to come up were being given an unplanned start? Or if all the land in the industrial estates meant for these units elsewhere had been fully and efficiently utilized already? Or who else had got or would get that real estate in the city?

The Master Plan did not limit industrial options for light and service industries to plots. A lot of such units were meant to be in flatted factories. The industrial space that was envisaged in this option could have accommodated 30,000 to 40,000 units of 50 sq. metres each (the size of the 300 flatted factory units allotted in 2000).[125] In reality, none of these flatted factories had been built in spite of having been proposed in 1962, strongly recommended again in 1974 in the mid-term appraisal, and proposed yet again in 1990. To get an idea of what happened to this land, take the case of the century-old Delhi Cloth Mills (DCM). In 1962, the Plan suggested that it be shifted and 27 acres of the land thus cleared in the heart of Delhi be used to set up flatted factories. This was enough for nearly 3300 units of 50 sq. metres each. DCM was to shift by 1965 or, latest, by 1967. It finally closed in 1989. By then, in addition to the 52 acres of freehold land that the Mill already owned at this site, DDA had given it 11.7 acres of leasehold land for expansion. In 1989, the then Lieutenant-Governor Romesh Bhandari ordered that DCM be allowed to use all the 63.7 acres it owned for its proposed project to build flatted factories and multi-storeyed housing. In 1991, the supreme court upheld DDA's claim to the leasehold land.[126] But in July 1994, the union urban development ministry directed that this land be restored to DCM.[127] The flatted factories that should have come up on the site in the 1960s were still not there in 2000. But who's to ask when they would come up and for whom after the clean sweep was done?

As per the 1962 Plan industries were allowed only in industrial areas. But in 1990, specified types of units were also allowed in planned commercial areas. Surely thousands of units could have been thus accommodated. When the revised plan was approved in 1990, work was under way on the design of one of the three urban extensions, Dwarka. Dwarka is in a different direction from the other two extensions (Rohini and Narela) and eminently suited to locating one of the two extensive industry zones proposed in urban extensions. Besides, it was also supposed to accommodate some of the proposed sixteen light and service industrial estates. Indeed, around 6 per cent of the area in Dwarka was reserved for industries. But the union government wrote to DDA to say that in view of the policy to restrict industries, industrial allocation should be curtailed and commercial allocation (in which light and service industries are also permissible) increased instead. Although proposals to amend the Master Plan to this effect finally did not come through, the industrial component in Dwarka was dropped.[128] But no one seems to have monitored the impact of this significant policy decision, taken while the matter of industrial land use was before the apex court.

On the other hand, there is perhaps no planned commercial area—in Dwarka or elsewhere—where Master Plan provisions for industries have been implemented. A notable case in point is a state-of-the-art community centre (commercial area meant as per the Master Plan to serve a local population of about 100,000) developed in the 1990s by

HUDCO, designed by a leading private architect and built by a leading corporate developer. In 1990, HUDCO was still supposedly focussed on low-income housing. But the union urban development ministry decided to get some exclusive housing built through it on a prime piece of real estate very close to South Extension, an up-market commercial area in South Delhi.[129]So splendid was the housing scheme HUDCO came up with that it must have found Master Plan norms for the community centre it was to build next to it rather tame. So, it planned a 'community centre' which had guesthouses, restaurants, a five-star hotel, a shopping arcade and a cultural centre.[130] Of course, such a plan had no place for messy industries, though the Master Plan permits 140 types of industries in a community centre. But who's to question the combined urban development indulgences of premier urban designers and developers in government, corporate and private professional sectors working in partnership?

There is also the matter of the land vacated by shifting of H-category industries. In May 1996 the court had asked owners of these plots to surrender two-thirds of the land to DDA for community use. Further, it said, 'the most important community need which is wholly deficient and needed urgently is to provide for lung spaces'.[131] On the rest of the land it permitted one-and-a-half times the floor area ratio (FAR) normally permissible to help owners 'meet the cost of relocation'.[132] When it was brought to the court's notice that several units would take advantage of this 'land use package' by selling the land and leaving workers to fend for themselves, it ordered six years' wages as compensation for the workers if an owner opted to close rather than shift.[133] As mentioned, this order was rarely complied with. A follow-up study also reported that most owners had enough capital and were simply not interested in paying.[134] Nor were they in any hurry to surrender their real estate to DDA. A 'grey area' was conveniently noticed in the order. Owners felt DDA should pay compensation and leave to them the choice of what land they hand over. DDA, on its part, saw no reason to pay compensation or be stuck with problematic sites, such as ones mired in court cases.[135] Four years after the order, not one square inch had been handed over to DDA. In May 2000, the court said the owners were not entitled to compensation beyond the extra FAR and ordered them to surrender the stipulated portion of land to DDA by 28 May, failing which DDA had to file applications before the district judge by 23 June. The district judge would execute the court's order of May 1996 and report compliance in four weeks thereafter.[136] On 24 June, by when DDA had filed one 'incomplete and vague' application, the district judge asked it to file site plans of the lands it wanted to take over. DDA filed a few site plans and twenty-six owners filed objections; DDA filed replies. The court overruled the objections through separate orders and some owners filed review petitions. On 3 August 2000 the court issued warrants for DDA to take possession of the land to be surrendered—for all of just nine factories which had been shut down.[137] Two days later the bailiff returned to say that the warrants could not be executed as the places were 'encroached and closed'.[138] Who's to ask if this is how we 'manage public land'—especially when it is real estate for the rich—even as we always seem to be terribly short of it when it comes to the poor?

But this is not the main point in the matter of the land spared by shifting H-category units at the end of the 1990s. The point to be noted is that those industries that existed prior to 1962 were to have closed by 1965 or latest by 1967; those that had come up during 1962–90 should not have come up at all, but in 1990 they were 'condoned' and given till 1993 to shift; and those that had come up after 1990 should also not have come up and had not been 'condoned' so far. In effect, industries that should not have begun operations after 1962 or, if existing before that, closed down latest by 1967 were being gifted precious industrial land as an incentive to close down at the end of the 1990s. The 1990 Plan document does not mention incentives (only a three-year limit for closing). In 1962, the Plan did suggest incentives, but these came with a time limit. Surely, even the oldest among these industries were not entitled to benefits beyond what they could have claimed latest till 1967. Many (including the nine against which the district judge issued warrants in August 2000) had been occupying space not meant for them in industrial estates meant for other industries. Their owners, instead of being penalized for prolonged misuse, were now being generously allowed to change to a conforming industrial activity on the same site if they so desired. In effect, 'yet-to-come-up' industries were being allowed a greater claim on scarce industrial land in Delhi while so many other 'old' ones were being unceremoniously closed or shunted out on the grounds that there was no more industrial land available.

The Master Plan says land spared by shifting H-category units is to be used for 'making up the deficiency, as per the needs of the community, based on norms' given in the Plan and if the land is not needed for this 'it will be used as per prescribed land use'.[139] From everything else in the Plan, 'community' is arguably meant in the sense of 'local resident community'. In the case of industries closed on sites not meant for them, the 'community' could be in need of 'lung spaces'. Equally it could be in need of schools or hospitals or flatted factories—all as per norms. In the case of industries closed in industrial estates, there is no 'community' as such, except perhaps workers in shanties badly in need of housing. The Master Plan also limits land to be left for parks and green buffers in industrial estates to 8 per cent in estates for extensive industries and 12 per cent in estates for light and service industries.[140] This is to be ensured on the whole while designing the layout (it is not the norm to be followed for each individual plot). Industrial land, it must be remembered, is precious for the city's economic well-being. Like commercial land, it provides workspaces at convenient locations and with necessary facilities. But unlike commercial areas, it can be 'saved' under zoning laws from the market forces that tend to overly commercialize work areas to the detriment of the convenience and efficiency concerns underlying land use decisions. To put more parks in industrial areas than are necessary to create essential buffers is sub-optimal use of public land. To do so when people in the streets are crying for a small piece of industrial land for units crucial not only to their but also to the city's economic survival is very poor planning indeed. But who's to ask when and how the colour pencils for modifying and use drawings all became green? Or when and why it was decreed that grass is more important than cows?

Planning for the Past

'The Great Terrain Robbery' is the longest playing film in the history of contemporary urban development. It is also one whose real storyline is seldom seen, what with so many other louder and lewder goings-on.

Up to a point the jamboree that grew around the matter of industries in Delhi was just another of these goings-on—portraying rank incompetence as benign humaneness, wanton contempt of law as considerate pragmatism and authoritarian greening as urban discipline. But by casting the Master Plan as the villain, the 'filmmakers' made this jamboree worthy of the climax scene in this 'film'. After all, *terrain robbery* could be defined as robbery only as long as there was a Master Plan to define who 'owned' the terrain, much like other robberies are definable only as long as there are defined rights to property. With the industrious themselves driven to raise slogans against the Master Plan that defines and protects their entitlements to the use of land in the city, land meant for them no longer needs to be robbed, just taken, from their kitty.

The master plan, like all plans and laws, is not perfect. More importantly, it is all that stands between precious public land remaining a public good and it becoming real estate in the hands of private individuals (including public figures), and between public landowning agencies (an oxymoron if there was one!) remaining custodians and becoming owners. But the difference between 'failure of the Plan' and 'failure of Plan implementation' was, perhaps, too subtle. As was the fact that those loudly blaming the Plan were precisely the ones who shouldered—even if they did not realize or feel—the collective guilt or failure of Plan implementation for all these years.

What happened to the Master Plan—indeed to the notion of planned urban development—in the capital in 2000 was a nightmare for many good old-fashioned town planners. Both the country's leading political parties were agitating on the streets against it. Many self-styled 'experts' in allied or unrelated disciplines had joined in taking pot shots at it. Much-encouraged politicians were announcing, also in matters other than industrial relocation, urban development decisions in the capital that had no basis in its statutory Master Plan. After all, with so many placards of so many protesters condemning it and nearly all of the rest of Delhi laughing at it, who would dare say, 'But the Master Plan does not allow this'.

Nothing trains planners to win friends and influence people the way only politicians and those with social skills that form NGOs can. Moreover, many planners, especially the ones who know the details, work for government and could say little as their political bosses became official spokespersons for and against the Master Plan, commenting on it only to reinforce their 'vision'. A few individual professionals did (try to) speak out in defence of the Master Plan, but they were no match for the anti-Plan tirade of the much more media-savvy politicians and NGOs. Institutional support for the Master Plan should have come from professional bodies, like the Institute of Town Planners, and schools of planning, like the premier School of Planning and Architecture. (Ironically both are located in Delhi.) But the former, like most professional institutes, is more a club of people with the same professional qualifications than an active platform for real professionals, and the latter, like most institutions of higher learning, is unfortunately not unduly agitated by the declining perceived worth of the profession. August 'professional' institutions all but played Nero while the Master Plan—the quintessential basis of the planning profession—all but burned on the streets of Delhi.

Planning for the future was well on its way to becoming passe. Planning for the past was hot, hip and happening, leaving those in charge free to have their cake and eat it too. They could become humane and pragmatic and 'regularize' those who had missed the bus to planned development and add to vote banks. Or they could become all disciplined and throw them out if they bothered someone who mattered or if the land they occupied began to look like worthwhile real estate, and thereby add to 'note' banks. Those in charge were already doing this in some measure—but only in some measure—in respect of unauthorized colonies, slums, farm houses, banquet halls, shops and showrooms, petrol pumps, etc. Now they could do it with gay abandon simply by rolling their eyes heavenwards and saying the words 'Master Plan' in an exasperated sort of way. The licence to amend the Plan at will was what they had gained out of just weeks of effort to undermine public faith in it (it could hardly have been more effective if it had all been carefully orchestrated).

This reduced the forthcoming exercise of revising Delhi's Master Plan, which was due for revision in 2001, to a redundant farce. But no one was asking to scrap it, only to amend it. The master plan—especially a 'flexible' master plan—is handy to flaunt as proof of planned endeavour for soliciting funding, besides which it provides necessary information to play the real estate markets. The master plan is not too bad provided you do not have to take the 'master' in it too seriously, provided planners with their colour pencils are willing to see that the future does not have to conform to the plan and, instead, that the plan can conform to the past. That, perhaps, was why professional planning institutions, despite their failure to adequately defend the master plan, were not asked to show cause why they should be allowed to continue occupying prime urban land or otherwise existing to a lesser or larger extent at the cost of tax payers. The master plan and those trained to make it still had their uses for the real and venal gods of Contemporary Urban Development.

■

Urban land (like all resources characterized by limited supply, high demand and competing and vested interests) calls for careful planning and rigorous plan implementation for efficient and equitable use. Thus far master plans have been largely careful in ensuring space for all. But failures in plan implementation have generally resulted in the powerful capturing more urban land than is their just due. Thus there are farm houses, large industries, big showrooms, etc., where none were intended. In the process, small homes and establishments have been pushed into slums and slum-like conditions. And large homes and establishments also contribute to slumming by leading to shortages of water, electricity, parking, etc., since (planned) infrastructure provision did not anticipate them. Indeed, urban equity and carrying capacity concerns are intrinsically connected and planned development of cities is, or should be, all about matching resources with needs with eyes set firmly on both these concerns.

Retroactive regularization or unplanned, hasty and sub-standard relocation of industries, slums, etc., cannot be a substitute for proactive planning. It only exacerbates slumming—not only by maintaining or recreating slum-like conditions for the 'poor' but also by encouraging lawlessness among the powerful by condoning (rather than correcting) the subversion of planned development.

With wilful planning for the past (in the service of the Great Terrain Robbery) becoming not only the accepted but the expected instrument of urban development, our cities have entered the fast lane to total slumming.

PART TWO

SHADES OF GREY—
CLOSE-UPS

3

Little People Rights

There was an impressive turnout of senior officials and representatives of friendly political parties, NGOs and donors at the Contemporary Urban Development (CUD) policy workshop that the Lord of CUD had convened. All quickly agreed on consensus starting points and key conflict/problem areas. The consensus was on two overall Urban Strategic Purposes (USPs)—first, to constantly celebrate CUD ideas (for a feel-good factor) and second to control land, etc. (for unhampered furtherance of CUD). The only conflict/problem was the demands on behalf of 'encroachers' that they be allowed to remain where they were or resettled and extended basic services. Participants quickly input their suggestions and comments on these issues on their networked computer stations and technical staff quickly did the needful, after which the Lord clicked Output.

When the default Old-fashioned Urban Development Option appeared, it said: 'Error: Inconsistent Input... Protesters' demands are entirely in line with consensus USPs... They all allow opportunities for creative minimalist interventions that can be celebrated and they require less land, etc. than required for settling "encroachers" in standard development... "Protests" are, therefore, not called for... Revise Input'. Everyone groaned and the Lord quickly clicked Skip to CUD Option.

A sigh of relief went round the room as a friendlier output began to appear. It said: 'Congratulations!... Protesters' demands are entirely in line with consensus USPs... Conflict can be readily resolved by conceding—without legislating—The Right to Stay, The Right to Resettlement and The Right to Minimum Services... Proceed on CUD as before, justifying all future actions on the basis of one of these new Rights for the People... Invite Protesters for consultations (preferably in luxurious locales) and try to win them over.'

The computer-generated policy approach was unanimously endorsed well in time for lunch. The Lord of CUD was very pleased—with the clever charter of rights, with the enthusiastic consensus, with the success of the workshop and with the positive brilliance of CUD.

Right to Stay

The Draft National Slum Policy for India circulated at the end of 1999 is clearly opposed to slum evictions. This was largely the result of NGO consultations, not just on this policy, but at several forums over many years. There is no doubt whatsoever that summary evictions— often in inclement weather and with authoritarian high-handedness— are acts of state that have no place in civilized, democratic societies.

The credit for drawing attention to the injustice of slum evictions goes to the efforts of several NGOs over two decades, besides of course to V.P. Singh for his dramatic intervention starting in the spring of 2000. Without such interventions and efforts, stories of victims of evictions—too caught up in the onerous task of day-to-day survival to become 'organized', too illiterate to become articulate, too exploited to have faith in seeking justice—would have remained unsung tragedies.

Protests against summary evictions initially were protests against violation of human rights. They have now grown to a clamour for the Right to Stay in the name of housing rights. The fact, however, is that housing rights are violated when people are forced—by failures of governments mandated (and constantly claiming to be committed) to facilitate housing for all—to settle in squalid and precarious conditions, not when they are evicted from them. Yet, NGOs, more than anyone else, have reduced housing rights to the right not to be evicted.

The story of how this happened is not the subject of this discussion, which focusses on what this right means to those on whom it has been conferred. Suffice it to say it followed the changing role of NGOs— from activism to convergence with government, from identifying problems to becoming partners in state-designed solutions, from giving voice to the people to becoming a hand for universalizing global paradigms, from minimal operations to massive fund-raising, from simple folk to celebrity.

Nearly all NGOs 'working in slums' are providing in-slum services funded by or through the state or directly by foreign donors or charitable civil society. They run street schools for slum children. They distribute STD drugs out of well-funded AIDS programmes. They mobilize communities for state- or donor-funded infrastructure improvements. They organize saving and credit groups for, among other things, recovery of state-provided loans. They also agitate against evictions. The last often ends up being quite glamorous because that is when they find greatest support from hapless people and can more easily take to the streets or go to court and, of course, to the media. But evictions, however painful, affect only a few out of hundreds of slums in any given city. All in all, NGOs 'working in slums' are already doing what the DNSP recommends—treating slum upgradation as a solution.

But surely, with all their 'grassroots insight' it could not have escaped their notice that this is not working and the Right to Stay which they want so generously bestowed upon the people is no great privilege. It may stop the occasional bulldozer but, for the rest, it does little beyond change the label from 'problem' to 'solution' with some creative jargon in small print.

∎

V.P. Singh's 'success' in turning away bulldozers from the slum next to the railway line at Wazirpur, for instance, was projected as the start of a struggle for wresting for wretched slum dwellers 'the right to live with dignity, work in security'.[1] But even with the bulldozers gone, slum dwellers continued to have to ease themselves in full view of passing trains. So much for dignity. And the slum remained where it was, with the last row of houses close enough to the tracks to reach out and touch trains, including ones that routinely transported inflammable goods. So much for security.

Barely a month after Wazirpur was 'saved', a fire gutted another trackside slum in Delhi. Fortunately, inflammable goods were not being transported at the time and the city was spared a major disaster, though several trains had to be diverted.[2] Earlier, days after Wazirpur was 'saved', 'large portions of south Delhi were plunged into darkness when transmission lines from a power station tripped when jhuggis underneath them caught fire'.[3]

In some such cases, slum fires cause inconvenience to others. But in all cases, they are as much or more devastating than bulldozers for slum dwellers and happen with greater frequency and suddenness. Huts made of inflammable materials, often with occupation-related hazardous materials stored inside, make many slums veritable tinderboxes. A short circuit, a fire in the winter to keep warm, the accidental bursting of a gas cylinder, carelessness—anything can make the huts go up in flames. And the narrow lanes make it difficult for fire engines to get there or to get there in time.

One of the first slum fires reported in the national media in 2000 was the one that destroyed over 400 huts in Calcutta in January. One eighteen-year-old was killed, ten others were injured and 3000 were left homeless.[4] Also in January, in Delhi, a fire in the riverside slum of Yamuna Pushta gutted 700 huts, seriously injuring two persons. It took twenty-five fire tenders two hours to bring the fire under control.[5] In February 2000, in another part of the sprawling Pushta, a four-year-old died in a fire that destroyed 400 huts. This time, twenty fire tenders battled the blaze for over an hour. [6]

Summer time, especially, is fire time in slums. In April, in Delhi, three days before the slum fire that plunged a part of the city into darkness, 600 huts were gutted and three persons injured in another slum fire.[7] Ten days later, a minor girl died in another fire in a slum that destroyed seventy huts.[8] Four days later, 200 huts were destroyed in yet another fire that took twenty-three fire tenders two hours to bring under control, injuring one fireman.[9]

After the fire that led to trains being diverted in May, Chief Minister Sheila Dikshit visited the area and announced payment of Rs 1000 to each affected family. In Chennai, after receiving twenty 'medium' severity calls and four 'serious' calls in 1999, the fire department created eighteen fire outposts, each with six men and a 10,000-litre water tank, to handle summer fires in slums. In May 2000, 'only' one medium and four serious calls were received.[10] In Delhi, an affidavit submitted by the fire department later in court—the matter, like almost every other area of civic services in the capital at the turn of the millennium, was the subject of a PIL—said we cannot effect fire safety compliance in slums.[11]

Come monsoons and it's flood time in slums—bulldozers or no bulldozers. Even if they are not near rivers, slums lacking decent drainage suffer water logging and related problems of infrastructure, health and hygiene. When they are located along water bodies and watercourses (which they often are because these are marginal lands that have little 'value' for the rest of the city), they get inundated. In Brahmarambapuram, a sprawling 'improved' riverside slum in Vijayawada, for instance, residents have 'door numbers' written on pieces of furniture because the houses, along with the doors, are washed away by floods every year.[12]

The 'almost ritual-like exodus' of residents who have 'got used to planning their lives around the ebb and flow of the river' makes a splash in national media when it happens in Delhi's Yamuna Pushta.[13] Every year in the history of this fifteen-year-old slum, its residents have been shifting to the capital's high roads, including its VIP routes, when the river overflows its banks and returning when the waters recede. Delhi does not normally have a flood problem. But when the neighbouring state of Haryana releases surplus water, the Yamuna rises. In June 2000, when Haryana announced it would release 200,000 cusecs of water, 200,000 slum dwellers of Yamuna Pushta prepared to move.[14]

Slum fires and floods, like the ones reported in the newspapers in 2000, have been going on for years with unfailing regularity. What made them a wee bit different in Y2K was what got reported alongside. On 31 January the fire in Pushta was reported alongside a news item of Chief Minister Sheila Dikshit launching a slum improvement project promoted by some NGOs.[15] On 17 April the fire that claimed a little girl was reported alongside V.P. Singh exhorting slum dwellers to wield lathis for their Right to Stay.[16] On 21 July the annual plight of Yamuna Pushta, Delhi's best-known slum, was reported alongside Delhi Urban Development Minister A.K. Walia's 'demand' that all slums be upgraded.[17] How patchy improvements by inexperienced NGOs or lathis to scare away bulldozers or a consensus on upgrading would save slums from fires and floods that regularly ravage was a question that did not seem to bother slum saviours.[18] After all, they lived in safe homes and their health and wealth was protected at tax payers' cost, far more than the Rs 1000 offered to slum dwellers as compensation.

■

Besides routine slum fires and floods, the media in 2000 also reported at least two slum-related 'urban calamities'.

In the middle of July, following a day of torrential rains in Mumbai, a landslide crushed Shivaji Nagar, a decade-old slum at the foot of a hillock in the suburb of Ghatkopar. One hundred and fifty shanties were destroyed. Over 100 people were trapped, sixty-nine died and several more were injured. When those outside government asked what happened to the Disaster Management Plan the city had prepared not so long ago, Chief Minister Vilasrao Deshmukh said, 'Such plans do not avert disasters; relief comes in later'.[19] State Home Minister Chhagan Bhujbal attributed the tragedy to weakening of infrastructure and urged the Centre to support the state in bringing about an 'effective check' on migration.[20]

Four days after the tragedy, with army and fire personnel still clearing the debris, Congress President Sonia Gandhi arrived 'especially to console'.[21] She described the incident as 'very unfortunate' and urged NGOs to help in 'relief measures and in the rehabilitation process'.[22] She visited the injured in hospital, and handed out the food and clothes already being provided.[23] Sonia Gandhi directed Vilasrao Deshmukh to rehabilitate the families and told reporters that the state would facilitate construction of houses for the displaced.[24]

In Mumbai two types of slum interventions were on-going at the time, both premised on the Right to Stay. In one, builders were offered incentives by way of greater floor space than normally permissible to build apartments on slum land. After accommodating slum dwellers, they could sell the rest of the apartments in the open market. In the other intervention, infrastructure was improved, such as constructing community toilets under a 'slum sanitation plan'.[25] However, no one asked how either intervention could possibly have averted the tragedy in Ghatkopar, just one of many slums on precarious sites.

During the same monsoon, 24 cm of rainfall in twenty-four hours in Hyderabad resulted in civic facilities collapsing and nearly hundred localities being inundated.[26] Environmental groups said the flood was 'man-made, if not government made', the result of decrease in rain water holding and draining capacities of various water bodies on account of encroachments.[27] Chief Minister Chandrababu Naidu also acknowledged this and set up two committees to look into the issue of encroachments.[28] No one asked why it needed a disaster to notice that encroachments, including slums, which come in the way of the natural drainage of water are risky. No one wanted to know why the state had allowed a citywide slum improvement project covering 811 slums, including slums in locations near water bodies, a decade ago in which Rs 450 crore was spent on housing, training and infrastructure. No one wanted to know why the state had launched once again, barely two months before the floods and in collaboration with the same donor agency, another statewide urban poverty project covering thirty-two towns and cities premised on the slum dwellers' Right to Stay.[29] Barely two months after the floods, for which the state sought Rs 300 crore from HUDCO for rehabilitating flood victims, the Centre approved a slum project proposal for which the Municipal Corporation of Hyderabad was expecting foreign funding.[30] The project premised on the Right to Stay had 'components like training, education, health, water, sanitation, women and child development, besides infrastructure development'.[31] On the lines of Mumbai, the corporation had also decided to relax building regulations for builders to build free housing 'with lift facility' for slum dwellers on slum land. This time, it seems, the corporation did not go seeking funds and 'international agencies were themselves keen to fund the program. The pace of development and the happening image of the city is said to have done the trick'.[32] No one asked—not even with the floods still fresh—how that made any difference to the fact that such approaches did not seem to work.

■

Foreign consultants and advisers who come with foreign funding can be forgiven for not seeing the real issues of slumming as they go about facilitating third world development from the most expensive hotels, cars, bars, planes and trains. But desi politicians and NGOs do catch glimpses of these issues, for example when they show up for 'relief work' or to dole out 'compensation' in the aftermath of routine and not-so-routine slum disasters. Yet they clamour for slum dwellers' Right to Stay—to be spared the bulldozers—only to be devastated by fire, flood or land slip. They clamour, ironically, for a right to live only to die.

In impossibly dense slums, and especially in those in precarious locations, upgrading is a waste of money—irrespective of whether the money comes from Indian or foreign taxpayers. It is also very unfair because people, encouraged by investments by or through the state, invariably make shelter investments of their own. In the DfID-sponsored slum project in Indore, a centrally located riverside slum was 'improved'. It does not take an urban planning genius to see that centrally located riverfront sites are not suited for low-income housing. It would appear that when the project started it was clear the slum would have to be relocated, but it was nevertheless decided to install infrastructure so that the slum dwellers were 'benefitted' in the meantime.[33] Unfortunately the residents of the slum were never informed of this—not when the British High Commissioner visited the slum in 1991 and again in 1992.[34] Not when infrastructure works worth Rs 1.5 million started in 1992.[35] Not when state officials visited the slum in 1994 when a cleanliness drive was launched with community contributions.[36] Not when people began investments in toilets and houses. Or in 1997 when they launched a widely appreciated community effort to de-silt the river (or rather drain), as a result of which, for the first time in years, the settlement was not flooded.[37] Not in July 1998 when the state decided to grant ownership rights in project slums under the tenure law that was already in existence since 1984.[38] Not, in fact, till October 1998 when the slum dwellers faced eviction as a result of a scheme for riverfront development.

On learning of the eviction, slum dwellers protested outside IDA's offices. The question resentful residents rightfully wanted answered was that while the state may have the right to bulldoze its own celebrated investments, what right did it have to undo investments made by the slum dwellers themselves against implicit and explicit promises of tenure? They refused to leave the site, saying they would not let the state carry out any development on it. (Incidentally, speaker after speaker at a meeting of V.P. Singh's Jan Chetna Manch in May 2000 voiced the same sentiment.)

Such a 'demand' from slum dwellers is tantamount to cutting one's nose to spite one's face. In Indore, it was made by slum dwellers living in squalor next to a stinking drain. It was made after they had 'benefitted' from the world's most celebrated slum improvement project and the first-ever state legislation granting tenure rights in slums—operating arms of the Right to Stay so to speak. This is as good as the Right to Stay can ever get. And yet, it is no good at all.

■

The Right to Stay, pretty dubious when seen from within slums, looks even more suspect when seen from without in a citywide perspective.

In Delhi, for instance, jhuggis accommodate 20 to 30 lakh people and occupy about 4000 hectares of land (almost all of it government land) out of approximately 70,000 hectares meant to be urbanized for a population of 120 lakh as per the provisions of the 1990 Master Plan.[39] The Right to Stay then translates into endorsing the inequity of one-fifth to one-fourth of the city's population living on just 5 per cent of the city's land. In other cities, with less public land available for 'encroachment', slum densities are even higher and the urban land distribution statistics even more inequitable. With or without 'improvement', these are not statistics to be proud of in a democratic welfare state.

It does appear that humaneness is just a clever cover-up for keeping large and growing numbers of (poor) people in (very little and very sub-standard) place. For the 'righted', such as squatter settlements, unauthorized colonies with tiny plots or industries in places not meant for them, the Right to Stay is tantamount to confinement and being shortchanged on the equitable benefits of planned development. The 'saviours', besides getting to look 'humane' (and at times honoured for some clever new idea for 'poverty' or 'governance' interventions within the ambit of the Right to Stay), get to control more urban real estate for their own benefit and the benefit of their cronies. Land meant for low-income housing, flatted factories, free schools, etc., can thus be spared for more lucrative forms of development, such as high-income housing, up-market commerce and elitist institutions. Of course, these are also 'unplanned'. But the very versatile Right to Stay can easily be extended to them as well—in the name, this time, of pragmatism and the very tempting 'revenue generation' through 'regularization fees'. In the capital, for instance, very posh but very illegal banquet halls, nursing homes, unauthorized colonies and farm houses have all been or are up for some sort of regularization.

Violation of urban laws has become not just the accepted but the expected way of city life and retroactive 'regularization fees' (incidentally, seldom actually recovered) has become a substitute for proactive urban planning. Such rampant contempt of law by people and its wilful modification by those in charge of law keeping through all manners of 'amnesty schemes' does not augur well for urban governance. Nor does 'regularization' do very much more than protect private investments made in (illegal) buildings as it does not—and at times can not—come with improvements in facilities like water, power, parking, etc.—necessary to make a meaningful difference to quality of life at the settlement level.

The Right to Stay has contributed immensely to the vote banks and note banks of politicians and indirectly benefitted those who benefit from politicians in ways not intended in the constitution. But the cost of these 'benefits' has been the slumming of our cities. The terrible price we have paid for them was graphically illustrated by none other than Mother Nature.

■

On Republic Day 2001 an earthquake, reported variously as measuring 6.9 or 7.9 or 8.1 on the Richter scale, struck Gujarat.[40] For weeks the tragedy and the politics of the disaster made front-page and prime time news. There were accounts of anguish, reports of rescue and relief, tales of typical tardiness and the terrible, terrible toll. There were comparisons with the Centre's response to the devastation caused by a cyclone in Orissa fifteen months ago. (It was reported that Gujarat was being treated better because it was rich and a bastion of the BJP, and because the quake occurred just before the annual budget.) There were explanations as to why foreign aid was being freely offered (earthquakes, unlike plague, are 'global' disasters and the Gujarati diaspora is powerful by 'global' standards) and accepted (our 'globalizing' nation was opening up).

In all this reportage, however, the one theme which is of relevance to the present discussion is that it was not the earthquake itself but the buildings that had taken lives.[41] This was, of course, something everyone had known all along. But this time urban India sat up and took note, because the buildings that collapsed were not humble huts in some previously unheard of place; they were the all-too-familiar tall and small residential and commercial buildings which dot the urban landscape of all Indian cities, the buildings we all work and live in. Plans to become state-of-the-art with 'specially trained staff and imported equipment to handle any type of disaster' did not sound impressive and urbanites wanted answers to questions about damage prevention.[42] What if a quake shook Delhi, Mumbai, Hyderabad, Pune?

Were the buildings safe? Not quite, we were told by the experts. Many of our cities are on shaky ground and most buildings were 'vulnerable'.[43] Why? Didn't we have the technology to build safe buildings? Didn't we have laws and guidelines to ensure this? We did have the technology and the laws, we were told. In fact, we could build buildings designed to withstand earthquakes of magnitude 10, our expertise in this was 'next only to USA and Japan', and in Japan an earthquake of magnitude 7.2 had not killed anyone.[44] Our first building code for earthquake-safe construction was dated 1962, our bylaws required structural stability certificates, our research agencies had guidelines for safe buildings. In 1997, a vulnerability atlas had been prepared and circulated for states to make special bylaws and disaster management plans where necessary. The epicentre of the Gujarat earthquake was an already identified hot spot and building height had been restricted there.

Once again earthquake experts were repeating what they had been saying for decades about safe buildings and safe building codes and guidelines.[45] Unfortunately, they were 'just' scientists and 'science is a political orphan'.[46] Politically more savvy 'urban experts' 'who cannot differentiate between the front end and back end of science' were in charge.[47] And it was in their charge that so many buildings had killed so many with many more waiting to do the same.

In Maharashtra, despite big earthquakes in Koyna (1967) and Latur (1993) and a risk assessment and disaster management plan (demonstrated in Ghatkopar) thereafter, most buildings are unsafe because of the use of inferior materials and neglect of zoning regulations.[48] In and around Delhi, where the risk of earthquake is 4 on a scale of 1–5 (5 being the most risk-prone), things are no better. East of Delhi, an entire township has forgotten it has been built in a seismic zone because officials have 'not received a copy' of guidelines for earthquake-safe building.[49] In a posh township south of Delhi, the state Town Planning Department often issues requisite certificates without verifying if norms have been followed.[50] In the rest of Delhi also 'people hardly show any respect for bylaws and have made deviations which have a bearing on the structures in case of seismic activity'.[51] In Ahmedabad, many of the collapsed buildings had poorer building material, greater number of floors, shallower foundations, fewer beams and columns, heavier overhead water tanks and bigger balcony projections than were permissible or required under the laws.[52]

High-rise buildings built by private builders were not the only ones to collapse and thereby kill, but they were the ones to do so in a most photogenic way. They contributed to a part of the toll, but they attracted total concern. In Delhi, Jagmohan, who had directed bylaw amendments immediately after the earthquake, ordered assessment of structural safety standards in (only) high-rise buildings in Delhi.[53] In Hyderabad, the corporation had already 'requested' (only) builders to submit structural stability reports on 'humanitarian grounds'.[54] In Ahmedabad, a leading daily launched 'a serialized campaign to expose guilty builders'.[55] In Gujarat, it was especially convincing to blame the 'builder–politician nexus', which was 'omnipresent' when the earthquake happened, with many in power being either 'builders-turned-politicians or politicians-turned-builders'.[56] In Ahmedabad, the development authority chairman was a builder and a political appointee. In Vadodara, the deputy mayor was a builder. In Rajkot, Surat and Bhavnagar, state ministers held 'considerable stake' in real estate.[57] Builders came to the aid of political parties in successive elections. And the parties came to the aid of the builders between elections, allowing them to build at will. State Home Minister Haren Pandya candidly confessed that 80 per cent of Ahmedabad's new high-rises did not have building fitness certificates and less than three months before the catastrophe, the government had issued an ordinance to legalize all illegal constructions in all the six major towns of the state.[58] The build up to the ordinance followed a by-now familiar path. Hearing a clutch of PILs, the high court had asked the government to enforce existing laws. The government knocked down a wall here, cleared a basement there, but left big builders alone. The court went on getting exasperated and directing action. The government went on being defiant and making excuses. The court initiated contempt proceedings against key officials.[59] Two days before the hearing, a Cabinet meeting was summoned to approve the ordinance, which had the support of the opposition and was approved by the governor the next day. The government, predictably, said 'pulling down of a large number of buildings is neither feasible nor desirable' and would cause 'hardship to large numbers', whereas regularizing them for a fee would generate revenue.[60] On grounds of pragmatism, humaneness and bonus revenue benefits— one-size-fits-all justifications for the Right to Stay—all illegalities were sanctioned. These included, for instance, a swimming pool on the tenth floor and a penthouse extending 16 feet, which fell off three months later, dragging down an entire block with it.[61] The rest, as they say, is history or rather, in this case, debris.

∎

The Right to Stay comes at a cost. The collapse of unintended, albeit 'regularized', constructions in Gujarat demonstrated this most graphically. But more subtle costs are borne even in less extraordinary circumstances. It's very likely that the excessive constructions that collapsed in the earthquake were already causing visual squalor and infrastructure stress; perhaps the booming and excessive real estate market that propelled it had driven others into slums. Indeed, the twin application of the Right to Stay for the poor and the powerful is connected in a vicious cycle perpetuating the slumming of our cities. 'Regularizing' wasteful use of land by some in unintended ways drives others to unintended sub-standard options, and 'regularizing' sub-standard options spares more land for wasteful unintended use. Seen from this perspective, squalid shanties and plush farm houses are responsible for slums in our cities in equal measure. And when unintended development and its regularization becomes the norm, slumming becomes the dominant urban motif.

The aftermath of the Gujarat earthquake also provided an insight into the politics of development, which thrives on the Right to Stay. The roulette style post-earthquake 'introspection' stopped at the 'deadly builder–politician nexus' with the certainty of a fixed spin. This 'deadly nexus' survived the catastrophe in Gujarat. Many, whose flats had collapsed, were not complaining as the 'very powerful' builders had either offered them free flats or intimidated them.[62] Officials were under pressure from the 'builders' lobby' to give 'a clean chit' to buildings that had developed cracks. The 'lobby' was also 'apparently now interested in the rebuilding work'.[63] Three weeks after the quake, in Delhi 'six national parties, together with sixteen regional ones, confabulated for three hours' about disaster management. Not once did they refer to 'the insidious builder–politician nexus'.[64] It was at the door of this obviously indifferent and seemingly invincible nexus that we, shaken but not stirred, had placed the blame for the devastation and were now politely waiting—for what? For it to obligingly self-destruct?

Meanwhile what about all the others without whose help the builders and politicians would not have managed to make the deadly Right to Stay a central tenet of Contemporary Urban Development? Quality of urban development is, after all, the collective responsibility of several professions and institutions. Politicians and builders, for instance, do not design (illegal and unsafe) buildings, architects do. They do not regulate urban-scape, urban arts commissions do. They do not whet project-planning details, planning and funding agencies do. They do not point out and fill up technical performance gaps, specialist civil society agencies do. What had they all been doing?

Architects were telling us on television and in newspapers about dangerous bylaw violations, inappropriate materials and elements, and the virtues of traditional buildings.[65] In Ahmedabad, they said, problems may also have arisen in buildings designed by 'local architects of world class'.[66] In Delhi, some were glad to say, 'now, people are willing to pay us considerably more to design quake-proof houses'.[67] Structural engineers did ask how architects had 'the expertise to hold forth on earthquake resistant buildings, when it is an extremely specialized form of civil engineering'.[68] More importantly, how come they failed to notice obviously unsafe features in buildings till after they had collapsed. After all, things like too much glass or too little column size, extra floors or larger water tanks than allowed, etc., are quite visible, especially to the trained eye. Had they complained to local bodies or to the Council of Architecture? Had they taken collective professional action against erring professionals? No. Instead, they waited for the buildings to collapse and then told us they knew why they had collapsed and how they ought to be rebuilt. The Council of Architecture even organized 'a demonstration of transit shelters' and invited a bunch of ministers for a look-see.[69]

The Delhi Urban Arts Commission announced it would study the 'damage potential' of glass in the event of an earthquake. After having cleared and cheered classy glass buildings for years, it now remembered glass was unsuited to the capital's climate and energy shortages and posed traffic hazard and environmental problems. Like a capricious sultan, it rejected the entire 'sudden rush' of a 'large number of proposals' for glass buildings. That was its post-quake contribution.[70]

Much was forthcoming from HUDCO which has a countrywide network of regional offices and 'building centres' for transfer of building technology from 'lab' to 'land'. It also runs training workshops in areas related to disaster mitigation. After the Gujarat earthquake (as after the Jabalpur one of 1997 and the Latur earthquake of 1993 before that), HUDCO announced (besides financial assistance) a 'technology package for building earthquake resistant houses'.[71] Commenting on the devastation, HUDCO Chairman V. Suresh said, 'It shows that building design norms were violated rampantly'.[72] And on Delhi's vulnerability, Suresh lamented the fact that the Master Plan (revised in 1990) 'does not recognize the fact that Delhi lies in the high seismic zone' (according to the atlas prepared in 1997).[73] Presumably HUDCO, even as it went about earthquake-resistant designing, technology transfer, training and funding had not noticed all this before the quake.

From NGOs we had the (honorary) director of Ahmedabad-based Disaster Mitigation Institute saying he had 'not seen a single building with any earthquake resistant features in these areas', leaving one to wonder about the role of his institute.[74] We also heard a lot of ideas about rehabilitation from the director of the Delhi-based Hazards Centre, leaving one to wonder who might be more interested in less glamorous prevention.[75]

All around us were 'earthquake experts' pontificating about buildings—and more eagerly about rebuilding. That these wise men and women had not shared their building wisdom before the buildings collapsed was partly because most had been busy otherwise pleading for the Right to Stay. Many architects, for instance, had been criticizing Jagmohan's demolition initiatives in Delhi. A member of the Delhi Urban Arts Commission (though not a planner) had been running the Master Plan down and arguing that industries be left alone. HUDCO, of course, had authored the DNSP, the greatest official advocacy so far of the Right to Stay. The Disaster Mitigation Institute had been playing an advisory role in Ahmedabad corporation's slum-upgrading project on the lines of the one in Indore. The Hazards Centre was making expert comments in support of unauthorized colonies, non-conforming industries and slums in Delhi. Just three days after the earthquake in Gujarat, the lieutenant-governor of Delhi, conceding 'the problem arises in case of unauthorized buildings', reiterated his keenness to regularize unauthorized colonies and said the government (yet to complete even routine 'development' in colonies regularized in 1977) would 'ensure that all safety standards are followed'.[76]

Brought up on Bollywood and tutored to trust the rest, the 'builder–politician nexus' is the one we like to blame. The fact, however, is that in the collective responsibility for quality in our cities, there are many other places where the buck could stop. But, with most partners in the business of development aligned together in favour of the very convenient and very fashionable Right to Stay, the buck does not stop anywhere, dragging the city ever deeper into the chaos of unintended ('regularized' or otherwise) development, making it ever slummier.

Right to Resettlement

Resettlement is the proviso on which those warring for (others') Right to Stay agree to peace negotiations.

The concept of Resettlement and Rehabilitation (R&R) is really one that has its origin in large regional infrastructure projects such as dams, highways, canals, etc., that require displacement of people already settled in places that are designated 'project sites'. Mandarins of nation-building design projects for greater common good and, say, villagers get labelled Project Affected Persons (PAPs) requiring resettlement. As the earthmovers and hammers and chisels of 'development' redraw the maps that society and nature have drawn, R&R is meant to soften the blows.

The style and standard of R&R has often led to enduring conflicts. Yet, the concept of R&R, as applied to settled communities that got in the way of development for the greater common good is, if the greater common good is itself acceptable, not flawed. But it makes sense only when applied to people who were settled in the past and need to be unsettled in the present for some future purpose. This description does not fit, for instance, urban slums.

Cities are not built over slums. Slums grow in cities. The genesis (but only the genesis) of slums lies mainly (but not exclusively) in work-seeking migration from rural areas. In a sense, those who come to cities to find work are already PAPs of lopsided rural development. Unsettled from their villages they come to the city in the hope of becoming (re-)settled, but end up remaining unsettled in slums for years, even generations, watching urban development pass them by. How can then one speak of resettling those who have not quite settled?

The distinction between settling and resettling the poor is not just a semantic fine point. It is, rather, the basis of a dangerous distortion of the equation between the welfare state that is mandated to take care of the needs (including shelter needs) of its citizens on the one hand and, on the other hand, the majority in the city. Willingness to resettle slum dwellers has the flavour of a favour. It implies that the state is willing to condone slum dwellers for having encroached on land meant for other (others'?) public purposes and even give them a puny place to live (though it may seem like 'rewarding a pickpocket'). Settling slum dwellers on the other hand would amount to admitting that the state and its partners have failed in housing supply to the point that backlog has exceeded cumulative supply and, as a corollary, that slum dwellers are not culprits but victims in lopsided urban development. This truism, for obvious reasons, cannot be admitted by slum saviours.

The Right to Resettlement that they are willing to bestow upon slum dwellers in lieu of the very suspect Right to Stay is thus founded on a distortion of facts. This distortion snowballs, like a growing carry-forward error, into distorted standards, sites and priorities for resettlement.

■

Let us consider standards first. In April 2000, addressing the thirtieth annual day function of HUDCO, Jagmohan drew attention to the appalling fact that 19 per cent of Indian families live in less than 10 sq. metres and 44 per cent in urban areas live in just one room.[77] Immediately afterwards, he and HUDCO resettled thousands of slum families from Delhi in 12.5 sq. metre plots in Narela. With full ground coverage and individual toilets and kitchen spaces, these can accommodate one small room at ground level. There is, of course, scope for vertical expansion and that alone justifies the label of 'solution' instead of 'problem'.

In the massive slum resettlement exercise in Delhi in the mid-1970s, plot sizes were 40 sq. metres to begin with and these did not include space for toilets, as community toilets were envisaged. Since then plot sizes for resettlement have been steadily declining. On the other hand, there has been a move to do away with the law that places an upper limit on urban land holdings, which the rich have been finding restrictive. Architects and planners, instead of crying foul over the 'flexibility' of the lower limit of habitable dwelling sizes, seem to take it as a 'challenge' to their creativity in being able to design tiny units. In Narela, HUDCO's design wing was quick to put up a 'demonstration house', presumably to 'demonstrate' that it could fit on the puny plot.[78]

The small resettlement plots do not even compare well with the space that people occupy in slums. The land under slum settlements in Delhi, as mentioned earlier, is around 4000 hectares and the number of slum families is variously estimated between 400,000 and 600,000. Even with the higher estimate of number of families, the gross area occupied per family on average comes to 66 sq. metres. In planned housing areas, the net residential area (which is the area under house plots and appurtenant services and excludes major roads and facilities) is about half the gross area. In slums, with little land under other facilities, net residential area tends to be even greater, on average well over 33 sq. metres. In other words, in our welfare state, the majority population in the city is only being resettled (instead of being settled) and that too in a manner in which its territorial share in urban land is reduced to less than what it held while it was unsettled.

Of course, this is justified on grounds of the alternative being 'better' because it is 'planned', which is normally understood to mean it is orderly with housing services in place. But this claim merits scrutiny on two counts. First, and most obviously, it is not entirely true. In almost every large-scale resettlement project there are protests about infrastructural inadequacies. In Hyderabad, reservations were being expressed in mid-2000 about Nandanayanam, a large-scale resettlement project on the outskirts of the city. It was said that for residents the transition was 'like jumping from the frying pan into the fire', the place was 'turning into a sprawling slum with garbage dumps and unhygienic conditions increasing by the day', and there had been 'three deaths in as many months' on account of snakebites.[79] Narela being Jagmohan's baby attracted more publicity and more flak. A lawyer filed a PIL on the lack of schools and later petitioned the National Human Rights Commission about 'inhuman conditions without any civic amenities'.[80] A federation of non-governmental and community-based organizations in Delhi visited Narela and came out with a report on which a newspaper account ended with the line 'altogether Narela is the new name of hell'.[81] An unfazed Jagmohan invited the press and parliamentarians to come see the good work, saying that 'teething troubles in Narela are the natural consequences of shifting and these occur everywhere'.[82] He had a point. Bus services, schools and other infrastructure do improve after a period of 'teething' even in higher income housing and no one was loudly protesting the small plot sizes that would remain unchanged forever.

The problems of Narela were, by no means, exceptional. In 1962, Delhi's Master Plan had cautioned that housing with sub-standard plot sizes was prone to deteriorating into slums. In 1990, the revised Plan noted this had happened in 'resettlement'colonies.[83] 'Development works' in these colonies ('developed' up to a quarter century ago) continue to remain on the agenda for political promises and parleys. In August 2000, for instance, with the spotlight fixed on problems in Narela, Delhi Congress general secretary alleged that the BJP-controlled corporation was not implementing development projects in resettlement colonies, which it considered Congress vote banks.[84] It is generally true that current slum resettlement projects usually end up looking not very different from the slums they replace. It is little wonder that most people resist efforts to resettle slum dwellers near their housing areas on grounds of 'proliferation of slums' in their neighbourhood. In a public meeting in July 2000 in Delhi, for instance, the general feeling was that villages on the fringes of Delhi were 'being given short shrift' by relocating polluting industries or slums to them.[85] Later, in another resettlement initiative in the capital, residents of the adjoining flats protested.[86] Earlier in Surat, the corporation's effort to shift a slum to Panchsheel Nagar was thwarted when residents of that area turned hostile.[87] In Mumbai, residents of Malvani formed a citizens' council to object to the proposed resettlement of slum dwellers from the Sanjay Gandhi Park to an area in their vicinity.[88] Why, even civic administrators speak of 'slums and resettlement colonies' as if they were the same, rather than, say, of 'resettlement colonies and other planned colonies'. This brings us to the second big hole in the claim of resettlement being 'planned' development. Sure, projects are planned, but by cutting corners on planning standards, the result of the planning is not what planners call planned.

Consider a resettlement area of one hectare divided into 12.5 sq. metre plots. Even allowing a generous half of the area for parks, open spaces, etc., this comes to a minimum of 400 plots, i.e., a density of 400 *families* (or 2000 persons counting an average of five persons per family) per hectare. 'Planned' densities recommended in the Master Plan for Delhi are up to 400 *persons* per hectare.[89] Developments that reach five times the recommended densities can only be called planned crowding, not planned development. And planned crowding, from the point of view of infrastructure and health, is no better than unplanned crowding in slums.

■

Next let us consider resettlement locations. All decent master plans make provision for low-income housing in locations all over the city. The original Master Plan for Delhi, for instance, proposed 'suitable sites in several zones' where the poor might 'put up cheap houses but the layouts would have to be according to standards'.[90] The underlying logic of this is that we do not expect or want the poor to stay poor forever. As their circumstances improve, we believe, they will be able to improve the condition of their houses, but the layouts have to match future standards from the beginning because they cannot be changed. For existing squatters, the Plan recommended they 'be relocated in various parts of the urban area so that they are integrated' and said that 'it is of the utmost importance that physical plans should avoid stratification on income or occupation basis'.[91]

In the 1970s (by when the proliferation of slums had become a conspicuous feature of urban landscapes) master plans even demarcated relocation sites. In Indore, for instance, nearly 400 hectares of land were specifically earmarked for rehabilitating squatters in 'resettlement zones' in various parts of the city.[92] In the 1980s, when the Master Plan for Delhi was being revised, it was again reiterated that housing 'should be integrated. The community (about 1 lakh population) may contain a complete cross section of the income groups' and should have at least '25 per cent as site and services development and about 45 per cent housing up to 2 rooms dwellings to provide shelter for low income families'.[93]

Besides such provisions in master plans, there have been other policy provisions regarding land reservations for the urban poor. But, like in the story of industries in Delhi, all or most of this land—especially in 'good' locations—has been stolen from the kitty of the poor and sizeable resettlement projects are invariably on city outskirts. In Hyderabad, recent relocatees complained that they 'have now to travel

20 km for doing our old job. Is it possible?'[94] In Delhi those who have been resettled say that in the places from where they had been shifted, they had 'many takers for their skills. At Narela, in the midst of empty LIG and MIG flats, they find themselves without any source of livelihood. The city is too far away and ill-connected for daily commuting.'[95]

Settling the poor in large areas meant only for them does not make planning sense. Integration of various classes of people in residential neighbourhoods has been the recommended option in master plans thus far because it has obvious advantages. For the poor it offers better access to livelihood opportunities as well as to quality infrastructure—roads, water, schools, hospitals, etc. For the non-poor it offers better access to the services offered by the poor. In general, it is in line with the principles of democracy. Segregation, on the other hand, has corresponding disadvantages, as demonstrated by the high incidence of all manners of ills—ranging from epidemics to riots—in large resettlement colonies.

Former prime minister V.P. Singh hit the nail on the head when he wrote in an edit-page article that Narela-style resettlement 'tears asunder the vital link between the place of residence and employment' and 'the relocated population is bound to sell their tenements at alternative sites and return to the city'.[96] Of course, this was not a new nail and it had been hit on the head for decades. More importantly, what V.P. Singh wanted was already provided for in Delhi's statutory Master Plan (just as more than what he was demanding on the policy side was already provided for in the DNSP). But slum saviours, once they decide to don that mantle, are in such a rush to save that they find no time to pick out weapons for such saving from the arsenal of existing laws and policies.

Instead of demanding that the Delhi Master Plan be implemented to the advantage of slum dwellers, V.P. Singh said, 'there is no denying the flawed nature of the Master Plan' and that it 'is biased in favour of the elite'.[97] This was also the view of several NGOs, who arranged and attended, along with several of 'their' slum dwellers, a convention on the Master Plan in June 2000 where they had invited V.P. Singh as well as Sheila Dikshit. Slum dwellers presented their 'problems' (including electricity billing and water problems). Sheila Dikshit reiterated her 'new' slum policy. V.P. Singh reiterated his demand for a slum policy.

All this had little to do with the Master Plan per se, which is mainly about land use planning. Yet everyone said or implied that the Master Plan was no good and, although they seemed to neither realize that the Master Plan already provided the basis for what they wanted nor had anything better to suggest, they gave themselves the mandate of making a 'people's master plan'.[98]

Jagmohan, on the other hand, was justifying Narela on the basis of his vision of having a Delhi as per the Master Plan. But this vision was only half the vision. While he saw that slums were on land meant for other uses as per the Master Plan, he failed to see what was happening on the land meant to house the poor in order to pre-empt slums (much like what had happened in the matter of industries). To add to the chaos, others joined in to react to the Plan-bashers with their own brand of defence of the Plan. In a rejoinder to V.P. Singh's article, for instance, H.D. Shourie, an eminent PIL lawyer, said, 'When the Master Plan was prepared it was never envisaged that our population would continue exploding'.[99] Shourie failed to mention that the Master Plan had envisaged a population of 12.8 million for Delhi in 2001, which had been overshot only by a few hundred thousand. And that included not just migrants in slums but migrants in, say, public sector undertakings, corporate houses, etc., that the Master Plan had suggested should come up outside Delhi to facilitate regional dispersal to limit the population of Delhi within its carrying capacity. What seemed to worry him about V.P. Singh's criticism of the Plan was its implied 'threat' that 'vast acres of land near India Gate in Lutyen's Delhi should be utilized for housing the poor', including 'acres of land attached to the bungalows'.[100] This, incidentally, is something the Master Plan (and not, say, H.D. Shourie) prevents us from doing. He argued his own planning logic for the slum problem and concluded 'These people have to be resettled in properly developed colonies. These can only be created at places where this will be practicable and feasible in the surrounds of Delhi, preferably near the towns that exist in the neighbourhood of Delhi; the government must organize transport facilities to enable the workers to come from these colonies to Delhi for work'. Ironic, that the eminent lawyer's views were completely at variance with the vision of the statutory Master Plan whose criticism he had set out to rebut.

What was being played out was a tragi-comedy. What Jagmohan

was doing in Narela was not in the spirit of Delhi's Master Plan. Yet he and his supporters were defending his actions in the name of the Plan. And those protesting them were bashing the Plan when they might have done better to demand its implementation. Narela was like any other usual resettlement project. But it became a unique missed opportunity. With V.P. Singh and Jagmohan—both men of immense stature—taking opposite stances on the Master Plan and resettlement, the spotlight was briefly fixed on the issue of resettlement locations. But when stars start writing their own stories, the plot rarely progresses logically.

■

Next let us consider resettlement priorities. The accepted practice of resettling slum dwellers (or, for that matter, industrial units) instead of settling them has led to a distortion in not only what they get by way of 'planned development' and where, but also whether they get it at all. Notwithstanding oft-repeated political and global commitments to shelter and planned development benefits for all, the majority in the city is not settled routinely, but only when 'special circumstances' make the Right to Stay untenable. Often, however, the reasons given for resettlement are themselves untenable. In the case of Narela, India's National Report for the Istanbul+5 UNCHS (Habitat) Conference 2001 says in a box titled 'Narela: A Happy Example of Relocation and Rehabilitation' that slum dwellers were relocated from 'the most untenable and disaster prone sites in Delhi'.[101] That, of course, is not entirely true as the same 'untenable and disaster prone sites' were found appropriate for non-slum development such as government housing, office complexes, etc.

A long-standing 'special circumstance' in which slums become 'untenable' is when a landowning agency, after years of failing to develop or protect its land, wakes up to a need to do so in 'public interest', requiring clearance of slums that have come up while it was napping. Reducing the welfare state to a poor manager of real estate, slum policies in major cities hinge on contributions of landowning agencies as and when they 'need' their encroached land. The All India Institute of Medical Sciences in Delhi was going to add a premier facility in 2000 only after paying Rs 12 crore to MCD's Slum Wing as landowning contribution towards resettlement costs to get 20 acres of its land cleared of 5000 huts.[102] Mumbai (and air-travelling populace elsewhere) heaved a sigh of relief when the Airports Authority of India agreed to pay Rs 32 crore to Mumbai Corporation towards the cost of resettling 2550 tenements on its land so that aircraft which had to take a longer runway in order to circumvent a thicket of slums could cut down taxiing time.[103]

This financial arrangement for resettlement means one government agency pays another out of public money. Moreover, the payment is seen as a favour to the encroacher, rather than as penalty for the agency's laxity in minding public land. The Airports Authority, for instance, while it had to shell out crores in Mumbai, got away scot-free in Jaipur when its land was 'cleared' to allow for expansion in order to make the airport an international one. The Authority had been allotted the land five years ago but had not barricaded it or done anything else to stop much of it being encroached. Yet, an obliging welfare state stepped in with free help to take care of the 'favour' to encroachers in, of course, the wider public interest of giving a boost to the state's key industry, tourism.[104] (Incidentally, a few weeks later, the Airports Authority's international airport in Hyderabad was served notice for attachment for non-payment of property tax dues.)[105]

Besides public interest activities of landowning agencies, court orders—often in PIL—also lead to 'special circumstances' for resettling slums. In the 1970s PIL was conceived as a 'strategic arm of the legal aid movement intended to bring justice within the reach of those who, on account of their indigence, illiteracy and lack of resources, were unable to reach the courts'.[106] In the years that followed, through PIL, citizens have found 'new ways of expressing their concern for events occurring at the national level and exerting their involvement in the democratic process'.[107] On the other hand, there has been criticism that 'the judiciary is overstepping the boundaries of its jurisdiction' and that 'PIL is being misused by people agitating for private grievances in the garb of public interest and seeking publicity'.[108] In cities, where problems are complex, conflict greater, efforts more 'visible' and 'experts' aplenty, PIL seems to be becoming a form of surrogate governance. (In Delhi, in 2000, so much of the government's activity in so many matters boiled down to securing compliance of court orders in PIL that one might have been excused for thinking of it as the court's bailiff.) Whether all this is in the spirit of what was the envisaged role of PIL is for the legal profession to judge.[109] The point here is that priorities for slum resettlement have lately been determined in no small measure by court orders, often as a result of PIL, seeking removal of slums. This has also extended to appeals to politicians to get slums removed in public interest.

In Delhi, in February 2000, residents invited Jagmohan to see the squalor around the Kalka temple and within days more than 5000 huts on the adjoining land (earmarked green in the Master Plan) were surveyed for resettlement.[110] In October, he inaugurated a park with 'modern concepts like rain water harvesting, meditation centre and jogging tracks' developed by HUDCO and the Central Public Works Department at a cost of Rs 1.62 crore on 4.5 acres previously under a slum and announced a similar park on another site from which slums had been shifted to Narela.[111] In November, 'to the relief of residents of about 150 group housing societies' who had been 'pressurizing the local administration', plans to shift four slum clusters on land meant for parks were announced.[112] In Ghaziabad, in September, the development authority removed 500 huts ('causing difficulties to local people') from the green belt.[113]

Indeed, a lot of slum resettlement has lately been triggered (through courts or otherwise) by a penchant for painting the town green. At the same time, governments ever-willing to throw out slum dwellers to add a dash of green have not been averse to taking away a dash of green as well. In 2000 there was talk about forest land being denotified, a development authority reportedly sold some forest land as residential plots (obviously not for resettling slum dwellers), and V.P. Singh said about the Sanjay Gandhi National Park in Mumbai, 'Mark my words, the land cleared of hutments will be given to private developers'.[114]

In 2000 with so much resettlement going on in Delhi and Mumbai, slums like Yamuna Pushta and Ghatkopar were not priorities. Those protesting the evictions and resettlement from other, safer slums said, 'Stop demolitions during the rains'.[115] But no one asked, 'Why not resettle Pushta or Ghatkopar first? What shade of green—of grass or of money—can mean more than the lives of people?'

∎

Obviously, the Right to Resettlement in its present form does not offer much to the 'righted'. Till not very long ago (before the ascendancy of the Right to Stay), however, it did attract a lot of funding and professional interest. As a result, one will find a resettlement project or two proudly sitting in the portfolios of many great or wannabe great Indian architects. The Aranya project in Indore designed by a team led by eminent architect B.V. Doshi is one of the best-known resettlement projects. It is also one of the most jargonized.[116]

Aranya's 'design philosophy', for instance, is based on six 'broad goals': vitality, imageability, equity, efficiency, flexibility and feasibility. 'Specific issues' explicated are: indigenous character of built form, innovative approach to sites and services, reconsideration of norms and standards, optimization of land use, marketability of land and cross-subsidy, economy of infrastructure and road network. The design addresses these 'broad goals' and 'specific issues' at 'various levels of hierarchy'—township, sector, community, cluster and dwelling—through 'checklists of detailed guidelines'. The result is a layout design for a site of 86.24 hectares in which 58 per cent of the land is under 6543 plots. Highlights are a mix of plot sizes with two-thirds of them earmarked for economically weaker sections, a town centre to provide a 'focus', and sector-level spaces designed as flowing pedestrian greens.

Implementation of the project by the Indore Development Authority started in the late 1980s. In 1990 HUDCO supported the designers of the project to fully 'document' it. In 1995 Aranya was honoured with the Aga Khan Award for Architecture for its innovative and sensitive planning and design for the benefit of over 40,000 poor people. Being widely acclaimed, besides widely documented, Aranya has become an essential case study for students of low-income housing design and it would not be an exaggeration to say many young professionals aspire to design just like that.

The truth about Aranya, however, is that its winning elements simply do not exist on the ground. There is no town centre, no flowing pedestrian greens and no 40,000 poor people living there. These exist only in the literature on Aranya and for more than a decade we have been celebrating a drawing, a design idea, that we are not sure will work because it has not yet been tested.

In the beginning of 2000, a professional architectural publication featured an article on Aranya as it really exists on the ground.[117] Nevertheless, the celebration of this non-existent wonder continues and in the beginning of 2001, in the midst of all the pontification that followed the devastation in Ahmedabad, there was also an eulogizing reference to Aranya. Yoginder K. Alagh, co-founder of the premier school of architecture in Ahmedabad, said of B.V. Doshi, also co-founder of the same and Ahmedabad's best-known architect, 'Doshi showed in his Aranya experiment that we have to help the community to organize itself'.[118]

The Aga Khan Award put Aranya in a class apart, but in the world of resettlement there are several other small wonders of architecture and creative English that look very different in literature and in reality. Besides professionals, such 'disconnect' between design and reality also owes to politicians who are given to announcing, to the accompaniment of glowing descriptions, resettlement projects for the poor and then never finding the time to look back and see whether they really worked. For instance, by 2000, a 'dream housing project' launched two years earlier by the prime minister for the poor in his constituency had turned into a scam, with the development authority allotting houses to the non-poor.[119] Narela, even as it is under way, has already made it in our country report as a 'happy' example. The fact, however, is that glamorous and glamorized resettlement projects for a few hundred or even a few thousand in cities with enormous housing backlogs only bring glory to slum saviours, not succour to cities fast turning into slums.

∎

Finally, let us consider a real urban resettlement—one meant for the well settled rather than for the never settled—as a case in point to show that at least some slum saviours do understand sensitive resettlement when it pleases them.

This 'initiative' came from an all-party house committee for accommodation for Lok Sabha Members of Parliament (MPs).[120] The committee had decided (following flak from the supreme court) that MPs who have lost elections must vacate official residences. But in April 2000, after 'sustained pressure from all parties', it decided that unsettling MPs settled in official housing even after they were no longer MPs was 'a very harsh decision'. MPs, after all, 'have their children in local schools, their families move here and there is a change of base' for them. Moreover, on being elected, every MP 'thinks he will be in Delhi for the next five years. But as has been seen in the past three tenures of the Government, no single House has completed the full term'. For that, naturally, one can't blame the MPs. Accordingly, for 'humanitarian reasons', MPs in the parliamentary housing committee decided that former MPs must be resettled in Delhi and, in order that they were not hastily unsettled, there should also be transit accommodation for new MPs.

This would mean that the capital would have far more Lok Sabha MP houses than the number of Lok Sabha MPs. The parliamentary committee picked up 3 hectares of prime land (costing Rs 8 crore), taking care to ensure that it was in the heart of Delhi so that the honourable MPs would not be inconvenienced too much by having to be driven long distances.

Here then is an example of good practice in sensitive resettlement for the direct and indirect benefit of those who had been rejected through due electoral process by the people of India. For the ordinary people of India (who also have 'children in local schools', besides no official cars to transport them), however, resettlement continues to happen in 12.5 sq. metre plots in some wilderness just outside the city, it happens rarely, it happens in lieu of settlement, and it happens as a favour.

Right to Minimum Services

In most Indian cities slums as old as the 'modern' urban planning passing them by can be found. In these you will find youngsters whose grandfathers (even great-grandfathers) set up home and whose fathers (even grandfathers) were at some point given a precious token or card as proof of their existence. Veterans here will tell you things about planned development that no development research would. They know because they were part of the process—as cheap labour in stone quarries, brick kilns, construction sites, hot-mix plants, industry, transport—although they are still waiting for a share in the product of planned development.

They are still waiting because slum saviours are still 'experimenting'. Governments announce the Right to Stay and then take it away when they 'need' to. Others demand the Right to Resettlement and then crib about the resettlement and demand the Right to Stay. Somewhere down the line, slum saviours bestowed upon slums 'the right to minimum services in the meantime'. The (valid by any standards) argument for this was that every citizen has a right to basic services. The logic of services being 'minimum' related to them being 'in the meantime'. But 'meantime' has become forever and 'minimum' has become the norm.

How this happened is, again, not the subject of this discussion, which focusses on what this right means to the righted. Suffice it to say it was linked to the ascendancy of (in place of the right to equal stakes in planned development) other rights already described. Besides, from the perspective of slum saviours, it is extremely convenient that still-waiting slum dwellers actually appreciate cheap minimum services occasionally doled out to them. There is also the vast institutional paraphernalia—across government, non-government, donor and lately even corporate sectors—that has 'developed' to deliver these services and it, too, has to be 'sustained'.

From the point of view of slum dwellers, however, minimum services in slums remain what they always were—inadequate, sub-standard options, good only 'in the meantime' and illogical and unjust as permanent solutions. Nevertheless, the minimalist notion of services for the poor has come to extend also to facilities meant for them even outside slums, as manifest in 'minimum' care of the schools and hospitals that only they use. And, lately, it has been stretched even further, with sites housing facilities for the poor being taken over (in the name of city asset management) and 'landless options' being extended to the poor (in the name of greater access and outreach).

■

First let us consider minimalization of infrastructure services within slums. Years ago many city governments started providing cheap brick paving and common water points and toilets to somewhat alleviate the miserable living conditions in slums. The provisions were 'cheap' because they were meant to be temporary and they were 'common' because, in addition, there was no space for individual facilities. Now, every couple of years, especially when an election is around the corner, brick paving is renewed and common taps and toilets are repaired, cleaned, added. Very likely there are many settlements where cumulative resource costs of 'temporary' works over the years far exceed the costs of standard works for the given population.

While slum saviours' perceptions of slums and services in them being 'temporary' are changing, constraints of space and high densities remain. However, as with diminishing plot sizes, slum saviours view these constraints as challenges to their creativity. Take the case of toilets. Even without, but especially after, experiments like Indore it is clear that individual toilets in high-density settlements with puny plots cannot realistically be expected to work. But public toilets (fine in public places or even as makeshift arrangements for a while) cannot become satisfactory all-time everyday options. Predictably, a nagging problem with slum infrastructure has been poor maintenance of public toilets and the impracticality of individual toilets.

The only real solution can be alternative settlement options in which individual toilets are feasible. Instead of working towards this, slum saviours have applied themselves to more creative thinking. Enter the much-celebrated concept of pay-and-use toilets. The idea might just have struck some jet-setting saviour while dropping a coin into the box placed outside public conveniences at some international airport. To pay to pee is all very fine there, but to have to forage for change each time nature calls is a bit much. But, by the time this realization might have dawned, the concept was already on its way to becoming a global paradigm and no U-turns are allowed on that one-way street. So there was more creative application of the mind to come up with more right answers to the wrong question. In some places women and children were allowed to use the pay-and-use toilets without paying. In some places monthly family passes were tried in place of each-time payments. In some places communities were involved in running the pay-and-use toilets. Efforts were even made to 'improve the demand' by 'making communities aware of the need' for toilets.

In 2000, in Mumbai, after decades of watching its public toilets quickly become dilapidated, the corporation was again working on making public toilets work. A 'slum sanitation programme' that had failed to take off in the past four years had now been 'modified' by Additional Municipal Commissioner Subodh Kumar. According to him, the scheme did not work earlier because different agencies were involved and it would work now because 'all these agencies will work together'.[121] The World Bank would provide Rs 40 crore, the state would chip in Rs 10 crore, and MLAs and corporators could also chip in from their development funds. The corporation would construct the toilet blocks. Residents, through community-based organizations, would deposit in advance Rs 100 per adult in a bank and take responsibility for maintenance as well as payment of electricity and water charges. The government was talking of identifying 'places where there is a demand', of 'need to first change the mentality of the slum residents to use the toilets' and of constructing toilets only 'where the slum dwellers have agreed to maintain' them.[122] All this cleverness, of course, does not change inherent problems. All it means is that next time public toilets become defunct, slum communities will have only themselves to blame.

Provision (in lieu of any standard shelter option) of sub-standard minimum physical infrastructure in slums, compounded by neglect of its maintenance (in the guise of community responsibility or otherwise) is the main reason for the persistence of squalid conditions in them. Further, the continuing debate on more creative and contemporary minimalist options also does not leave much time for actual provision. In Delhi, in 1999–2000 for instance, Rs 6 crore was allocated for providing water and sewer facilities in resettlement colonies and slum clusters. The allocation was later increased to Rs 13 crore. But till January 2000 only Rs 4 crore had actually been spent.[123] Obviously, in the pursuit of the Right to Minimum Services for slum dwellers, activity gets precedence over impact, ideas get precedence over activity, the fashionable prevails over the sensible and the slumming of our cities continues.

■

Let us consider an example of how shortchanging the poor on basic services extends to minimum care of services meant for them even outside slums.

In many cities, government schools serve mainly (if not only) slum dwellers and are in a shocking condition. In the capital, we came to know exactly how shocking the conditions were in mid-2000 when a special session of the deliberative wing of the MCD followed a special survey. Delhiites learned that 1818 MCD-run primary schools catering to 900,000 predominantly poor children functioned out of 1264 school buildings. There was a shortfall of about 2224 classrooms. Around thirty-five schools ran entirely out of tents and several others were partially tented. Twenty-five school buildings had been declared dangerous and most others were poorly maintained. Five hundred and twenty-one buildings received no water supply or very little water owing to low pressure; 628 had no arrangement for water in toilets. Provision of toilets was inadequate and their condition usually deplorable. One hundred and forty-four school buildings had no electricity due to non-payment of dues, 85 had no electricity meters, 255 had defective meters, 466 had defective wiring, 650 had defective fans and 771 had defective tubes and bulbs. In some places, the approach road was in bad shape and in some water logging in the monsoons was bad enough to require suspension of classes. There was a shortfall of 1.58 lakh dual desks and students usually sat on floor mats. In many schools teachers were forced to do the same as there was a shortfall of 12,000 chairs.[124]

Half a century after free and compulsory primary education was enshrined as a directive principle in the Constitution of India, these statistics came up in the capital at the first-in-over-three-years special session of MCD following the special survey that followed—you guessed it—court orders in a PIL. In 1998, the All India Lawyers' Union had sought the Delhi High Court's intervention to improve the condition of MCD-run schools. The 'BJP-controlled' MCD had predictably passed the buck to the Congress government, saying it needed Rs 47 crore to improve the schools and in April 2000 the court asked it to file a report on the status of amenities in them.[125] The Delhi government filed an affidavit saying Rs 23 crore had been allocated to MCD to change tent schools into pucca schools. Of this Rs 14 crore was unused, another Rs 10 crore had been forwarded to the MCD for the current session, and Rs 90 crore had been allocated for education during the current financial year. The government claimed it had never denied that MCD required funds. In May 2000 the court directed the chief secretary to prepare a status report on the condition of MCD schools.[126]

The court was also hearing a related matter arising out of an incident in February 1999 in which a girl was shot in her school premises by an assailant who had entered through one of several collapsed portions of the boundary wall. Still, repeated letters from the principal to the education minister and the Public Works Department asking to mend the wall went unanswered as did representations to the police about anti-social elements around the school. The parents of the victim then petitioned the high court and it was then, more than a year after the incident, that the police instructed a beat constable to patrol the area around that school during school hours.[127] It was even later that the Delhi government on the court's directions prepared a status report on the condition of boundary walls in all 433 government girls' schools. It turned out that 203 schools had no walls or broken walls or walls made of tin-sheets. In July 2000, the government told the court that it would raise the height of the boundary walls.[128] Around the same time, a section of an MCD primary school building under construction collapsed on the first day of the academic session after summer vacations.[129]

Meanwhile, the Delhi government had priorities other than the obvious. In January 2000, 'after analyzing the problems' Sheila Dikshit's government, in its inimitable style, had 'come to the conclusion that both teachers and students seem to be lacking in "motivation".[130] Delegating financial powers to principals and a three-week training were on the anvil to 'motivate' teachers. Sheila Dikshit also spoke of 'incentives' like free uniforms and scholarships, especially stipends for the girl-child, to 'motivate' students.[131]

Also in January 2000, half way through winter, MCD was getting down to distributing 50,000 uniform jerseys amongst its 900,000 students. (Its suppliers were supposed to have delivered 200,000 jerseys in December 1999, but the chairperson of the education committee said, 'we don't want to discourage them by announcing penal action'.) The MCD planned 'different colours of uniforms in different MCD zones' in the next session.[132] Decisions on 'different colours' were expeditiously taken and announcements to supply uniforms to all students made.[133] But our elected representatives continued to squabble over awarding the contract for uniforms.[134] In December, with three months of the academic session remaining, Municipal Commissioner S.P. Aggarwal said firms given the contract for 5.13 lakh jerseys would deliver by 22 February 2001.[135] Again, students had to wait till the end of winter for jerseys and till the next academic year for uniforms.

School bags promised by the MCD also remained just a promise after the prime minister presented the first bag in 1998 at a function to mark the fortieth anniversary of MCD.[136] In September 2000, MCD announced it would start distributing bags to all primary students from 14 November (Children's Day).[137] In October, the municipal commissioner said four firms would supply 8.9 lakh bags at a cost of Rs 8 crore.[138] But till December end only 1.5 lakh bags had been supplied.[139]

Likewise, even as allocations under the centrally sponsored mid-day meal scheme have been increasing, distribution has been deteriorating. In 1996–97, Rs 8.31 crore out of the Rs 9.5 crore budgeted was utilized. The corresponding figures were Rs 8.47 crore out of Rs 14 crore in 1997–98, Rs 7.8 crore out of Rs 12 crore in 1998–99 and Rs 4.85 crore out of Rs 18 crore in 1999–2000.[140] The number of days (out of 210 school days) on which meals were provided on average in these years were, respectively, 153, 150, seventy-two and thirty-seven.[141] The 'meal' had been reduced to biscuits—at times so sub-standard that children were throwing them 'into the gutter because they caused stomachaches'.[142] The Delhi government, given to lateral approaches to solving problems arising out of its own lapses, was considering 'decentralizing' the scheme. School principals (lacking in 'motivation' to teach) were to be made responsible for procuring and distributing mid-day meals (comprising 'nutritious and fresh items') with involvement of (largely non-existent) parent–teacher associations. This was to be tried out on an 'experimental basis' in 2001.[143]

Meanwhile, performance of MCD school students in school-leaving examinations was, again, poor in the results announced in June 2000.[144] In August, a month after schools had reopened after the summer vacation, it was reported that only 50 per cent of the maintenance and repair works that were to be carried out during vacations had been completed.[145] It was also reported that there was a shortage of at least 1000 teachers.[146] At the same time, cyber-savvy Sheila Dikshit inaugurated a computer education laboratory in one school to launch her government's programme to impart computer education in government schools.[147] At the end of August, Sheila Dikshit 'expressed her dissatisfaction' with the department's performance. She did pull up officials in the matter of constructing rooms in schools but was reportedly 'more upset' about the progress of the computer education programme.[148]

In September, MCD conducted a survey and found over 100,000 out-of-school children.[149] Normally about 25,000 children enrol in MCD schools every year. After its survey, MCD 'established an all-time record by taking its enrolment figures to over 80,000'.[150] Officials said that the introduction earlier in the year of English as a subject (besides the promise of free uniforms, bags, books and mid-day meals) had motivated people to send their children to MCD schools.[151] Councillors continued to fret about shortage of teachers and space and condition of school buildings.[152] MCD said its school buildings had place for only 55,000 students and officials had been directed to assess where double shifts and tents were needed.[153] Meanwhile, especially since fresh enrolments were not necessarily to schools with surplus space, children just had to be crammed into already overcrowded classes in many schools. Efforts were also being made, in compliance with court orders, to improve amenities, though much remained to be done.[154]

Clearly, for the poor, the government seems to view enrolment and incentives for enrolment as an end in itself rather than as a means for universalization of primary education.

In urban areas, where slum children and their parents and teachers are exposed to—even if they are excluded from—a quality learning environment, decent school buildings and teaching is really all the 'motivation' that is needed. Yet our governments are keen on more contrived 'incentives' like free uniforms, books, bags and meals. For those in charge, such schemes add to vote banks (as they are converted to political largesse) and to note banks (through typical tendering procedures in currently corrupt urban India). But for slum children these 'benefits' do not mean much—not merely because they normally do not materialize.

■

Lately the prolonged neglect of school buildings has been doing more damage than denial of reasonable quality learning environment. It is adding school education to the shelf of 'landless' options on offer to the poor. NGOs have been running shanty schools, even street schools, in slums.[155] Now even governments have taken to doing the same or similar.

In August 2000, the MCD, 'taking a major initiative', decided to set up 'extended schools' with community help.[156] In these schools the 'community' provides accommodation and MCD provides teachers, textbooks, uniforms, mid-day meals, etc. Necessitated by the decision to enrol 80,000 to 100,000 students with infrastructure to accommodate only 55,000, this was based on a 'suggestion' of the State Council for Educational Research and Training (SCERT), which felt 'children should not be deprived of education due to lack of infrastructure'. SCERT and an NGO called Navjyoti coaxed MCD into opening one such school in Yamuna Pushta. Even though the 'Congress and BJP leaders had been fighting over who was going to inaugurate' it, the school was nothing great. It had the usual problems of MCD-run schools, with just a headmaster and one teacher to take care of 150 students, no water and toilets, and students beginning to drop out within two months. And it had the additional problem of a learning environment that included, among other things, an uninterrupted view from the classroom of groups of men (not just local residents) taking drugs.[157]

In a similar, much larger exercise in Indore in 1999 the government 'opened' 103 schools in slums by writing school in chalk on the doors of community halls built under the ODA slum project.[158] This was part of a larger exercise of 'rationalization' in which, it was claimed, poorly attended schools were being closed and merged to optimize teacher–student ratios. (Similar 'rationalization' exercises seem to have been on elsewhere as well—possibly as a result of a consensual paradigm of the type that emerges in sectors with a lot of foreign funding—such as in Srinagar in 2000.)[159] In Indore, however, availability of readymade community halls made it possible for the government to claim that new schools were being opened where they were needed. The administration was proudly claiming these were 'no-cost' schools and appealing to charitable organizations to contribute floor mats, etc. (In a similar vein, in Delhi in 2000 the mayor was asking citizens to help make municipal schools in their areas better.)[160] But the inadequate, unequipped and run-down community halls in Indore could hardly attract (or accommodate) the ninety-odd students necessary to justify (on the basis of a desirable teacher–student ratio) the two teachers posted to them. Most had fewer students than the schools closed down on grounds of poor enrollment.

It is not clear why those who can think of asking the 'community' to find a pathetic site and civil society to charitably contribute other essentials do not think of asking fancy private schools that are given public land at throwaway prices to share their facilities with government schools instead. In Indore, one of the government schools closed due to 'rationalization' was running out of a private school that had earlier been allotted land on the condition that a government school would also be run from the same premises. In Delhi, private schools are allotted land at cheap rates and the lease clearly states they are to offer free seats to the underprivileged in lieu. Although most schools close by afternoon and their buildings and playgrounds could easily be used afterwards in the spirit of this, it does not happen unless the school chooses to do so, not out of a legal obligation but out of charity. On the other hand, several private schools use their premises after school hours for activities for the benefit of their own students or even for others and charge a fee for the same. In effect, many private schools in Delhi are making money out of the land allotted cheaply to them while failing to do by poor children that for which it was allotted cheaply. Yet, those in government and non-government committed by mandate or choice to universalizing primary education (and, presumably, themselves parents of children attending private schools) set up pathetic 'extended schools' on illegal community land in slums rather than enforce legal land lease provisions for the same in well-equipped schools.

From the point of view of slum children, who do not have many opportunities to come out of the squalor around their homes, location of their schools within their slum is worse than almost any other alternative. For others, such as the land mafia, it is better for not using real estate. After all, even many government schools occupy sites that have become prime land which many feel are wasted on the poor.

In Delhi, the attempt of an unscrupulous builder to grab a school site made news in May 2000.[161] In Indore nearly all the schools closed in 1999—though they had varying levels of enrolment and dilapidation—were centrally located. For schools that were not closed but which occupied commercially valuable land, the administration, in order it said to pre-empt encroachment by others, decided to carry out commercial development on part of the site on its own. The difference between illegal encroachments by others and commercial development by the state, the state said, was that the latter would raise much-needed resources for education. This was being done even as available resources were not being fully used and the revenue raised in similar manner on at least two earlier occasions had not been ploughed back into education.

In seminars the idea of putting part of the premises of poor children's schools to commercial use in order to 'raise resources' for educating them may appear clever or practical or radical. In the real world, it can look rather shameless. A government girls' school in Indore, for instance, has (as a consequence of such a 'radical' measure) outside it one Ding Dong Bar, purportedly rendering indispensable assistance for raising revenues so that we might be able to educate our daughters. Also in Indore, as testimony to the kind of choices we are learning to make, on 18 October 2000, an eighty-six-year-old TB sanatorium that had served the poor well was demolished to make way for an Indian Institute of Management (IIM) for more futuristic public good.

The events leading up to this bordered on the bizarre.[162] In February 1998 the state decided to hand over the sanatorium land to IIM by shifting the sanatorium with its 159 inmates. This was despite the fact that 125 acres—more than what most existing such campuses elsewhere occupied—in the vicinity had already been allotted to IIM, which had now asked for some more. In March, a PIL was filed against this decision. In its reply, the state said the land would not be given to IIM without first creating 'an equal or better' sanatorium on '22.654 hectares'. The court dismissed the PIL on 20 July. On 18 July (two days before the court order), the secretary, human resource development, informed the chief secretary that the PIL had been dismissed and patients should be transferred or discharged. In November a contempt petition was filed. In December three patients filed a separate petition. On 3 December the court ordered status quo. On 23 January 1999, the state issued orders to stop transfer and discharge of patients. The court dismissed the contempt petition and disposed of the patient's petition in view of these orders.

In July 1999, a house-building society made a representation to the collector against allotment of the 20-acre alternative site that the state had identified for the sanatorium. Ten months later, in May 2000, a PIL was filed on substantively similar grounds. On 26 June the court ordered status quo on the site for the proposed sanatorium. This precipitated a PIL praying that the existing historic sanatorium be modernized. On the other hand, pressure from IIM was growing. On its first convocation in March 2000 its director said if the land promised to it was not allotted soon, the board would consider shifting IIM out of Indore.

In August the state forcibly discharged most patients. This created a furore. The local press reported on it for days. The 'star' was Satish Pathak—a sputum positive, multi-drug resistant TB patient who had started living at the railway station after being forcibly discharged. The petitioners, who had approached the court for allowing the sanatorium to remain on the original site, approached it for intervention. On 17 August the court ordered status quo. On the other hand, on 20 August, Union Minister for Human Resource Development (the ministry that takes care of IIMs) Murli Manohar Joshi and his Minister of State Sumitra Mahajan (also MP from Indore) visited IIM. Joshi said 'hurdles in the way of establishing IIM would soon be removed'.

On 8 September the court directed that the state 'will not refuse to admit any patient and shall admit the discharged patients and also shall not transfer the patients' from the sanatorium. On 12 September Bhagwandas came to be admitted, but was told the authorities had no instructions. Along with others like him, he settled down outside to wait. On the evening of 13 September he turned critical. On the morning of 14 September he died—not quite outside the sanatorium (for he was kindly allowed in), but not quite inside either (for he was neither admitted nor treated).

After his death late Bhagwandas shared news space with IIM, which was threatening to leave Indore. On 16 September the director of IIM called a press conference and announced a deadline—the IIM board meeting of 3 October. Politicians across party lines joined in the mayhem to persuade it to stay and blamed one another for the 'crisis'. On 23 September the chief minister arrived in Indore to personally intervene. Also on 23 September more patients were discharged from the sanatorium. On 26 September an intervention was filed in the court, praying for the stay on the existing sanatorium to be vacated in the context of the forthcoming IIM board meeting. On 28 September another intervention was filed, alleging that the other was by those wanting to be spokespersons for the government. A third intervention was filed by Raju, Om Prakash and Santosh, patients who had been discharged on 23 September against their wishes. On 29 September, the court declined to admit any of these interventions and modified the interim relief to say that patients would 'be looked after better at M.R. TB Hospital'. This court order restored bonhomie between the IIM and the state. At the board meeting on 3 October, far from talking of leaving Indore, the board thanked the state for its efforts to resolve the land dispute in IIM's favour.

On 13 October Raju, Om Prakash and Santosh, along with others, filed a fresh petition to challenge the court's order of 29 September. Among other things, it was argued that the sanatorium occupied less than a twentieth of the land to be given to IIM and that IIM had already been handed over more than 170 acres, but had not started construction. It was prayed that IIM be directed to start construction (estimated by IIM to take two years) on the rest of the land and the state be directed to build the 'equal or better' alternative sanatorium (estimated by the state to take one year). Once the new sanatorium had been constructed, the existing sanatorium could be shifted and the remaining land handed over to IIM in accordance with the state's undertaking of 1998. On 16 October the court dismissed the petition in the first hearing, though it did direct the state to admit Raju, Om Prakash and Santosh in M.R. TB hospital 'for best care'. (Incidentally, M.R. TB Hospital was not being able to provide the court-directed 'better' care on account of its capacity constraints. Even with 'special' court orders for 'best care', Raju, Om Prakash and Santosh were refused admission. Eventually two of them were admitted but, since there were no beds, had to settle for their 'best care' on the floor in the corridor.)

On 17 October the court vacated the stay on the sanatorium site while disposing of the PIL that had sought modernization of the sanatorium in its present location. The court order said, 'TB patients can be better looked after by a chest centre' that the government now proposed within the 6-acre compound of the M.R. TB hospital. Within hours of the court order the state that had taken nearly a week to act on court orders for re-admitting patients in September, resulting in the death without treatment of Bhagwandas, made arrangements for demolition of the sanatorium. On the morning of 18 October a large police force and bulldozers were deployed. Despite the claims of the government about the poor structural condition of the eighty-six-year-old building, explosives had to be used. By evening, the state, in a remarkable display of efficiency, was done with its work for the good of Indore.

Later, less than a month after the state had dramatically demolished an eighty-six-year-old building whose heritage worth had been highlighted in the court, Jagmohan would visit Indore and declare it a 'heritage city'. Raju would die of TB receiving his court directed 'best care' on the floor in the corridor of M.R. TB hospital. The petition he and others had filed would go to the supreme court.[163] The IIM would say it needed the hilltop that the sanatorium had occupied to build an ultra-modern complex, complete with a glass 'skywalk' that was disabled friendly.

But all that is not part of this story. This story ends with the good old sanatorium that had to go (even though it was vintage and sweet and even though it occupied only a twentieth of a site that was twice as much as what other older IIMs have) to make way for a shiny new IIM. The shiny new IIM will be a monument to what the rights of the Little People can achieve for the Big People. The sanatorium enjoyed the Right to Stay—in utter neglect—for as long as there was no need to do anything about it. It was then given the Right to Resettlement the minute a fancy IIM came to town and started demanding more and more land like a petulant child. Then the Right to Minimum Services was invoked, downsizing 22 hectares to 20 acres to a part of 6 acres unlikely to be delivered, simply by discharging most patients and then claiming the rest did not justify a full-fledged sanatorium.

■

For the urban poor minimal 'landless' options—outreach services instead of hospitals, street education instead of proper schools, slum upgrading in place of housing—have all become very fashionable. They are also one-way streets. Once all urban land is lost to less essential, more glamorous uses there will be no turning the slumming clock back. After all it is impossible that an IIM built on an excessive 200 acres or a new-fangled cyber park or any of the plush farm houses large beyond land ceiling limits will ever be dynamited to make room for a TB sanatorium or a municipal school or a low-income housing project if and when our welfare state happens to change its mind about what is needed for urban welfare and to stop urban slumming.

4

Big People Rights

The CUD policy workshop that the Lord of CUD had convened had a more impressive turnout of senior officials and representatives of friendly political parties, NGOs and donors than his last CUD policy workshop.

All quickly agreed on consensus achievements and promising initiatives. The consensus achievement was the Charter of Rights for the People—the Right to Stay, Right to Resettlement and Right to Minimum Services. The promising initiatives were beginnings already made to strengthen and streamline synergy amongst CUD actors—a task force to flexibly define options for the poor, a fund for strengthening partnerships, and a policy of ignoring/distracting critics (while trying to win them over). Participants input their comments at their networked computer stations, the technical staff did the needful and the Lord clicked Output.

As usual the default Old-fashioned Urban Development Option appeared. It said: 'Error: Invalid Input… Rights do not match constitutional rights. Change Input or Disable Frame-of-Reference'. The Lord clicked Disable. All screens said, 'Old-fashioned Option cannot Disable Frame-of-Reference = Constitution'. All groaned and the Lord quickly clicked Skip to CUD Option. All screens said, 'Sorry. Old-fashioned Option cannot pass to CUD routine… Constitutionally invalid Input… To proceed to CUD you must delete Old-fashioned Option routine permanently (without Undo option)… For this all terminals must confirm. Delete?' All said 'Yesss!' and entered Y.

A sigh of relief went round the room as a friendly Output began to appear. 'CUD rating of input: Excellent!' (This was the default rating). And then, 'Suggestions for sustaining excellence… In place of case-by-case task force, fund, etc., assume on continuing basis Right to Define and Redefine, Right to Align and Realign, and Right to be Ostrich with Pet Red Herring.' The Lord said, 'Looks like we have a Charter of Rights for ourselves as well. Do we agree?' All did.

The Lord clicked Continue. The pre-programmed output triggered by the deletion of the Old-fashioned Option appeared. 'Special Opportunity… Discarding Old-fashioned Option is The Greatest Opportunity for furthering CUD… Followers of the Old-fashioned Option must be systematically phased out.' The Lord asked, 'Any comments?' An earnest lady representing a premier donor said, 'I fully agree. Followers of the Old-fashioned Option do not have the right development attitude. They dwell too much on past mistakes.' A clever looking man representing a group of NGOs added, 'They do not understand that all can work on everything and it is not necessary for roles of professionals, government and NGOs to be rigidly demarcated'. Criticism of the Old-fashioned Option flowed freely. The Lord of CUD was quite flattered. He turned to the chairman of his premier public sector undertaking and asked, 'What can we do to marginalize the Old-fashioned Option?' The bossy man replied, 'We can put up a CUD gala, a continuing CUD circus to showcase and celebrate CUD ideas, projects, people. All can set up some permanent exhibitions and we can work out a calendar of special events…' All applauded and began to make plans as they moved towards lunch.

The Lord of CUD was very pleased—with the clever Charter of Rights, with the consensus against the Old-fashioned Option, and with the enthusiasm about the planned circus.

Right to Define and Redefine

In the beginning of January 2000, trucks, excavators and cranes of the Municipal Corporation of Delhi (MCD) 'rumbled out of the workshops' to remove hawkers and encroachers to clear right of way on the roads. This New Year gift for the city had been approved at 'a high-level meeting'.[1] (A similar New Year gift was announced on 1 January 2001.)[2] Hundreds of unorganized sector platforms and kiosks were demolished.[3] Later in the month, Minister for Social Justice and

Empowerment Maneka Gandhi released the Dave Committee report that had proposals for bringing the unorganized sector under pension schemes.[4] In March, a day after MCD had demolished more minimum establishments, Delhi Social Welfare Minister Krishna Tirath announced a raise in minimum wages.[5] MCD's drive continued and in May Lieutenant-Governor Vijai Kapur promised strict action if encroachments came up.[6] Also in May, fifty vendors petitioned the Human Rights Commission for compensation of loss of earnings on account of having been forced to shut shop for a month when the city was 'spruced up' for Bill Clinton's visit in March.[7] MCD's drive continued till October, when it distributed *tehbazaris* (licences) to hawkers in line with the Chopra Committee report.[8]

Meanwhile, in Mumbai, in May, the original 'demolition man' bureaucrat G.R. Khairnar, barely two weeks after reassuming office in the Brihan-Mumbai Municipal Corporation (BMC), came down heavily on hawkers. Hawkers responded by blocking the road, shouting slogans and pelting stones.[9] Khairnar responded by deploying a commando force for the job, which he said was difficult as hawkers 'enjoy patronage of [the] civic license department and other senior officials' and are 'controlled by powerful syndicates enjoying protection from the underworld'.[10] Hawkers threatened agitation from June 1. On that day, forty-three days after his reinstatement, Khairnar retired. On his last day in office, after nearly a month of ruthless crackdown, he announced a 'scheme' wherein hawkers could remain, albeit in a disciplined manner. He now said hawkers are only 'earning their living' and 'are a social necessity'.[11] In July, the Bombay High Court—whose intervention had been sought through the ubiquitous PIL—gave directions for implementing earlier supreme court orders for marking out hawking zones.[12] BMC (which had been trying such schemes since 1983) realized only a fourth of the city's hawkers could be so accommodated and the rest had 'no option but to find an alternative source of income'.[13] Also in July the Bombay High Court dismissed a writ petition filed on behalf of hawkers to challenge Pune Municipal Corporation's (PMC) decision to cancel their licences to ensure smooth traffic on city roads. PMC had offered alternative sites in segregated hawker markets which hawkers did not find lucrative from the point of view of business, but which PMC and the court held were convenient from the point of view of the general public.[14]

Meanwhile, in Delhi, four shopkeepers' associations in the flourishing Janpath market in the heart of New Delhi protested against tehbazaris to hawkers opposite their shops, which the New Delhi Municipal Committee (NDMC) had granted earlier in line with the Thareja Committee report.[15] This, incidentally, followed NDMC's announcement (quite likely the result of the untiring efforts of the market associations) to give the shopkeepers themselves (of course against some payment) ownership rights over the shops that they so far had on rent.[16]

The swinging of the pendulum between ruthless evictions and accommodating schemes by the government, protests and PIL for and against them by civil society, and report after report by committees that affected hawkers in India's premier cities in 2000 were just continuing acts in a long-playing drama. Caught in the midst of great governance in which the left hand does not know what the right hand is doing and retirement brings an entirely different kind of wisdom, hawkers have been hawking—and paying *hafta* (protection money) to minions of the big guys whose 'patronage' they 'enjoy'—for decades. For decades the Big People have been defining and redefining them—as encroachers who hassle and as poor guys who serve—just as they have been defining and redefining all Little People.

■

The Big People are supposed to address *all* urban issues—unorganized trade, traffic, crime, poverty, power theft, garbage, pollution, runaway population, etc. But even as they never tire of reiterating their commitment towards the poor and problem solving, they have mastered the art of blaming the poor for all urban problems.

On 8 March 2000 (Women's Day) Sheila Dikshit was on television blaming poor migrants for crime in Delhi.[17] She was drawing an association between migrants, slums and most problems of the city and would have us believe that migrants stress our cities, migrants live in slums, and hence slums stress the city.[18] Stretching this 'logic' to the limit around the same time, the Congress government in Maharashtra was seriously considering enacting a law to stop influx of migrants and ban slums in Mumbai.[19] Later in Delhi, Health and Urban Development Minister A.K. Walia said that 'a large number of HIV-infected people migrate to Delhi for seeking jobs'.[20] Various governments were also working out schemes in slums to check power thefts.[21] And the apex court's remarks had led us to link slum dwellers with pickpockets and small industrialists with hooligans.

All this vacillating defining and redefining of the unpeople of India by their elected, appointed and self-appointed saviours has blown our minds. Forgetting our national pledge of all Indians being brothers and sisters, 'we' constantly wonder about 'them'—hawkers, slum dwellers, small industrialists, migrants—even as we really have no right to 'judge'. 'We' wonder if hawkers hawk to serve us or to block our roads. 'We' wonder if slum dwellers are victims or culprits in problems of garbage, power shortages, etc. 'We' wonder if small industrialists are hooligans or indispensable cogs in the wheel of economic progress. 'We' wonder if migrants are driven in desperation off the rural development road to nowhere or wickedly come to 'our' cities to slum them and kill us with AIDS and more. 'We' wonder because whenever we look we find Those In Charge always and still wondering about long-standing problems, as if there was no yesterday, no law and no data (though it is copiously collected) to tell us—as if we had nothing except their pathetic pontifications.

Consider Delhi's hawkers for whom successive governments alternately deploy and withdraw removal vans. The city's statutory Master Plan says informal sector ('working without a roof, including small *khokha* on roadside') 'needs full consideration as it provides much needed employment to the unskilled and semi-skilled' and 'it is of utmost importance' that it should be 'integrated in the physical planning process'.[22] It further says, 'it is possible to create lively shopping areas by suitably introducing informal sector' and even speaks of 'few standard efficient and colourful designs'.[23] It notes that these 'units locate themselves strategically near work centres, commercial areas, outside the boundaries of schools, colleges and hospitals, transport nodes and near large housing clusters'.[24] It spells out in great detail standards for integrating space for hawking in planned development.[25] These standards are in line with the natural propensity of hawkers to locate in various places and are meant to deal with the performance–nuisance conflict that is inherent to hawking activity. The Plan requires that 'at the time of sanction of building plans, the provision of informal sector trade units should be ensured'.[26] These comprehensive and arguably adequate statutory provisions for hawkers have not been implemented. Yet 'we' wonder about 'them'.

Consider the mysterious migrants, supposedly all in slums. For cities like Delhi and Mumbai statutory regional plans were prepared decades ago precisely to ensure that city-ward migration is spread over a larger area. It is also well known that people do not migrate from lovely hinterlands where urbanites take vacations to live in urban slums. They come to *work*. Accordingly, regional development strategies hinge on dispersal of workplaces, not on forcible relocation of the poor. One has only to look around in government or MNC or public sector offices (many of which should be in satellite towns) to see that migrants are not found only in slums and the ones in slums stress the city the least. Yet 'we' wonder about 'them'.

Consider crime and the poor. It is very likely there are no statistics to show that poor migrants in slums are responsible for most crimes. There is no basis to paint one class as a criminal class. No penal code bases punishment on class of offender, only on gravity of offence. It is wrong to punish a pickpocket more because he is poor and a murderer less because he is rich. The poor, if only because of their circumstances, are less capable of grave crimes than the rich. A belatedly but well-understood case in point is of power thefts. For years power theft by the poor has been touted as the main reason for distribution losses and our electricity departments have targetted much of their 'action' in this regard at slums. But power supply has not improved. In 2000 the capital was leading in transmission and distribution (T&D) losses with a tally of 60 per cent. More power was being lost than supplied for use and the losses amounted to Rs 2500 crore annually. Nineteen per cent were 'technical losses' and the rest thefts. Several employees, even as they carried out 'drives' to check power theft by others, were themselves caught stealing power. In all, a fifth of all 'thieves' seemed to 'steal' half the 'stolen' power and these fellows (including 'powerful babus') do not live in slums. Slums account for a measly 5 to 6 per cent of the power stolen—something that should have been obvious from the fact that they occupy a measly amount of city space and that their consumption patterns simply do not allow enormous amounts of power use.[27] Yet 'we' wonder about 'them'.

Consider A.K. Walia who, worried about AIDS-carrying migrants, mounted an AIDS campaign *in slums* in June 2000. This was called 'Family Health Awareness Fortnight' (to 'ensure that the stigma attached to AIDS does not drive people away', explained the minister).[28] But, perhaps not wanting dollar daddies doling out AIDS funds to miss his effort, he gave away his clever secret to the press beforehand. With seventy NGOs the health minister was offering slum dwellers check-ups and medicines for sexually transmitted diseases at that time of year when water- and vector-borne diseases are rampant in slums.[29] Had he some alarming statistics showing higher prevalence of AIDS in slums? Had he some alarming micro-studies suggesting higher incidence of high-risk behaviour in slums? Even before his campaign started, he admitted he had neither. What, then, was the basis for his insistence on going ahead with a campaign that did stigmatize slum dwellers and very likely also diverted precious resources to oddly targetted interventions that were non-priority or useless? The basis was the minister's personal view that slum dwellers 'are more prone to contracting HIV/AIDS because of their suspected sexual behaviour' based, in turn, on his personal profound assumption that people camping in Delhi for petty jobs visit red light areas![30] Yet 'we' wonder about 'them'.

Reducing law and policy making and all manner of research and data collection at taxpayers' cost to an end in itself, city and slum saviours constantly reinvent—or just creatively and contemporarily rename—the wheel. All that changes in the games Big People play is who gets how much hafta or funding or how many brownie points or media coverage. The poor stay poor. The rich stay rich. Hawkers keep hawking. Slums keep growing.

The Right to Define and Redefine is effectively deployed by those who have given it to themselves to show that saviours are busily running the show, so that nobody sees those being saved aren't getting anywhere. It is also deployed to downsize national commitments. Defining how less is good for the poor (under, for instance, the rights described earlier) is one form of such deployment. Another is redefining who exactly the poor are.

Notions of 'poorest of the poor' and 'most vulnerable groups' help saviours engage with as little as pleases them. Thus, despite a constitutional commitment to universalization of primary education, development dons speak of elementary education for the most vulnerable and, in their enthusiasm to get there, look at *gali* (street) schools with pride, not shame. Despite having failed to provide—even facilitate—jobs, schools, dispensaries and housing for slum dwellers, they ask slum women (both 'more vulnerable' and 'more potential') to form self-help groups even though contemporary urban development has nothing to offer them after they are so 'empowered'. Despite the dissatisfaction with urban poverty definitions based purely on income criteria, they come up with schemes for those below poverty line (BPL) knowing full well that 'clean' implementation of such schemes is impossible.

In March 2000 former prime minister V.P. Singh (ending his political *sanyas* in Wazirpur) demanded special ration cards for the poor so that they could get rations at half price.[31] In November 2000 Prime Minister Vajpayee (celebrating his seventy-sixth birthday) announced a scheme for India's poorest families to get wheat at Rs 2 per kg and rice at Rs 3 per kg.[32] Critics said the scheme would increase the subsidy burden by Rs 2300 crore a year and made no sense given that the government had recently slashed food subsidy by Rs 3000 crore. A parliamentary standing committee went so far as to describe the scheme as 'Tughlaqian' and wanted to know if the finance ministry, the Cabinet and the Planning Commission had been consulted before announcing it.[33] Supporters, on the other hand, said 'it makes good sense for the Government to target its abundant food stocks at the poorest households'.[34] The Centre asked states to identify families that figured amongst the poorest and said the scheme would start functioning by end of February 2001.[35]

In January 2000, Yoganand Shastri, food and civil supplies minister in the Congress government in Delhi announced that 500,000 jhuggi ration card holders in Delhi would get wheat and rice at Rs 4.65 and Rs 6.15 per kg respectively under the Targeted Public Distribution Scheme (TPDS).[36] TPDS, introduced by the Centre in 1997 for BPL families, had not been implemented in Delhi because the Delhi government wanted all residents of slums and resettlement colonies to be considered BPL while the Planning Commission insisted on annual family income of less than Rs 24,200 as the criterion for being identified as BPL.[37] The Delhi government's stand was that slum dwellers are 'most obviously poor' and 'already have distinct jhuggi cards'.[38] The logical thing for it to do would have been to get the Centre to modify the scheme for urban areas to use residence in a slum rather than income as the criterion for entitlement for cheap rations and then apply it to existing slum ration cards. But logic does not drive governance and certainly not political responses to leaders of other political groups demanding and announcing cheap rations for the large vote bank of the poor.

The Delhi government 'launched' in February, typically at a rally, TPDS for all jhuggi dwellers. Yoganand Shastri, reiterating the government's firm commitment towards jhuggi dwellers, told them they would get 'new' ration cards.[39] For 'new' cards they had to sign a form and get the 'old' cards stamped. In February 2001, hundreds of thousands of jhuggi dwellers in the capital were putting their signature or thumb-impression on 'the form' and taking days off from work to queue up to deposit it and get a precious stamp on their 'old' card (naturally, if they had one) to make it a 'new' card.[40]

'The form' was an undertaking that their combined annual family income was less than the magic figure of Rs 24,200! Many, if not most, jhuggi dwellers in Delhi could not have signed such an undertaking with confidence (as their incomes are often irregular) or with honesty (as their incomes are often greater). But they were signing up in hordes, because many could not read or understand what 'the form' (at times in English) said and because recent political announcements had led them to believe they were all entitled to a 'new' card. Yoganand Shastri was reported saying that the declaration was 'just a bureaucratic formality and does not mean anything' and, although it says legal action will be taken against anyone giving false information, 'no one would face any action'.[41]

Here, then, was the quintessential scheme for the wilfully defined 'poorest of the poor'. Jhuggi dwellers were led to signing false affidavits that, obviously, gave corrupt government functionaries a new tool for extortion. (Their access to cheap rations, on the other hand, did not improve in real terms because making rations cheaper did nothing to change the fact that ration shops mostly remained out of stock.) The government was spared the tedious effort of identifying the poor *and* scored a tidy tally of brownie points. Everybody else hated jhuggi dwellers for 'increased subsidy burden' and agreed that giving them free plots indeed amounted to rewarding pickpockets.

Right to Align and Realign

The global paradigm of partnerships as a panacea has led to the ascendancy of civil society in development. In 2000, throughout the country, elected governments were 'partnering' with selected others.

These efforts were at their prolific best in the capital. From saying 'no' to polybags to saying 'no' to river pollution, from court orders on litter to court orders on vehicular emissions, from rain water harvesting to bus accidents, Chief Minister Sheila Dikshit had found a one-size-fits-all mantra—school children, residents' welfare associations (RWAs), corporates, celebrities and NGOs. Her government never tired of reiterating its commitment to making Delhi a model city; nor of reiterating this could only happen through collective effort.

In January, her penchant for participatory problem-solving was institutionalized in her government's 'concrete plan' for *bhagidari* (partnership).[42] By February, her government had brought out a 'strategy paper'.[43] In March, she inaugurated 'a large group interactive event' with government officials and twenty RWAs. Participants engaged in an 'intensive dialogue' in 'small face-to-face table groups'.[44] Problems and solutions were documented for analysis (even as matters discussed had been and were being anyway documented and analysed by a plethora of more professional research, training and policy-making bodies).[45] Meanwhile, at the end of the workshop, Sheila Dikshit announced plans to provide some funds to RWAs.[46] In June, there was a second bhagidari workshop with seventy RWAs. She was also talking to other prospective *bhagidars* (partners) such as at 'a half-day brainstorming' with scientists/technologists on bhagidari possibilities and while launching 'a series of lectures on burning issues concerning the Capital' for members of the elite India Habitat Centre.[47] The second RWA workshop, 'conceptualized' by an NGO on the basis of western experience, involved thirty-five tables shared 'under the maximum mixing (max-mix) principle'.[48] Inaugurating it, Sheila Dikshit reiterated that 'without complaints and suggestions, participation and cooperation, government cannot move forward'.[49] Two hundred and ten representatives of RWAs and 200 officials identified solutions.[50] At the end of the workshop Sheila Dikshit asked officials to go to the field for first-hand knowledge of problems.[51] She said RWAs now saw her difficulties with 'multiplicity of agencies' and the administration now knew what RWAs expected (though 'complaints' from RWAs related to well-known problems like water shortages, garbage not being collected, etc.).[52] She outlined a follow-up 'strategy' consisting of chief ministerial instructions to departments, departmental instructions to officers, officers' meetings with RWAs, etc.[53] In August, she held a meeting to review progress. Departments had 'identified' areas where RWAs could play a role and announced some plans—roadside plantation, rain water harvesting in ten colonies, checking leakage and thefts from water mains, re-carpeting roads, installing garbage bins. Sheila Dikshit said there would be 500 bhagidar RWAs by next year and once again urged all to come forward to make Delhi green.[54] RWAs had already done 'a tremendous job' of planting 300,000 saplings. Eighty RWAs 'in partnership with the corporate sector' had also agreed to maintain eighty parks and in 'another significant development' some had agreed to switch streetlights on and off.[55]

But the best benefit of bhagidari had come before and had little to do with Sheila Dikshit's plans. At the time of the workshop with RWAs in June, Jagmohan's bulldozers had been targetting unauthorized additions in DDA flats, RWAs of many of which were bhagidars. At the workshop, Sheila Dikshit had said field visits by officials could have checked illegal constructions and RWAs had demanded powers to fine those who did not follow civic rules.[56] Afterwards, RWAs and federations of RWAs and the apex association of federations of RWAs of DDA flats were writing to the press and the prime minister to ask for protection of illegal constructions by their members. Their stand was that 90 per cent of the flats had illegal additions (to meet growing *needs*) and so these should be regularized.[57] Actually, it is unlikely that 90 per cent of the flats are even occupied, leave alone altered. Many flats have not been altered—for lack of need or resources, because they have been rented, or even just out of a respect for the law. Many residents are also opposed to illegal additions and several had written to Jagmohan earlier to complain, congratulate, thank. Now Jagmohan gave in to their (not quite representative) RWAs.[58] He gave law-breakers a reprieve and asked RWAs to define 'minor and major alteration'.[59] Thereafter, bhagidari, purportedly for making Delhi better, took off more firmly in the direction of unintended development.

RWAs, which had so far 'been existing under the cloud of non-recognition', had tasted 'success' and wanted more—more cooperation, more recognition, more tree-guards, more tankers, more power, separate funds, fax machines.[60] They wanted more tube wells and got them even where there was a ban on ground water tapping.[61] They wanted more hospitals, colleges and Delhi Haats and got them even though the Master Plan did not envisage them.[62] Bhagidari had elevated chosen bhagidars above questions about what these wilful gifts meant for the rest of the city, its ground water, its hospital waste, the land requirement for housing the poor and the whole notion of planned development as opposed to slumming.

As the government, mandated to equitably deal with the whole city's civic problems, got 'busy ironing out snags' to ensure 'better co-operation from different agencies' for RWAs of ninety well-off areas out of several thousands in Delhi, many others must have felt rather disoriented.[63] Even among bhagidars, expected to 'help' in all manner of things, many old-fashioned ones (who believed their responsibility ended with paying their taxes and the rest was the job of government servants suitably selected, trained and paid for the same) must also have felt rather disoriented.

But they were not the only ones whose developmental roles were changing.

■

Consider celebrities. Till not long ago our singers sang, designers designed, players played, beauty queens went to Bollywood and so on. Once in a while one of them took to charity. Nowadays they are *all* expected to have a cause before they can claim to be a celebrity. In October 2000 there was even a UN meet to reflect on the role of celebrity advocacy. 'Nobel laureates, athletes, actors, musicians, authors, scientists and media personalities from 20 countries' participated.[64] Miss Universe Lara Dutta and Bollywood actress Manisha Koirala represented India.[65] The previous year another Miss Universe had addressed an international conference on urban management. One wonders if these lovely ladies (like tax payers) are disoriented by these additional responsibilities.

Consider also the corporate sector. Till not so long ago our welfare state was rather wary of the profit motive of the private sector. Corporates were expected to make profits, ensure economic growth and pay taxes so government could look after welfare. Any direct role was through law that obliged them to, say, provide housing for employees or leave land or houses for the poor in their housing projects. Their track record in getting around such laws was often used to deny them a larger piece of the developmental action. Now things—or at least the *perception* of the role of the private sector— have changed. Already in every city in India one can find on tree guards and planters, streetlights and railings, benches and dustbins little legends proclaiming corporate contribution in making cities clean and green. Now even urban planners after completing postgraduate studies (for which they get a generous stipend) find openings in corporates, including MNCs, as they go about greening and cleaning or property development or just brokering.

We do not know if the worth of all this corporate contribution is anywhere near the value of corporate tax default in the country, but we do know that the former is getting more visible. In Pune in June 2000, at an international consultation on 'tripartite partnerships for poverty alleviation' between governments, NGOs and international donors, 'everyone was rooting for the fourth partner: the private sector'.[66] A delegate said, 'In the era of globalization it would be in the interest of the corporate sector to collaborate with NGOs to reduce poverty because it would then get a bigger market for its products'.[67] In April, reflecting a 'drastic change in its "attitudinal landscape" from the "socialist ambience" of the 1970s', the Jawaharlal Nehru University wrote to top industrial houses requesting them to contribute to its coffers.[68] The Delhi government was also writing to various corporate forums and federations like the Confederation of Indian Industry (CII), the Punjab, Haryana, Delhi Chamber of Commerce and Industry (PHDCCI) and the Federation of Indian Chambers of Commerce and Industry (FICCI) to seek 'a better response' for its bhagidari invitation.[69]

In July 2000 at the South Asian Forum on Environmental Cooperation between Government and the Private Sector, Minister for Environment and Forests T.R. Baalu called upon the private sector to invest more into improving the environment.[70] At the same time, in what was seen as 'a precursor to the establishment of private forests', the Andhra Pradesh government was working on tie-ups with industrial houses for tree plantation, starting with plantations spread over 10,000 hectares, on a 'pilot basis'.[71] The Rs 380 crore World Bank-aided AP Forestry Programme was ending and the 'state does not have funds to continue with its social forestry and forest regeneration programmes'.[72] An official of the environment and forest department had already toured the US to study private forests there and two more top officials were scheduled to make similar trips for fine-tuning the government policy on private participation in forestry.[73] In Delhi, the US ambassador planted a tree to mark his commitment to the environment (and presumably to private participation therein) in a 'children's educational park' developed as part of an 'ambitious project' jointly being carried out by civic authorities and the corporate sector.[74]

Also in July the findings of a study on corporate sector responsibility (based on a survey of 600 companies) were presented at a seminar organized by CII, a union ministry and a UN agency. The survey found that for most corporates 'social responsibility' translated into a focus on employees, suppliers and other stakeholders, was driven by reasons of government goodwill, image, employee morale and philanthropy, and was 'overwhelmingly' limited to writing out cheques and to CEO-driven efforts.[75] Indeed, in Ahmedabad in the mid-1990s, Arvind Mills had embarked on a citywide slum upgrading project on the lines of Indore out of, they claimed, not charity but 'enlightened self-interest' to have a slum-free city in order to attract the best global partners.[76] However, after improving one slum (mainly inhabited by their employees) and having won a place in the Habitat II Global Best Practices as an example of slum networking (their effort being limited to just one, obviously un-networked, slum notwithstanding), they withdrew. One wonders, in the light of such experiences and surveys, if corporate captains (like tax payers and the lovely ladies, etc.) feel disoriented by the great expectations of, for instance, the Draft National Slum Policy.

∎

The role of NGOs, the oldest 'partners in change', is also changing. In January 2000, the director of Charities Aid Foundation (CAF), a Delhi-based NGO, was reported saying, 'India perhaps has the largest number of voluntary organizations with the estimates ranging from 30,000 to a million. Over the years, as availability of foreign and government funds increased, many fake and self-seeking organizations emerged.' CAF had begun a process of rating NGOs on the basis of 'a thorough analysis' of their financial statements.[77] In March, MCD decided to cancel its contract with Sulabh (the NGO that is to pay-and-use toilets in India what Hoover is to vacuum cleaners and Xerox to photocopiers) following detection of irregularities in Sulabh-run toilets.[78] Around the same time a 'scam' surfaced in Lucknow where it seemed several NGOs, in connivance with officials of the state urban development authority, had siphoned off during the last four years Rs 80 crore meant for the National Slum Development Programme.[79] In April, in a PIL filed by a former chairman of the Juvenile Welfare Board, the high court directed the Delhi government to submit a list of children homes being run without licences by NGOs.[80] In May, the Ministry of Human Resource Development stopped grants to some NGOs on account of their failure to submit utilization certificates to the ministry.[81] In September, Union Minister of State for Social Justice and Empowerment Maneka Gandhi blacklisted a number of dubious NGOs and put the details on her ministry's website.[82] In the beginning of October, Minister of State for Home Vidyasagar Rao told the media that NGOs had received foreign contributions amounting to Rs 3402 crore last year and the government was considering a legislation to regularize use of foreign contributions by NGOs.[83] In mid-October, the National Human Rights Commission was reported to be 'contemplating serious action against' fake human rights groups.[84] At the end of October, in a PIL claiming that more than Rs 7500 crore released as government grants to over 30,000 NGOs had not been accounted for, the Delhi High Court directed the union government not to release any more grants to NGOs until they produced utilization certificates for previous grants.[85]

For a deeper insight into the issues underlying such events, let us digress a bit to consider what came to be called the Sahyog episode. In Almora, then part of Uttar Pradesh and now part of the hill state of Uttaranchal, an NGO called Sahyog brought out a booklet titled 'AIDS *aur hum*' ('AIDS and us') in September 1999. Funded by the McArthur Foundation, Sahyog, on the basis of 'research' consisting of 'interviews and focus group discussions', had brought out the booklet 'to enhance awareness about AIDS'.[86] It reproduced 'comments and observations of those interviewed on sexual practices and customs prevalent in the Almora region'.[87] Later Sahyog said it had 'quoted people verbatim to make the report authentic' and 'in any case, the material was meant for a select audience, that of NGOs and policy-makers'.[88] But not-so-select subjects of the 'scurrilous "research"' got to see it and did not take at all kindly to the 'graphic literary style' in which it made sweeping statements about widespread sexual promiscuity, homosexuality and incest in the region.[89] The research was labelled offensive, obscene and downright pornographic.[90] They said it was an attack on the culture of the hills, meant to spoil the image of the region for foreign funding.[91] In April 2000, all hell broke loose.[92] An 'irate mob' attacked Sahyog's offices on 20 April. The police sealed the offices, confiscated copies of the booklet and arrested eleven staff members and trainees—five for 'breach of peace' and six on more substantive charges of 'obscene publications' and 'public mischief'. The sub-divisional magistrate increased the bail amounts for the former. The Almora Bar Association announced that no one should represent the accused. Almora and Ranikhet remained closed for two days as a mark of protest. On April 22, a show cause notice was issued to Sahyog. Its landlords asked Sahyog to vacate their property. An apology and withdrawal of the booklet on April 26 was of no avail. On May 1 the Allahabad High Court rejected application for bail. On May 4 the four men in judicial custody were handcuffed and paraded through the market along with the women. On May 9 the National Security Act was invoked on four members of Sahyog. In an uncharacteristic show of unity, local politicians as well as local NGOs and eminent citizens all condemned the booklet and the NGO. On May 17 the issue was raised in the state assembly through an adjournment notice and, 'rising above party lines', members 'expressed anguish' over the 'objectionable report'.[93]

What, perhaps, drew national attention to the episode was the intervention of NGOs from outside the region. Soon after members of Sahyog had been arrested, NGOs in Delhi and Lucknow started meeting to 'condemn the police action' and rushing to Almora to lobby for their release.[94] Later, several NGOs demonstrated outside UP Bhawan in Delhi and presented a memorandum to the Uttar Pradesh governor to protest the invoking of the National Security Act.[95] For days there was a spate of edit-page articles in national newspapers.[96] All these conceded that (i) Sahyog had muffed up on its 'research' and reporting and (ii) it reflected poorly on its credentials that after years of 'working' it hardly had any local support. A few (not written by NGO-walas) were unconditionally critical on these counts, but the rest, having said this, hastened to add that what was done to Sahyog was far worse than what was done by Sahyog.[97] This argument hinged primarily on 'police excesses' and on the 'human rights' and 'civil liberties' of Sahyog (and was most succinctly presented by an eminent PIL lawyer, complete with legal precedents against denial of bail, handcuffing, denial of legal services, preventive detention, etc.).[98] The authors putting forth this argument were especially upset that the harassment of Sahyog continued even after it had apologized and had offered to withdraw the booklet (which, according to the eminent lawyer, was the 'equivalent of a self-imposed forfeiture order').[99] Commenting that everyone makes mistakes and that Sahyog had learnt from its, they said the way in which Sahyog workers had been treated— like 'goondas, porn-pushing criminals and, to top it all, as a security risk and threat to the nation after being handcuffed, humiliated and jailed'—did not augur well for the morale of NGOs.[100] Many felt Sahyog had been made a scapegoat at a time when considerable flexing of political muscle was going on with statehood for Uttarakhand imminent and that the 'public protest' was 'carefully organized and orchestrated' with the entire local political spectrum and civil society 'ill-disposed towards Sahyog' and the local media campaigning against it for a month before events had taken this nasty turn.[101] The articles even said that had the booklet not been about AIDS (or rather sex) and had the region not seen a high degree of mobilization against 'outsiders' as part of its statehood movement, this wouldn't have happened.

Be this as it may (or may not), the unsavoury Sahyog episode, even though it happened in the hills and not in a city, did throw up some general, serious and fundamental questions about the competence of NGOs in their chosen areas of work and the accountability of NGOs to their chosen constituencies.

■

A third issue relating to the role of NGOs, namely, the precise definition of their role in the larger set of 'development' roles, also continued to simmer on a backburner. Not too long ago, governments had begun to solicit the support of NGOs in development activities. Since then NGOs have come a long way from delivering to disparaging to designing to determining interventions.

The year 2000 also saw our governments turning to NGOs for all sorts of help. In the capital, for instance, in January, the government gave up trying to improve the running of government-run homes for beggars and juveniles and decided to hand over their management to NGOs.[102] Then it decided to let NGOs operate from government-run schools and also asked corporates to chip in with an awareness campaign through 'both audio-visual and print media' to help with the constitutional commitment to universalizing primary education.[103] (Somehow, in this spirit of informal bhagidari, it did not think of asking corporate-owned private schools to share infrastructure with ill-equipped government schools in the spirit of the formal land lease conditions they had signed.) In March, with no immediate possibilities for augmenting water supply in sight, the government roped in an NGO to create awareness (through RWAs and, of course, with support of government engineers) on water conservation and rain water harvesting.[105] In May, 'in a radical departure from the existing practice', Delhi police even asked NGOs (seven, to begin with, including one started by a senior police officer) to help them in the investigation of rape cases.[105] In June, an NGO 'conceptualized' Sheila Dikshit's bhagidari workshop for RWAs. In August, states were asked to utilize the services of NGOs to ensure inclusion of disability data in the census.[106] In September, Delhi Health Minister A.K. Walia at an NGO-organized 'Perfect Health Mela' (in which the Delhi government put up more than thirty stalls) 'encouraged NGOs to enter into the arena of health awareness'.[107] (In June, about seventy NGOs had already participated in Walia's 'Family Health Awareness Fortnight' for slum dwellers.)

It does appear that NGOs have become quite indispensable for the government as it goes about delivering, especially to the underprivileged, services it is mandated to deliver. Why, there are even agencies of government that deal with people only through NGOs.[108]

Of course, NGOs were do-gooding even without being asked to by the government. An NGO was going to build a centre in South Delhi for mentally handicapped children with Japanese funds and another, likewise, was going to provide basic education as well as vocational training to poor children in West Delhi.[109] One was going to set up 'the city's first pay-and-stay old age home for middle-class senior citizens'.[110] Several new and old NGOs, singly or jointly, with or without school-children and celebrities, were planting trees and saying 'no' to polybags.[111] And many, many NGOs had added to their collection of 'issues' (or had been started with) the artistically twirled red ribbon (indicating support for AIDS awareness) that was attracting perhaps the biggest bags of funding ever.

And, of course, NGO doings were not limited to delivering services. (In any case, as any NGO 'activist' knows, service delivery is actually about social justice and empowerment.) NGOs were also blowing the whistle on government inaction (such as through previously mentioned PIL seeking removal of industries, slums and litter, etc.) and action (such as through protests against relocation of industries and slums, revival of a waste incinerator, etc.). [112]

On the proactive front they were doing research to see what the government was unable to see. Being action oriented, NGO research priorities lie to some extent in areas where funding for further work is available. This is perfectly fine, provided it does not end up in selective reporting to improve funding prospects. This, for instance, is what was widely alleged about Sahyog's research and, indeed, appears to be not uncommon in research on possibilities connected with the very funded and very mysterious HIV virus. Just before Sahyog reported its research on AIDS possibilities in hill communities, a Delhi NGO reported its research on AIDS possibilities in the Wazirpur industrial area. [113] The emphasis was on 'possible impact of the HIV/AIDS patients in the workplace in terms of labour wages and cost, employment security and discrimination, etc.' [114] Actually, in Wazirpur, the study found no impacts of HIV/AIDS for the simple reason that it did not find any HIV/AIDS. But, undeterred, it went ahead to study the 'possible impact' of possible HIV/AIDS. The 'survey findings' were, in good measure, by way of unsubstantiated gossip on who thought who was having sex with whom and how often. These opinions were 'reported' in anecdotal Sahyog-style, projecting Wazirpur as a dirty little, naughty little place. The report was discussed at a round table meeting attended by representatives of trade unions, the ILO, academicians, women's groups and other NGOs. Leading national dailies reported on it with headlines like 'Wazirpur industrial area on the brink of an AIDS disaster', 'A crisis waiting to happen' and 'National policy on HIV demanded'. Of course, in the absence of any usable empirical data in the 'study', the round table could hardly have come to any informed conclusions. Participants concluded what was needed (as always for everything) was to have a national policy, to call on the chief minister, to organize community meetings, to prepare campaign material, etc. As an 'immediate' strategy they felt it would be a good idea for employers to distribute free condoms with salaries.

Of course, NGO research is not limited to such work. In mid-2000 there was a path-breaking study in which volunteers from several NGOs came together under the aegis of an international NGO to spend several nights counting and interviewing the homeless in Delhi. Around the same time a forum of eight organizations was taking a critical look at the Master Plan for Delhi that was officially due for revision.

Based on their experiences with service delivery and their criticism of government and their research, NGOs were also engaging (besides in serious seminaring) in designing comprehensive interventions. In January, Sheila Dikshit launched 'a unique project which aimed to develop, test and demonstrate a new approach to urban development and improve quality of life in slums by involving people's participation' in Delhi.[115] The project, Promoting Linkages for Urban Sustainable Development (PLUS), initiated by an international NGO (with Indian expertise mainly in rural interventions), involved a group of Delhi NGOs and hoped to cover thousands of slum clusters in the city over the next five years.[116] Naturally, it started in a few 'pilot' slums. In April, a Town Enrichment Action Movement (TEAM) Project—a joint initiative of the United Nations Development Programme (UNDP), the British High Commission and an NGO—was launched in Gurgaon. The synergy purportedly happened since Haryana has 'a large number of children out of schools' and 'female literacy as low as 41 per cent' and since 'getting children out of work and into schools, with a special focus on the girl child, is a high priority for UNDP'.[117] The project hoped to create 'necessary momentum' for enrolment of all children into schools, as well as addressing 'issues such as provision of a platform for local NGOs and industry to join hands'.[118] Naturally, it started with one slum. In the coup in this category, in June, the forum of eight organizations, with their fresh insight into master planning, convened a convention inaugurated by Sheila Dikshit and concluded it by giving themselves the mandate to prepare a 'people's Master Plan'. By November, this forum (by now comprising forty organizations) had already put together some sort of a draft and had forwarded some suggestions to the DDA.[119] In March 2001, this forum co-convened with the MCD's Slum Wing another meeting between NGOs, slum residents, politicians and the adviser dealing with slums in the Planning Commission. At the end of a day of acrimonious blame trading and anger venting it was decided that the Planning Commission would consult the forum convenor before finalizing the Commission's report on slums.[120] Also by March 2001 the NGO that had studied the homeless in Delhi had drafted, on the request of the government, national schemes for the homeless and had also been invited to contribute in this matter to the Tenth Plan document being prepared by the Planning Commission.[121]

The Planning Commission, incidentally, was made the 'nodal agency' for NGOs in March 2000.[122] Obviously NGOs were flying high.

■

Let us pause in this account of the ascent of civil society in general and NGOs in particular to reflect on how this came about. After all, opportunities to engage in citywide interventions or a piece of action in the Planning Commission don't normally come knocking on the doors of even the most committed activists or brilliant professionals in billion-strong India. But they do come knocking on the doors of certain sections of civil society in a process driven not just or necessarily by commitment or capacity but by 'civil politics' involving, much like electoral politics between elections, some mobilizing at the bottom and a lot of manoeuvring at the top.

Most big league NGOs also have big time clout. The chief minister launching a citywide slum project to be implemented by NGOs that were till then working in non-slum interventions or were even non-existent without so much as spelling out how this connected to the government agencies duly mandated for taking care of slums in the capital is just one example. Besides, at launches of their interventions and inaugurations of their seminars, NGOs flex political muscle by 'honouring' politicians and bureaucrats for working for the people. (In June 2000, for instance, the Rotary Club of Bangalore conferred a Paul Harris Fellowship on the chief minister of Karnataka in recognition of his 'service to the State'.)[123] Lately there has also been a trend of NGOs bringing their 'community' to meets where politicians and bureaucrats sit on the other side of the table on the dais, almost as if

NGOs were liaison agencies between the people and their governments.

This subtle politicization of civil society is matched by the NGO-ization of government. Government increasingly turning to NGOs for all sorts of things is just the manifestation of this. Individual politicians and even political parties have been floating NGOs. (In October, for instance, it was reported that the RSS had set up an NGO to avail government funding.)[124] And the 'movement' of bureaucrats—who know best the 'intricacies involved in actually getting access to funding'—from the government sector to the non-government sector is reminiscent of the movement in the 1980s of technology graduates to postgraduate management courses for enhanced career prospects.[125] (Two of Delhi's best-known NGOs, for instance, are 'owned' by senior police officials. Both were involved in the survey of the homeless in which, incidentally, police brutality featured as the most widely reported problem.)[126]

When politicians and bureaucrats play favourites on awarding tenders or buying arms, they are condemned for being corrupt. But when they play favourites with NGOs or other civil society bhagidars they are applauded. The Tehelka expose using hidden cameras to show who takes money in defence deals shook the nation in March 2001. But so many pictures openly taken and splashed in newspapers showing bureaucrats, politicians, donors, NGOs and the private sector sharing in odd and changing alliances, so many platforms to discuss the plight of the poor have never stirred us. This is only because in such circumstances money does not directly change hands, and 'social work' is pious and by global reckoning civil society is very fashionable. But all this is still about playing favourites and civil politics, and therefore has serious implications for the ethics of governance, more so since civil politicians are not tied down by strings of accountability that still connect electoral politics, howsoever murky, to the people.

Ascendancy of civil society has also had a more direct impact on quality of urban development. Old-fashioned urban (or any) development recognizes three broad, equally important roles—planning, implementation and monitoring. While it expects all development actors to synergize based on their inherent strengths, they are expected to contribute primarily to particular areas.

Planning is best led by trained professionals because they have the requisite expertise and the objectivity needed to keep longer term objectives and wider perspectives in focus. Implementation is best led by agencies of government because they have greater wherewithal as well as, theoretically, greater accountability. Monitoring is best led by grassroots organizations because they have a greater grip on ground reality to see if intended benefits are accruing or if adjustments in planning or implementation are needed. Of course everyone is expected to work together. Planning must take into account implementation constraints and monitoring feedback. Implementation must take into account explicit as well as implicit intentions of plans as well as areas where implementation has to be shared—not so that government can abdicate responsibility but because grassroots organizations are better suited to certain tasks. Monitoring and evaluation must provide timely and constructive support to implementation and feedback for planning.

In Contemporary Urban Development the lines separating these roles have become blurred. Professionals (being, except in individual cases, least political) are becoming increasingly marginalized in planning. Government agencies (being government agencies) are surviving but becoming increasingly wilful in implementation. Civil society (being currently most fashionable) is usurping other roles without having the inherent strengths needed and at the cost of the monitoring role that it is most suited to.

As an example of loss in planning quality consider the national schemes for the homeless which were being drafted by NGOs in March 2001. These included schemes for temporary community shelters, crisis centres, drug deaddiction, etc., but not housing (though the campaign was called 'Aashray Adhikar Abhiyan' or Housing Rights Campaign). These 'priorities' for national schemes were based on the findings of research in Delhi. That housing was not a priority for the homeless was a very significant finding which would have sounded a loud alarm to any professional researcher. If the homeless do not want housing, we are overestimating housing shortages. If they do and are not mentioning it, we need to understand why. In this case one did not have to look beyond research design for the reason for the missing response. The survey had elicited priorities through a single unprompted question on problems faced at sleeping places (which returned responses like police brutality), although useful information on such matters requires many direct and indirect questions. Also only 690 persons had been interviewed out of 52,765 that the study had counted and these were entirely randomly selected. This, by any standard, was a rather inadequate sample. The very well-meaning researchers (volunteers who actually spent whole nights on the survey) were obviously very moved by the very visible distress of the homeless. But a heart that melts at the sight of the problem is not quite a substitute for a head that can come up with real solutions. Meanwhile, schemes that speak of 'shelters' and 'half-way homes' to meet the immediate needs of the homeless carry the real danger of diverting attention from the urgency of providing proper housing for them. And schemes that highlight drug addiction among the homeless carry the danger of erroneously connecting homelessness and drug abuse in the minds of others.

As an example of loss of quality in implementation consider any 'citywide' scheme by any NGO. These tend to supplant rather than supplement less glamorous government efforts. What is worse is these NGO initiatives themselves seldom move beyond 'pilot' phases.

As an example of neglect of monitoring responsibilities consider the forum of forty organizations working on a people's Master Plan for Delhi. Their presentations at their 'meeting' in March 2001 as also the leaflet they circulated in V.P. Singh's rally on 27 February suggested they were not opposed to the provisions of the Master Plan, only to the fact that these had not been implemented.[127] It was not really clear why they wanted to make an alternative Master Plan when they found the Plan prepared by planners not too bad after all. More importantly, it was not clear why they had not used their insight into the pro-people provisions of the Plan in order to get those implemented rather than stake a claim to prepare another plan. Why had they not demanded at any point since 1990, when the revised Plan had come into force and the matter of relocation of industries was already being heard by the supreme court, that its provisions for non-conforming and new industries be implemented? Why had they not pointed to its low-income housing provisions all over the city while protesting distant relocation in Narela? Why had they not objected to the orders for removal of hawkers before implementation of Plan provisions for settling them? Did none of the forty organizations represent small industries, slums and hawkers? Then whom did they represent and what mandate did they have to prepare a 'people's plan' when they were not interested in implementation of the statutory Plan for the people? Would they monitor their—and only their—plan?

NGOs seem to have decided (rather unilaterally, one might add) that they—and they alone—will decide and invent and re-invent the wheel as often as they please. Professionals and government agencies are equally to blame for this as they have not taken their roles seriously enough to defend them. Government agencies, of course, are notoriously manned and wo-manned by those unwilling or unable to do more than that required by their job descriptions. The failure of the professional community—especially professional bodies which seem to have become politics-ridden forums for collective action for individual good rather than individual action for collective good—to protest the marginalization of professions in the emergent development scenario is more unforgivable.[128]

∎

The foregoing is not to say that all NGOs, corporates, RWAs, etc., are wicked, but only to make the point that with no clarity on roles, we are looking development anarchy in the face. It is hardly surprising that even after years of greater civil society participation, reality has not changed very much for the urban poor. Systemically, 'non' government and government no longer seem as different as they were made out to be. Ratios of good to bad, efficient to inefficient, committed to corrupt are more or less similar in both. As are circumstances—including well-appointed offices and assorted freebies and the not uncommon absence of substantive grassroots understanding of problems or any real vision for solutions.

To say time and again that the politician–builder nexus or the donor–bureaucrat nexus or any other nexus is subverting an otherwise fine 'system' is an inaccurate oversimplification. What seems to be the case is that there is no 'system' any more and all the wicked nexuses are only manipulating anarchy. In cities, a central motif in such manipulation is the subversion of planned development (meant to benefit all) in the service of vested interests. And an inevitable consequence is the slumming of our cities.

Right to be Ostrich with Pet Red Herring

The greatest and most elegant of the rights of slum saviours is the

Right to be Ostrich with Pet Red Herring. Protests by commoners—through letters or phone calls (including urgent faxes and distress calls on their elected representatives' cellular phones)—are handled with stunningly simple silence. It is as though there were a 'do not disturb' sign outside the door behind which governance purportedly goes on. It is especially amazing how our elected representatives get away with constantly spending more time on themselves and one another than on us, except when they have to renew their mandate. Perhaps their bluff has not been called because a 'none of the above' option does not appear on the ballot paper and public ire only translates into anti-incumbency benefit for the next guy rather than into forfeiture of all security deposits in elections.

Government officials and professionals and other development *bhagidars* in civil society who do not derive their development mandate directly from the people are even freer to engage with people at will and be ostrich for the rest. Those in politics (including civil politics) are, of course, obliged to keep up some pretence of listening. But, naturally, they do not really have the time or the inclination to actually listen since they are more keen to be heard themselves. So, what they do is replace the 'do not disturb' sign with a diversion sign and let loose a pet red herring. The commoners are told the diversion is the real issue and the only way their problem—any problem—can be solved is for them to join hands with their saviours by attending a rally or joining some *manch* (platform) or bhagidari or some other esoteric initiative suggested by the saviour.

The ostrich syndrome is obviously difficult to document, as one knows of it only through one's own limited experiences and to it we shall return a bit later. The pet red herrings, on the other hand, are very public—almost like cine celebrities—and worthy of being commented upon in that vein. If there were to be a pet red herring awards night, the honours might be somewhat as follows.

The Hrithik Roshan award for the most savvy and rapid ascent from debut to super-stardom would go to IT. Of course, we all love IT and there is no doubt that IT is a great help. But in state after state our elected representatives have bought themselves laptops and logged on and would now like us to wait with them for IT to solve all our problems. That's what brings IT to this award function. The message from Andhra Pradesh—one of our original cyber states—seems to be: 'Never mind if our farmers are committing suicide; our development indicators on laptop purchases, internet connections, software development and hardware production are very buoyant and the donors are very impressed.' The message from Madhya Pradesh— very happening on e-governance—seems to be: 'Never mind if we closed a couple of schools and blew up a sanatorium, our website on education is raising lots of funds and the IIM will take us further on the IT expressway. See, we've even managed an international award for our Gyandoot e-governance project in less time than it takes to troubleshoot hardware.' The message from Delhi—the new kid on the IT block—seems to be: 'So what if our school buildings are collapsing and our children don't get their jerseys on time, we've all bought our laptops and we are even installing computers in some of our schools. We don't have any idea of the exact numbers of polluting industries, slums, illegal farm houses, etc., but once our GIS gets going it will give you all the data at the click of a mouse. No, we don't know what is the GIGO principle.'[129]

The Amitabh Bachchan award for evergreen lifetime super-stardom getting shadier with age would go to Environment. Of course, we all care for The Environment. But most of us have this uncomfortable feeling that The Environment has been made into a convenient term to push other agendas—a worthy nominee for a red herring award. The message is pretty clear: We are a developing country, so please don't dwell on impractical things like cleaner fuel or industrial waste sites or ground water levels. Please appreciate we are planting trees wherever we can and with whoever will join us. No, we did not know that space amounting to another earth is required for the number of trees needed if nothing else is done to save The Environment. And no, we have never actually said grass is more important than cows.

The Asha Bhonsle award for enduring versatility would go to Good Governance. Of course, we all desperately want Good Governance. But what we are getting is a double-speaking red herring. The Delhi government claims to be plagued by a multiplicity of agencies but wants to set up new agencies at the drop of a hat, such as under its new slum policy, its plans for villages, etc. Many municipal agencies do not find the time to use up budget allocations but are always short of funds. Illegal developments are demolished in the name of 'discipline' and condoned in the name of 'humaneness' or 'pragmatism' in the same place at the same time. And so on.

The Govinda award for popular cinema without lasting impact would normally go to whoever manages the greatest rally tally, but for 2001, in just the first quarter, Gujarat's builder–politician nexus and Bangaru Laxman on the Tehelka videotapes have set fairly high standards.

The Mani Ratnam award for slick direction would go to International Awards. Without being armed with their international trophies many might not have managed to gun down whistle-blowers (armed only with evidence of ground realities and/or an eye for the large picture) and the red herring film industry would be history.

There are also other pet red herrings. Soon after Tehelka.com released its videotape of the BJP president accepting a wad of currency notes (allegedly for a defence deal), Congresswoman Renuka Chaudhary got on television and coyly said, among other things, that voters had got what they deserved. Obviously she was part of a small minority that had failed to notice that for quite some time voters have not been getting what they deserve. (Unless, of course, she meant a Congress president doing the same might have looked better on television.) In Indore's celebrated slum project fake success is professionally attributed to community participation and real failures to the community in the same breath. Obviously promoters of the project have not figured out you can't have your cake and eat it too—not for long, in any case. After the Sahyog episode, Sahyog members said they were victims of small-town mentality. Obviously they had forgotten that being in a small town was part of the trade-off they had willingly made for being well funded and in a balmy climate. Friends of Sahyog were concerned about the 'rights' of Sahyog that people had infringed. Obviously it did not occur to them that if the 'rights' of NGOs need to be defended against the people whose rights NGOs are supposed to be protecting and whose interests they are supposed to be serving, we must be skating on terribly thin ice. Such red herrings enrage rather than engage people, renew rather than divert attention. They are forgettable extras that will never make it to any red herring awards night.

So let us turn to ostriches. The rest of this is in first person because, as mentioned, ostrich sightings are limited to one's own experiences and those of friends. And—to balance the seemingly anti-NGO tirade of a bit earlier—I recount here only non-NGO experiences.

■

In October 1998, Indore's slum project bagged the Aga Khan Award for Architecture (AKAA). This was the second time (after Aranya in 1995) that a project for the poor in Indore had won the AKAA, the profession's highest—or at least best-known—award.

In December 1998, at the fifteenth national convention of the Indian Institute of Architects (IIA) in Visakhapatanam, I was an invited speaker. My presentation—made to architects from around the country—included slides of Indore's slum project and an appeal to IIA to do something to draw attention to the tragic truth.[130] A promo and lunch sponsored by the same sponsor followed my presentation. I suspect everyone soon forgot my presentation.

A year later I learned IIA's sixteenth national convention was to be held in Indore on 25–26 December 1999. By then I had shown my slides of both the AKAA winning projects in Indore in a number of architecture classrooms and was working with Jhuggi Basti Sangharsh Morcha (JBSM), a group of individuals and organizations in Indore's slums. I saw the forthcoming convention as a significant whistle-blowing opportunity and got in touch with IIA to ask if they would visit the AKAA winning projects, and with JBSM to suggest they approach delegates for professional support.

On 9 December I received an e-mail from the convention organizers saying they would visit Aranya. However, in Indore on 24 December, after several phone calls, I got the distinct impression that no such visit had been scheduled. On 25 December I sat outside the convention in protest and distributed a flier I had got printed the previous night.[131] Some reporters, after reading it, came and told me they had also raised the matter at IIA's press conference on 23 December. They took it up again in the inaugural session. In the afternoon a few members of JBSM came and circulated a polite little appeal to delegates to visit the winning slum project and suggest solutions to the problems created by it. IIA ignored us all.

On 26 December, a few of us with placards and parodies of film songs demonstrated outside a different exhibition venue (where delegates spent three hours looking at tiles, jacuzzis and suchlike) to protest IIA's refusal to see the AKAA winning projects even after being requested (and even as it was deliberating a 'Vision beyond 2000' at its convention). Drummers hired by IIA were instructed to play loudly each time we raised slogans. We went inside, where delegates were having breakfast (hosted by the builder-owner of the venue). Architects from IIA Indore threw us out and other architects watched us being thrown out. Less than a dozen of the 500 'distinguished delegates' bothered to speak with us and fewer bothered to go and see their profession's most celebrated projects.

IIA nevertheless continued to wax eloquent through the press and in 'technical papers' (in its convention souvenir on the convention theme of 'Vision beyond 2000') about social responsibility, the urban poor, etc. Perhaps it had its reasons for not speaking with the 'poor' standing in flesh and blood outside. Perhaps it did not realize that the image of the profession was built not through talks inside convention halls but through actions outside them. Maybe it missed the fact that perhaps for the first time in its history its convention had been noticed by the host city. And if the press coverage (other than its own releases) is anything to go by, the majority in the city may well have written off the profession just as it has written off the profession's most honoured projects. From where I stood in Indore in December 1999, IIA looked less like a professional institute and more like a club of people with similar professional qualifications.

In January 2000 I wrote to the Council of Architecture (CoA), the statutory body that is supposed to regulate the architectural profession in the interest of society. I asked about implications of architects working in slums even as their code of professional conduct does not make them accountable to 'beneficiaries' who are not paying clients. I also asked about implications (on professional image and quality) of IIA's style of functioning, as sadly demonstrated in Indore. I got no answers. The abbreviation CoA could also, I believe, well expand to Consummate ostrich A-class!

■

In August 2000, in support of the local protest against discharge of patients from the TB sanatorium in Indore, I started an e-mail campaign. This was not a sign-and-forget campaign. Many who joined it responded to updates with ideas and suggestions. When, for instance, a leading national daily reported that Satish Pathak living at the station 'spoke like a rehearsed actor' and, days after Bhagwandas's death, that 'IIM Indore was being killed by the sanatorium', many wrote letters in protest to the editor.

When the IIM director set the date of the board meeting of the institute as the deadline for the state to settle the 'land dispute', those who were part of the e-mail campaign decided to write a letter to the board members. The joint letter, including views of about thirty professionals (including a number of very senior ones) from the fields of architecture/planning, management and healthcare made several points. One, it was a matter of concern that IIM's aggressive stand was being seen as the cause for the distress of the sanatorium patients and maybe even the unfortunate death of a patient. Two, IIM should lead from the front in resolving this conflict instead of walking away from it (especially in view of its claims of wanting to contribute to local and regional concerns). Three, 193.5 acres was in excess of what was really needed for IIM Indore since fully established IIMs had much less as also what was required by the design scheme for IIM Indore itself. Four, a design solution could be found wherein the sanatorium and IIM could coexist without hindrance to each other and, furthermore, investing in upgrading (rather than in destroying) the vintage sanatorium would go a long way in lending credibility to IIM's social concerns. Five, IIM should not take a rigid stand against occupying a site in proximity to a sanatorium as there is no medical basis to suggest it poses any threat to the well-being of others. Six, if IIM was opposed to the idea of having a campus near a sanatorium, in all fairness, it should accept an alternative site since the sanatorium—also a public institution—was there first. Seven, IIM should take the lead in ensuring this conflict was resolved through informed participation and to the reasonable satisfaction of all stakeholders and not be seen as blackmailing the state to its own advantage as that was not in the spirit of democracy or in the spirit of responsible management. This letter was sent via e-mail or fax to most board members to their offices in various cities and to Indore so as to reach them all before the meeting on 3 October. Not one of the board members responded.

In the matter of IIM and the sanatorium there were other ostriches as well. After the discharge of patients, the death of Bhagwandas, the stay being vacated on 17 October and demolition becoming imminent, and when the demolition started on 18 October, appeals were sent to some of the highest offices in the country. But all the king's horses and all the king's men could not— and did not—stop the sanatorium from being demolished. Simultaneously, and in between, requests were also made to leading newspapers to take a look. Besides the one to which we had to write protest letters, only one national daily reported the matter after sending a correspondent to Indore at the end of August.[132] A premier news channel did air on 25 September footage it had taken a month earlier. The national media was obviously too pre-occupied with details of a prime ministerial knee replacement and a union ministerial post-mortem diagnosis to be concerned about ordinary mortals like Satish Pathak or Bhagwandas or Raju or Om Prakash or Santosh or a sanatorium meant for the likes of them.

Then on 20 October, two days after the sanatorium had been dramatically demolished, a national daily had a 'story' from its Bhopal correspondent titled 'M.P. HC clears land for IIM at Indore'. This 'news item' did not even mention the demolition. It reported that 'the October 16 judgement has proved to be a boon for TB patients too. In place of the demolished sanatorium, Indore will get a National Institute for Chest Diseases'.[133] It further suggested that 'the NGOs who espoused the TB patients' cause in the IIM–sanatorium row' were quite satisfied with the judgement and quoted one 'Ramadhan, a social activist' in this regard using excerpts from the memorandum with which the e-mail campaign had started. There was no Ramadhan on the e-mail campaign. There was no Ramadhan amongst the petitioners whose case had been dismissed on 16 October. Neither the petitioners nor those on the e-mail campaign were satisfied. I had painstakingly kept this newspaper informed about the developments for nearly two months through no less than ten faxes starting with the memorandum at the end of August to an obituary for the sanatorium just the previous day. I now had four questions for the editor. One, how did their correspondent file a report on a controversial court judgement without speaking with the petitioners? Two, how did he use, late in October, material circulated at the end of August without confirming the contents from the source? Three, who was 'Ramadhan, a social activist' and what was the validity of his opinion? Four, how could a leading mainstream newspaper print a report from a regional correspondent even when it was contrary to the views received at exactly the same time directly from those who would normally have been the 'sources' for the same? Through several faxes and phone calls I asked these questions for the next three days. Later I was sent a 'rejoinder' from the correspondent that had his views on related and unrelated matters but no answers to my questions. Twice again I sent faxes. Then I just gave up.

So many like the eighty-six-year-old TB sanatorium that passed away in Indore on 18 October 2000 are so obviously caught on the wrong side in the war between the rich and the poor, the new and the old, the glamorous and the hapless, those who matter and those who do not. Litigation, demonstrations, protest letters, e-mail campaigns, appeals and whatever else to have their viewpoint be heard seem like home remedies that cannot possibly cure the terminal ailment that has turned systems meant to respond or redress into uncaring ostriches. That development processes have come to ignore so many so consistently has serious implications for planned development, which is meant to leave equitable room for all. Anything else directly or indirectly only abets slumming.

■

One of the oldest and loudest of my whistles is reserved for the maddening universalization of the slum upgrading paradigm. It is in this area that I have also encountered the most stubborn ostriches. I was senior consultant on one of the first comprehensive assessment studies in India of some of the largest slum upgrading interventions made till then. I have, since, written against slum upgrading in professional journals (which are hardly read by anyone) and in newspapers and talked against it in professional colleges to students (who can, naturally, not influence decision making). But, despite my efforts, I have not found an opportunity to really engage in professional debate. I'll mention here just four ostriches in this matter.

First, a premier research and training institution. During 1997–99, HSMI prepared on behalf of the union ministry the Draft National Slum Policy through what was touted as a widely consultative process. Earlier I had been a consultant to and, for over a year, a Senior Fellow in HSMI. Later, I must have been amongst the very few to send extensive comments on the draft to the ministry and HSMI. To date I only have an unofficial copy of the policy and at no point did I receive a response to or even acknowledgement of my comments. To date, therefore, I have no idea (and I suspect neither do the 'policy makers') on what conceptual or empirical basis could the upgrading paradigm have been extrapolated into national policy. In June 2000, when A.K. Walia mounted an AIDS campaign in Delhi's slums, I wrote to the various authors of the slum policy—which had drawn this luscious connection first inasmuch as the only 'disease' mentioned by name in their slum policy was, if you please, 'STD/HIV'.[134] My former 'boss' in HSMI actually called back this time, but only to say that the policy was just a document which they had prepared because the ministry had asked them to. Well, well.

HSMI is part of India's premier techno-financial habitat organization, HUDCO. We now learn there are some sorts of inquiries going on against V. Suresh and against the two chairmen before him. V. Suresh is someone I have known personally and he was highly regarded in the institution when I was its employee. He had not become CMD then. In April 1999 when I was making a presentation on Indore's pro-poor interventions—including, besides the celebrated slum project, others that HUDCO had been widely celebrating such as Aranya, etc.— at the Institute of Town Planners India, Suresh was giving the 'keynote address'. He referred to 'successful' interventions in Madhya Pradesh and held up a spiral-bound document to say HUDCO was working on a slum policy. The chairperson of the meeting, who knew the content of my presentation, passed him a slip of paper saying I had a different view. Suresh made some flattering remarks about my professional credentials and said he could not stay to hear me, but 'to answer my burning question' he assured me everything in Indore 'can be replicated'. I followed him outside to tell him *that* precisely was my fear and to beg him to spare some time for a reality check. Later, I wrote to him about Indore. Still later I wrote to him about the slum policy. In July 2000 (when HUDCO was closely associated with the resettlement in Narela) I also met him about these matters. A much former CMD had also written to him about Indore after reading an article I had written. But the CMD of our premier habitat institution, instrumental not only in getting Indore's slum project globally celebrated but also in extrapolating it to national policy, remained too busy to substantively engage with one who had carried out its official impact study surveys and who had been consistently begging for its reconsideration ever since. He remained busy even after he visited the project in November

2000 along with the minister. Well, well.

Then there are the international agencies that wholeheartedly promote slum upgrading in third world cities. Besides giving feedback from my study in Indore to DfID, I subsequently wrote to all those who had been involved in celebrating it as a successful intervention through their various honours. Only one of them did not respond. Others said things like my information was very useful for the future award processes, they would be pleased to place in their archives any material I would like to send them, they would like to include me in their visit to their next award project, they had diplomatic immunity, etc. Well, well.

Lastly, I would like to mention the national media. When the Indore slum project won the AKAA, the national media reported on it widely, but not from Indore. Through October and November 1998 I kept asking newspapers, newsmagazines and TV channels that were eulogizing the winning project to please check out Indore, if only in the name of principled reporting. In March–April 1999, when there was a spate of summary slum evictions in Indore, I kept asking them to go and see what was happening in the purportedly slum-free city where a state tenure legislation was in place. Again in July–August 1999, when 'no-cost' schools were opened in community halls built under the celebrated slum project and other schools closed, I kept asking them to check out the shadow of the winning project as it grew longer. In December 1999, after the IIA refused to check out the winning projects, I asked the national media to check out the IIA as well. In 2000, after the Indore project had been veritably extrapolated into a draft national policy, I once again requested them to please take a look... Off and on I still keep asking because I believe the slumming of our cities is not so much a class issue as a corruption issue and the media has an important role to play in exposing the slumming scam. But obviously the media— at least the mainstream media—does not share my opinion.

The difficulty of drawing media attention to any issue without a politician, celebrity or at least an NGO in the foreground is becoming an especially worrying trend. Most of the slumming stories chronicled in this book made news. But still this book had to be written to chronicle them because they never made complete news. The slumming of our cities touches the lives of so many urbanites being informed by so many newspapers, newsmagazines and news channels that claim to tell, analyse and debate the whole truth. But in most of the cases chronicled here, the media has reported the truth as seen by the Big People and played ostrich regarding the truth as perceived by the Little People, although the latter is often the more 'real' truth.

■

The ostriches mentioned so far were all being so on high-profile interventions. Others playing ostrich on everyday next-door happenings also contribute to the slumming of our cities. The following are recent experiences from where I live, a flatted housing area called Vasant Kunj at the southern edge of Delhi, close to the Delhi Ridge, being developed since the mid-1980s by DDA for about 100,000 people.

As mentioned earlier, in May 2000 Jagmohan had trained his bulldozers on unauthorized additions in flats like these. The RWA of my pocket of flats (one of nearly thirty pockets of flats here) issued a circular. The circular said that in 'this hour of *crisis*' when we were all spending 'sleepless nights', the RWA was making all 'efforts to ensure that no demolitions take place in our colony'. I drew the RWA's attention to the fact that there were several like me who were not spending sleepless nights and did not see this as an hour of crisis. I reminded it that residents had unconditionally mandated it only to carry out routine cleaning, greening and securing activities and it had to seek our permission before making any other 'efforts' on our behalf. I suggested, instead of making any 'efforts', we might try and get a grip on the types of additions that were safe, acceptable to neighbours, etc., and ones that were not in order to inform a sensible process of modifying the law. Eventually, this is what happened at the instance of Jagmohan, except that RWAs, without consulting all the people they represented, decided that almost everything was a 'minor' change. Meanwhile, my RWA, in these wonderful bhagidari times, did not even respond to my comment. Here, then, was a microcosm of the larger 'debate' on unintended urban transformations that invariably ends in quick-fix amnesty schemes rather than in any sensible process of trying to distinguish between violations stemming from inadequacies in the law and ones stemming from the wilfulness of those violating them.

In January 2001, the Delhi Jal Board at the behest of our MLA, on the request of our RWA, began digging bore wells near my house. There is a ban on ground water tapping here—to protect ground water levels around the Ridge in the interest of the city and to protect us from catastrophic consequences of excessive ground water withdrawal. In the midst of winter, we were getting water only through tankers. Obviously the 'legal' water meant for Vasant Kunj was being diverted (the MLA perhaps knew where exactly, though the rest of us could shrewdly guess). Besides the 'illegality' of bore wells and its underlying environmental implications, I was also concerned about the quality of water coming out of them. An expert had told me that according to data from the Central Ground Water Authority (CGWA) sweet water in the area was available only at a depth of around 150 feet and further below was water which was not potable. The boring near my house seemed to be hitting water way below 150 feet. I kept asking everyone if we had special permission from CGWA and if we had tested the water. Everyone just seemed to find me a nit-picking imbecile and kept saying how we all needed some water and how the MLA was being so very helpful. I wrote to CGWA and after several calls and reminders finally received a response saying special permission had been given for four bore wells in all of Vasant Kunj. Eventually, with this special permission for four and a lot of help from our helpful MLA, dozens of bore wells were dug. Some residents got the water tested and found it laced with all sorts of things definitely injurious to our health. But in bhagidari, as we went around planting trees to establish our pro-environment credentials, we were thanking—not lynching—our MLA for being so kind as to help us dig illegal bore wells so that we could get non-potable water to drink while doing unspeakable damage to our environment by excessive ground water withdrawal in a duly notified critical area. But my 'concern for the environment' was easy to belittle. After all, I had never ever contributed to the onerous task of hiring, firing or supervising *malis* (gardeners) to mind our parks. Worse, on at least one occasion, I had actually supported some children who wanted a park to be left as a playground rather than be used for ornamental horticulture. My horrific track record on 'environment' was basis enough for my RWA to ignore my concern for it. And what happened to me for 'complaining' to the CGWA? I became a snitch and some of my neighbours even thought I should not get a share of the 'hard' water they had arranged through their hard work. Here, then, is an insight into the real nature of citizens' environmental and developmental concerns being nurtured through bhagidari.

Meanwhile, claiming benefits of bhagidari, the RWAs had also taken to picking out plum pieces of vacant land and saying 'we want'…hospital, college, fancy crafts market…even though Master Plan norms did not permit these for the number of people planned for in Vasant Kunj. The site for the hospital gifted to us in the bonhomie of bhagidari was very close to my house. As a planner, I considered it a singularly inappropriate site in terms of location and access, not to speak of hazardous hospital waste that we had been reading a lot about in the newspapers lately. Besides, there were (much better) planned sites for health facilities that had still to be developed in Vasant Kunj and I had a sneaky suspicion that DDA was delaying their development for speculative reasons. In November–December 1999 and January 2000 I wrote to DDA to ask if this and other (unplanned) bhagidari benefits were in accordance with the Master Plan and approved zonal and layout plans for the area. In February I got a terse reply saying the hospital was part of the approved plan. This was odd, considering the site fell in an area earmarked for green belt in the Master Plan, an area for which the zonal plan had not been prepared, an area not covered by the approved layout plan of Vasant Kunj. I was not told about the other bhagidari benefits, nor have I been able, despite requests, to get a copy of the (latest) approved layout plan(s). Here, then, was an example of populist interference with planned development through a 'nexus' between, well, everybody.

■

While RWAs of DDA flats which are ten to fifteen years old were managing well to corner more than what was due to them under the law (and in the process adding to long-term problems of urban stress), much older residents living in the Vasant Kunj area (not included in government's bhagidari with citizens) were having an entirely different experience. The meanest ostriches I encountered were during a 'slum' demolition. At 12.30 pm on 5 July 2000 a bulldozer and a large posse of policemen arrived in Rangpuri Pahari, a fifty-year-old 'slum' settlement just west of fifteen-year-old DDA-developed Vasant Kunj situated in an area earmarked for green belt in the Master Plan. For two-and-a-half hours residents were given to understand that the bulldozer was headed elsewhere. During this time, the cops had cold drinks and cigarettes at a local shop, housewives hospitably gave them cold water to drink and the 'visitors' amiably chatted with several residents. Suddenly at 3.00 pm the bulldozer started razing their homes. Residents pleaded for time to remove their belongings, but were only abused and beaten. The MLA was contacted but said he could not help as he could not contact the concerned officials. By 5.00 pm fifty houses at the southern end had been razed. V.P. Singh arrived afterwards and made calls to stop further demolitions.

I met residents of Rangpuri Pahari for the first time the next day and have come to know them well since. But I cannot possibly imagine what they would have felt that night as they stood around the rubble that was till hours ago all they had painstakingly built and collected over the years. But I know what I had felt when I heard about the demolition late that evening and called several people—in the DDA, the union ministry, the Delhi government, the Slum Wing—and everyone just said they had not ordered it and so there was nothing they could do. I felt sick. Barely six months ago the union government had brought out a draft slum policy clearly opposed to summary evictions. Barely six weeks ago the Delhi government had announced a slum policy promising no demolitions. The Slum Wing looks after listed slums (including this one). DDA earmarks land for resettlement and low-income housing (which it has not adequately done in Vasant Kunj) and was not meant to have or permit any 'schemes' here (the area being reserved for green belt). Barely a fortnight ago slum evictions in Mumbai had been suspended in the monsoons in view of earlier supreme court orders. Less than a fortnight ago Jagmohan had given illegal additions in flats in Vasant Kunj a reprieve during the monsoons. Even before I knew what the bulldozer and the police had done in Rangpuri Pahari, I knew they had no business being there under existing policy, etc. After I heard what they had done, I called up the National Human Rights Commission and to my immense and very pleasant surprise the Commission started an inquiry on 7 July. On 18 July, in response to my representation outlining the inconsistency between the demolition and current slum policies, etc., Jagmohan also granted written permission for reconstruction. But no one responded to the residents' requests for assistance or even clarity on the purpose of the demolition or future plans. In what was seen as an extremely callous response, Sheila Dikshit said, when residents went to meet her a week after the demolition, that they must have put the notices which must have been served to them in their pockets and forgotten. And a senior official in her government suggested that instead of asking the government for relief I might try taking 'them' to a gurudwara or dharamsala. In September, the Delhi government arrived with a World Bank team in Rangpuri Pahari to do a survey 'for their benefit'. The residents asked the reasons for such concern after the demolition. The officials asked, 'What demolition?' In February 2001, DDA started getting the soil on the land abutting this settlement tested. According to the plans being used by the surveyors, more flats were to be built here, although this scheme had no basis in the statutory Master Plan for several reasons. One, it fell in an area earmarked as green belt. Two, the amount of upper-income housing permissible under Master Plan norms in a residential area the size of Vasant Kunj had already been constructed and the 'housing backlog' was only by way of cheap plots. Three, in the spirit of Master Plan provisions for 'non-conforming' uses, such as the Rangpuri Pahari settlement which pre-dated not only Vasant Kunj but Delhi's Master Plan and DDA itself, integration of existing unplanned settlements was a priority over new development. But repeated letters from the residents of Rangpuri Pahari requesting cheap plots and objecting to eviction to make way for an 'unplanned' scheme (both with reference to the statutory Master Plan) elicited no response from the DDA (the custodian of the Master Plan).

By the first half of 2001, beginnings made by Rangpuri Pahari in the second half of 2000 had drawn several others into the effort to ensure planned development in Vasant Kunj. When, in January 2001, the lieutenant-governor of Delhi (also ex-officio chairman of DDA) ordered removal of hawkers, I told hawkers near my house about Master Plan provisions for them. By February 2001, nearly 400 hawkers from Vasant Kunj had written in groups to the lieutenant-governor, with copies to DDA, the police and municipal officials, requesting that spaces be earmarked for them in DDA markets, etc., as per statutory provisions and removal be held in abeyance in the meantime.

A group of slum students wrote to the dozen up-market schools in Vasant Kunj (in the context of land lease conditions requiring them to reserve free seats) to allow them use of their premises after school hours. When officials in the education department, whom students went to meet after the schools did not respond, said that if they were given such permission they would 'grab' the school facilities, the children wrote to the chief minister. They also wrote to the DDA requesting space for a playground in their municipal school, which is on a site that is half the size recommended in the Master Plan for a primary school.

Numerous flat residents also came to appreciate that there was a convergence between their interests and those of the 'others' in Vasant Kunj. They came to appreciate that it was in their interest that slum dwellers be settled here rather than resettled far away—not only because they provided domestic services, but also because otherwise land meant for them would go to more up-market and infrastructure-stressing uses. They came to appreciate that space for hawkers was in their interest—not only because hawkers provided cheap goods and services and, perforce, passed on costs of extortion on account of 'illegal' locations to customers, but also because local markets were otherwise becoming infrastructure-stressing non-local commercial areas. They came to appreciate that there was a synergy between the concern of slum students (rooted in violation of lease conditions relating to free seats) and their own concern about traffic chaos outside and commercialization of local schools (rooted in violation of lease conditions about local enrolment). Flat residents, through a number of RWAs as well as their federation, also began to engage with DDA to question departures from planned development.

Residents of village settlements that had been engulfed by the development of Vasant Kunj on their agricultural land began to ask DDA about implementation of Master Plan provisions which were meant to ensure their integration in the new development, including priority development of facilities for them on proximous sites.

What was shaping up in Vasant Kunj in the first half of 2001 was different from other 'struggles' relating to urban development in two salient respects. First, it was not about people asking for regularization of violations and, in the process, claiming that the law was bad, but about people requesting DDA to do its job of implementing the Master Plan. Second, it was not a 'class' struggle but a protest against the politics and corruption in development that is reducing planned development in public interest to real estate development on public land for profiteering resulting in slumming. Residents were engaging on different dimensions of subversion of the Master Plan—selling of local shopping space to big companies leaving local commerce on the roads, allotting of sites for local schools to big schools to the exclusion of local children, building of costly flats in place of developing cheap plots leading to proliferation of jhuggis, wilful unplanned schemes at the cost of necessary outstanding planned development and adding an unintended up-market population with no regard to the critical water situation. The commonality of purpose that the residents of flats, jhuggis and villages were seeing was demonstrating that planned development can provide the basis for a synergetic and conflict-free society. The synergy was demonstrating the connection between equity and carrying capacity concerns of planned development. The ostriches were of course ignoring all of this.

People wrote about their concerns to the vice-chairman of DDA (custodian of the Master Plan), to the lieutenant-governor (ex-officio chairman of DDA), to the urban development minister (head of the ministry in charge of DDA and a man known for his faith in the Plan) and to the chief minister (chairperson of the bhagidari scheme). But all the hype about public participation in planned development notwithstanding, their efforts cut no ice with anybody.

Ironically, also in the beginning of 2001, DDA's office for Master Plan revision was set up in Vasant Kunj (in a block of six flats, although Jagmohan had said only months ago that such misuse of DDA flats would attract cancellation of allotment for others). In effect, planners in charge of the planned development of Delhi were sitting right here in Vasant Kunj, perhaps the only place where public faith in the Master Plan, which had lately become a convenient whipping boy for all and sundry, was being so openly demonstrated. But they did not see it as necessary or desirable to draw useful and timely feedback on Plan implementation from those who lived right next to where they were working on revising the Plan.

Our elected representatives—a Congress MLA and a BJP councillor—were too busy with the politics of feudal favours, besides the passing-the-buck games between the Delhi government and the central government that are the bane of Delhi's governance, to engage on issues relating to planned development. With them, the going was much easier for those seeking unplanned development benefits (illegal boring, extra hospitals, etc.) or 'routine' interventions as favours (hawking licences on roads, renewal of brick paving, etc.). This sort of 'development' is easy to dole out, has instant impact that potentially adds to vote banks, and plenty of scope for adding to note banks. What so many people in Vasant Kunj on the other hand were asking for did not fit in with the governance games currently being played. It was a matter of right under existing law and, therefore, not amenable to reduction to political largesse. It pointed a finger at both governments for their role in subverting planned development and, therefore, not material for the blame-game. Also, it was being asked for without leaving space for anyone's favoured NGO or consultant or party worker to take credit (for themselves and their 'patrons') for the people's initiative. It called for a lot of work, a lot of firmness, a lot of self-discipline, a lot of democratic behaviour on the part of our representatives, which was, perhaps, too much to ask. After all, tall claims about decentralization and power to the people notwithstanding, our politicians prefer to be fairly feudal and very self-serving even (or, perhaps, especially) in the capital of the world's largest democracy. Quite understandably, our elected representatives steered quite clear of what was going on in their constituency vis-à-vis the Master Plan.

■

Competing interests in urban resources make planned development a fundamental *need* of urbanites, calling for a high degree of responsibility on the part of those in charge of urban governance. Unfortunately, the vast majority of our public servants and public representatives seem to consider the vast majority of urbanites 'inferior' and not worthy of serving and representing. Whatever they do for the people increasingly seems to be purely incidental to what they happen to be doing for themselves, even though it is invariably given the flavour of a favour. It is as though the school of urban governance drama were left with only two roles in its repertoire—the feudal patron and the stubborn ostrich. Unfortunately, a royal bird with long legs is a singularly inappropriate mascot for the type of urban governance system necessary to meet the fundamental needs of planned urban development in order to save our cities from slumming.

Epilogue

Writing on the Wall

Perhaps I am too cynical. Perhaps I over-react. Perhaps I lack the right attitude towards development. Perhaps I am an idiot. But I can still see—even without glasses.

I see tailors and wannabe tailors applauding one another for fashionably clothing the emperor, and the still naked emperor walking through the great CUD circus, bewildered and cold. I see Sickly Cows feeding on garbage and Fences eating grass as they mind meadows for milch cows and imported pigs. I see Big People piously pleading for the wrong rights they have given the Little People and righteously fighting for the wrong rights they have assumed for themselves. I see every monument to CUD standing on building blocks guaranteed to produce slummier cities and more and more people falling off the CUD expressway, watching askance the great CUD race continue in the name of those it has miserably failed. And I do not understand, nor has anyone been able to explain to me how, if I see what I see, is CUD so great. So I posit it is not.

Not being a proponent of CUD I do not have yet another 'original' theory for a new, improved model for urban development arising out of my limited understanding just to pander to my own desire to be original. I only suggest that since the path we have taken in the last few years does not seem to be going anywhere we want to, we should just get into reverse gear and reach a better point to trace a new path and face a changing world with different challenges. I only plead for restoring the correct rights, clearer responsibilities and, thereby, systemic sanity in development systems that seem to be hurtling at breakneck speed towards complete anarchy.

Not as a 'solution' but merely as an 'example' of imperatives logically arising out of the chaos chronicled in this book and out of possibilities already available in existing laws and policies, reproduced here is most of an informal note I had sent in early 2000 to a senior government official (who had asked for it in the context of critical comments I had been making through letters and newspaper articles about the DNSP, Indore, etc.).

The first thing is land. If we are the state we claim to be, we cannot allow the inequity of a majority of the population having to live in a measly proportion of land. Many things need doing, starting with taking a different view of 'public purpose' and 'greater common good'. (After all what can be greater than the majority population!) There just has to be land reservation for the poor in all layouts with very strict enforcement of the same. I personally feel exemplary punitive action for omissions on this count is called for.

I am convinced some land can also be found within existing layouts. It may sound bizarre but 'employees' housing can be sensitively designed in some unused, 'leftover' spaces in upper-income housing/other areas (where legal/policy provisions anyway required housing for city service personnel to have been ensured), 'employers' being residents/users of those (inefficient) layouts.

A related thought is on unutilized public land. If an agency has not used what it was meant to, must it get an 'extension' for continuing inefficiency/speculation/whatever, especially if its own 'employees' (including 'indirect' ones like coolies/hawkers on stations) live in slums?

Something must also be done to restrict inefficiencies in non-poor/non-slum developments so we can economize on all land rather than just keep downgrading plot sizes for the poor. I recall the National Housing Bank had come out with guidelines on these lines.

Also, we need to get serious about voluntary resettlement. Try asking slum dwellers to apply for reserved plots in new developments, 'employees' housing as above, etc., instead of shifting entire slums to 'planned' enclaves of the poor, which can never be truly 'integrated'. After such de-densification some existing slums may actually become 'tenable' for upgrading!

The second thing is planning and design. Right now we seem to be applying all our creativity to somehow making the poor fit into tiny units in both resettlement and low-income housing. This is a self-defeating exercise because all it leads to is a different kind of slums!

Over the years, professionals have glorified certain minimalist design paradigms without waiting to test their impacts. Sadly, these have been extrapolated into education and we have an entire crop of professionals who swear by them. I personally think those who wrote these Emperor's New Clothes fairy tales should quit—but that of course is just a fairy-tale ending!

On the other hand there are less pretentious low-income housing projects that don't look so impressive in drawings but have worked. Perhaps we need to 'replicate' these simpler options rather than all the fancy designer low-income housing that has failed at great cost. The Master Plan (as revised in 1990) also seems to think so!

The above also applies to low-cost/cost-effective construction technology.

The third thing is institutional aspects. Some transparency (and before that clarity) is needed on who's going to do what and when. At present the whole thing seems to be in the nature of a free-for-all, no-holds-barred sort of effort!

There just have to be measurable indicators for progress—and so there has to be a strategic plan, rather than just a policy. Also that must come from government agencies. Right now anyone seems to have the right to prepare an alternative slum strategy or even master plan. This is a sure recipe for anarchy—after all everybody has a noise level and a nuisance value.

NGOs must be involved, but cannot be allowed to call all the shots. Their strength is their grassroots ethos, which makes them great for monitoring and implementation (including project formulation). To let them take over policy and planning levels—to the exclusion of professionals—is justifiable only after stopping expenditure on professional education. At the rate we are going, we will welcome even open-heart surgeries by NGOs simply because they care! Also there are good and bad NGOs and we must distinguish between them. It is not enough to check accounts or otherwise assess 'activity'. We need to assess their 'impact'.

Elsewhere also, confusing of activity with impact must go. I hate to say this, but many 'professionals' in many premier agencies seem to have been reduced to 'babus' and 'babuains' in a job, not a vocation. The problem is partly personal but partly systemic. After all, performance nowadays is measured in terms of, say, number of times bottoms occupy chairs in training, number of publications in research, number of awards in projects, etc. Almost all heads of premier agencies I am familiar with spend all their time improving these 'performance indicators' of activity and no time on assessing impact or building a purposeful vision.

We also need to get much more serious about what we consider 'good practices' worthy of 'replication'. All big-time firms and agencies are too quick on the draw to glorify what they have done—and then there is no looking back. The Indore slum project is an extreme example but it is by no means the only one. The 'disconnect' between claims and ground realities is growing and this does not augur well. Systematic impact assessment has to be institutionalized. For starters, can we stop celebrating projects for the poor before they are completed/occupied and subjected to impact assessment, including user feedback? This is especially necessary because codes of professional conduct do not make professionals accountable to 'beneficiaries' who are not paying clients. And 'globalization' of the habitat agenda has made it incumbent upon agencies to competitively report 'best practices'.

Most importantly, urban development agencies have to make 'backlogs' a priority in master plans (many of which are due for revision in and around 2000). They must put all except the most necessary new development on hold till those who have missed the bus of planned development are taken on board. Fancy 'world-class' commercial complexes and flyovers for future traffic counts can wait a few years. But the majority in the city cannot be left to enter the new millennium without any share in the benefits of our half-century-old planned development. They have already waited too long and, as our president lately reminded us, their patience must be running out.

■

The problem is not with identifying what to do. The problem is with how to make it happen. And this is not about 'resource constraints' or 'technology constraints' or 'organizational constraints' or 'vested interests' or 'population excess' or other oft-flogged dead horses. This, in my opinion, is a problem arising from two fundamental flaws in our thinking.

One is that we have rather conveniently taken quite seriously Lord Krishna's exhortation to Arjun on the battlefield to do his *karm* (duty) without dwelling on its *phal* (result). Planting trees for all, digging bore wells for ourselves, running gali schools for others' children and suchlike are not enshrined in our constitution as fundamental karms. Yet we have made them our karm in our view of development even as the phal (both good and bad) affects others as well. Almost every NGO, corporate, celebrity, 'activist', professional, bureaucrat transferred to a 'development'-related post, or politician come to power seems to want to do more and more 'original' developmental karm. They seem to have become original thinking generals, fighting battles of their own choice in their own way for their own victory. But the Mahabharat is a poor analogy for urban development. In urban development, victorious generals cannot a victory make because the desired phal is about changing the battlefield and not about winning a battle on it. Yet in our chosen *karmbhoomi* (battlefield) we are all running in different directions, scoring little victories and claiming to do our karm. Is it surprising that we are running only to stand still?

The other, and in my opinion greater, flaw in our thinking is that we do not put enough premium on equity. We teach our children to say yes to trees and no to polybags, but do we teach them to say yes to equity and no to inequity? We use efficiency and capacity as criteria for appraising, monitoring and evaluating interventions (whenever we do these things), but do we use equity as a yardstick ever? We don't. If we did, we would not have to fight wasteful interventions going on around us on contrived 'technical' criteria. Flyovers that our politicians are gifting to city after city would flunk on grounds of pandering to the wants of the rich even as the needs of the poor have yet to be met. Resettlement in puny plots in faraway locations would flunk in comparison with plot sizes and locations of those doing it. Slum improvement 'successes' would flunk on the criterion of land share. Analysis of financial statements (on items like proportion of money spent on travel) as a basis of rating NGOs would flunk for not including a comparison between improvement in the status of the saviours and the saved. But, in reality, all these don't flunk. They not only make the grade, they also set standards for the future. The wall of inequity we are building (meanly claiming to do so with the wholehearted participation of those left on the other side of it) is growing higher.

And the writing on the wall is clear, though we miss it, because it is writ, after all, on the other side.

∎

In the beginning of 2001, when I started writing this chronicle, slum dwellers near my house (who had been there since before the government 'developed' the area and built flats like the one I live in) were writing to ask the government to stop 'development' of more flats before first settling them. They were also writing to the chief minister to change the procedure that was forcing the majority of 500,000 families in Delhi to sign false affidavits just so they might keep their ration cards. Hawkers near my house, who had just learned that for ten years there had been statutory provisions for their benefit, were writing to the government to ask it to implement laws for settling them before implementing laws for removing them. Slum dwellers in Indore were writing to the Aga Khan Foundation (which was to again give its triennial honours) asking that nominations for settlement projects be first put up for public objections by their intended beneficiaries. All these people and others too were clearly angry. And in their anger I see most unpleasant glimpses of the future. Lest you think these are freak personal instances, consider the following calendar of what I consider significant events in the year 2000, along with examples of the reactions I know they evoked.

In January, addressing the nation on the eve of the golden jubilee of Republic Day, President K.R. Narayanan cautioned: 'Many a social upheaval can be traced to the neglect of the lowest tier of society, whose discontent moves towards the path of violence'. He warned that the fury of the patient and long-suffering people would be unleashed if the three-way fast lane of liberalization, privatization and globalization failed to provide 'safe pedestrian crossings' for unempowered India.[1] (I mentioned this a year later in the fifty-year-old 'slum' near my fifteen-year-old government-built flat. An elderly lady said, 'Perhaps we should write to the president and tell him the government has not noticed us for fifty years...and wouldn't have noticed us for another fifty if the value of this land had not gone up.')

In February, Bangkok prepared for a week-long UN conference. Thailand's prime minister said the meeting must address 'impact of globalization' and 'widening gap between rich and poor countries'. As he spoke, workers were lining up hundreds of potted teak trees and ferns to hide a slum across the street, presumably to ensure that delegates would not have to see the gap between the rich and the poor in Bangkok.[2] (A friend from Indore said, 'The same will be necessary in Indore if the UN ever decides to hold a conference in what it believes is a slum-free city on account of a project it believes is a global best practice. More necessary, in fact, because slum residents here will most certainly protest.')

In March an irate mob of around 5000 slum dwellers from Sanjay Gandhi National Park vandalized the Bharatiya Janata Party and Congress offices in Mumbai to protest against demolition of their houses. Days later, more than 300 of them created a ruckus in the Bombay High Court and, after trying in vain to pacify them, the division bench had to order the police to evict them from the courtroom.[3] (A colleague from Mumbai said, 'I wish they'd done this to politicians for helping them settle there instead of for failing to help them remain. That might have reminded politicians that their job is to help people get what is rightfully theirs, not to help them break the law to keep them open to electoral blackmail.')

In April, former prime minister V.P. Singh, in an hour-long address to 2000 jhuggi dwellers facing eviction in Delhi exhorted them to wield lathis for their rights. He said the government was deaf to pleas and would attend to their problems only if they got united and showed their might.[4] In an unprecedented development, Sahyog, an NGO, became the target of public ire in the hills and, in an uncharacteristic show of unity, local politicians and eminent citizens all condemned it.[5] (An old teacher said, 'Fifty years ago we needed to get united and show our might against foreign rulers. Now we need to do exactly the same against our own governmental as well as non-governmental organizations. It is sad that we don't have options for better uses for strength in unity.')

In May, in Mumbai, well-established but still unauthorized hawkers shouted slogans and pelted stones at a BMC demolition squad. Police had to resort to a lathi charge. Though no one was injured, the windscreen of one encroachment removal van was shattered. BMC only decided to intensify its removal drive by deploying more people, including commandos.[6] (I mentioned this a year later at a meeting of hawkers in Vasant Kunj while discussing the draft of the report they had commissioned for DDA. Someone said, 'Is that what they spend so much money to train commandos for? What do we live in…the world's largest democracy or a police state?')

In June, the year's summer time health intervention (made jointly by the Delhi government and dozens of NGOs) in Delhi's slums covered not water- and vector-borne diseases but AIDS awareness. There was no real basis to suggest either that slums were a priority for AIDS interventions or that AIDS was a priority for health interventions in slums. The minister in charge of both health as well as urban development portfolios had a personal opinion about the 'suspected sexual behaviour' of slum dwellers. (Slum dwellers were reported saying of the NGOs involved, 'These people come and sit here for the money. They do not care whether we are sick or not.' Others, affronted by the minister's remarks, were demanding that he 'apologize from the heights of Qutub Minar to the poor in Delhi for categorizing them as scum'.)[7]

In July, RWAs in Delhi, having got a reprieve in the matter of illegal additions to flats, told Jagmohan they would help him by forming an 'anti-squatter forum'.[8] (By then, in the drive against 'urban indiscipline', parliament was later told DDA had 'taken action to remove 2790 unauthorized constructions, 70 illegal constructions in flats and 107 encroachments on plotted area'. On the other hand, more than 10,000 squatter families had been relocated.)[9] (In the fifty-year-old 'slum' of Rangpuri Pahari, where fifty houses had lately been demolished with notice even as illegal additions in the neighbouring fifteen-year-old flats had been given a reprieve, someone said of flat owners showing such enthusiasm against squatters, 'Who do they think they are? Will anyone let us form an "anti-illegal-additions forum" against them?')

In August, when we celebrated fifty-three years of independence, in Indore, patients of the TB sanatorium were discharged to make way for a management institute that would train bright managers for the future. In Delhi it was reported that several secondary schools had built facilities to run management colleges, etc., on land meant to be used as playgrounds, even as lease conditions requiring schools to offer free seats to poor children in lieu of cheaply allotted public land were nearly never met. [10] (It struck me as being rather sad that we seemed not to be able to manage our management studies without compromising the rights of others. I approached some schools with suggestions on sharing their infrastructure after school hours. None responded positively and in one very expensive and very well-appointed school I was told 'We do not indulge in such things'.)

In September, a number of DDA employees were suspended when it came to light that they had connived with property dealers to sell at premium rates in the open market thousands of flats that ought to have been allotted at cost to the general public.[11] (In Rangpuri Pahari, where residents had begun to write to the DDA for cheap plots in the vicinity under Plan provisions, someone said, 'That's why DDA prefers flats to plots. That's why we "need" to be shifted from places where flats will sell well. Obviously, DDA cares more for its corrupt employees than us or its law.')

In October, the sanatorium in Indore was demolished. In a warlike operation, explosives were used and a massive police escort deployed to complete the job within a day, which started mere hours after the court had vacated the stay. (A friend who called in the morning to let me know, tearfully said, 'They have already started… It had taken them days to start readmitting patients after the court had ordered that… But this time they have already started…')

In November, the industrious in Delhi took to the streets and protested not just the closure of their units but also the entire urban development process (especially the Master Plan) that had brought them where they stood. The apex court only said they were 'hooligans'. (Being a planner specialized only in housing, I had to refer to the Master Plan to understand this. I ran my analysis through senior colleagues and later through some lawyers. To my dismay, they did

not fault it. I was left wondering how this could be happening then...
What kind of welfare state have we become?)

In December, while those whom DDA had failed (industries, slums
dwellers, etc.) continued to be punished, only seven DDA officials were
arrested in the 'housing scam' and Jagmohan said DDA had illegally
expanded a golf course.[12] In another case of this weird 'disconnect', two
months after it had dramatically demolished an eighty-six-year-old
sanatorium, Digvijay Singh's government in Madhya Pradesh bagged
one Global Development Network Award (out of 267 entries from
over fifty countries) for some 'innovative effort' for 'improving health
and medical services in partnership with the people'.[13] Also in December,
while our parliamentarians were considering giving themselves a salary
raise, the comptroller and auditor general's (CAG) report on four
government programmess targetted at the poor said that despite
Rs 13,790 crore being spent every year, intended benefits seemed to
have failed to reach the target groups, and that 'unless effective remedial
measures are taken, the non-existent relationship between input and
output is likely to continue'.[14] (Commenting on the news reports about
the CAG report, a disgusted slum resident said, 'Why don't they just
stop spending on us? We get nothing worthwhile anyway. At least that
way we'll not be blamed for being a burden on the exchequer.')

■

Isn't it obvious that the boat is leaking, the captains lying? Isn't it
obvious that urban development-walas must set their house in order?
Isn't it obvious that we must make urban development a vocation
instead of a business and get down to it in earnest? Isn't it obvious that
it is more urgent to roll the wheels we have than to invent new ones
that may or may not be better? Isn't it obvious we (whether in politics
or professions, in corporate or voluntary sectors, in government or
activism, in media or consultancy) must realign so it becomes clear
who all have an (vested) interest in problems and who all have an
(real) interest in solutions?

What are we waiting for? A bloody revolution?

Notes

FOREWORD

1. See McKissack, Patricia C. and Fredrick McKissack, *Sojourner Truth: Ain't I a Woman?* Scholastic Inc., 1992.
2. Shah, Idries, *The Sufis*, Anchor Books, 1971.

THE EMPEROR'S NEW CLOTHES

1. Much of this section was published as a paper by the author in *Habitat International*, Vol. 24, March 2000, pp. 91–117.
2. 'Gandi bastiyon ke liye chaubis crore ki yojna' ('Scheme worth Rs 24 crore for slums'), *Nai Duniya*, 8 October 1987.
3. 'Slums typically cover only about 5 per cent of the land area of cities... It is thus possible to have a massive impact on the city and its infrastructure by working only in these very small areas. Concentrating resources in these neediest areas is thus very cost effective.' (Diacon, D., *Slum Networking: An Innovative Approach to Urban Development*, Building and Social Housing Foundation, Coalville, Leicestershire, UK, 1997, p. 11.)
4. 'ODA project par antim hastakshar' ('Final signatures on ODA Project'), *Nai Duniya*, 8 March 1989.
5. 'ODA project ke bad ki zimmedari nigam uthayega' ('IMC will take over maintenance responsibilities after the ODA project'), *Nai Duniya*, 19 May 1989; 'Gandi basti or nadi paryavaran sudhar yojna ki swikriti' ('Slum and river environment improvement scheme sanctioned'), *Nai Duniya*, 3 December 1989.
6. 'ODA project ke antargat isi mah 6 bastiyon mein kaam' ('Works to start this month in six slums under the ODA project'), *Nai Duniya*, 3 January 1990.
7. 'Tang bastiyon mein samudayik vikas ka silsila shuru' ('Community development works started in slums'), *Nai Duniya*, 17 March 1990; 'Pehle samudayik bhawan ka udghatan 29 ko' ('The first community hall to be inaugurated on 29th'), *Nai Duniya*, 28 August 1990; 'Samudayik bhawan mein gatividhiyan shuru nahin hui' ('Activities have not started in the community hall'), *Nai Duniya*, 14 November 1990; 'ODA yojna ke tahat 40 BVM gathit' ('40 Neighbourhood Development Groups formed under the ODA project'), *Nai Duniya*, 29 December 1990.
8. 'ODA project ki samiksha hetu samiti' ('Committee for reviewing ODA project'), *Nai Duniya*, 15 February 1991.
9. 'Data chust "pata" sust' ('Donor brisk, receiver lethargic'), *Nai Duniya*, 8 November 1990; 'Jhuggivasiyon ne rally nikali, gyapan diya' ('Slumdwellers took out a rally, submitted a memorandum'), *Nai Duniya*, 1 April 1991; 'British dal swasth gatividhiyon se asantusht' ('British team not satisfied with health activities'), *Nai Duniya*, 17

November 1990.

10. Based on the author's notes of a workshop attended as an observer as part of a consultancy to develop a training manual for future workshops on Action Planning for Urban Poverty Alleviation under Indian Human Settlements Programme, HSMI, New Delhi.

11. 'British adhikariyon ne pradhikaran ki prashansa ki' ('British officials praise IDA'), *Nai Duniya*, 29 January 1992; 'British adhikari ODA project ki pragati se santusht' ('British officials satisfied with the progress of the ODA project'), *Nai Duniya*, 28 May 1992.

12. 'Jhuggi bastiyon mein nirman aur sajawat ke kai karya' ('Many construction and decoration works in slums'), *Nai Duniya*, 22 January 1993.

13. 'Jhuggivasi vikas karyon ka shre John Major ko dete hain' ('Slum dwellers give credit of development activities to John Major'), *Nai Duniya*, 24 January 1993.

14. 'John Major ko rijhane ke liye nakli swarg' ('Fake heaven to impress John Major'), *Nai Duniya*, 23 January 1993.

15. *Nai Duniya*, 23 January 1993.

16. From his remark in the register of one of the slums visited by him.

17. 'ODA project ki avadhi 95 tak badai' ('ODA project term extended to 1995'), *Nai Duniya*, 27 July 1993.

18. 'Bhim nagar ko adarsh basti maan kar vikas karya karen' ('Carry out development works considering Bhim Nagar a model slum'), *Nai Duniya*, 12 January 1994.

19. The author got to see this unedited tape when asked to help with transcribing and translating.

20. 'TV set community hall ke bajaye makan mein' ('TV set in house instead of community hall'), *Nai Duniya*, 11 August 1993.

21. 'Pradhikaran ke karyon ki janch karvayen' ('Institute an inquiry into the works by IDA'), *Nai Duniya*, 3 August 1992.

22. 'Tang bastiyon mein swasthya shiviron ka ayojan' ('Health camps arranged in slums'), *Nai Duniya*, 1 June 1993; 'Jal mal nikas ki vyavastha hoti to hadsa tal sakta tha' ('The disaster could have been averted if there was a system of sewage disposal'), *Nai Duniya*, 31 May 1993.

23. 'Kab badlegi taswir' ('When will the picture change?'), *Nai Duniya*, 19 June 1993. This was a more than half-page article in 'Focus', a section that carries a box at the top with the appeal: 'If you consider this matter important please send this clipping with your endorsement to whoever you consider the most powerful public representative.'

24. Diacon, D., *Slum Networking* (Note 3 above), p. ix.

25. Ibid., p. 68.

26. 'Ghatiya samagri ka arop' ('Use of sub-standard material alleged'), *Nai Duniya*, 1 April 1994. (Incidentally, this allegation came from one of the 'showcase' slums of the IHIP); 'Dhanrashi ki barbadi' ('Waste of money'), *Nai Duniya*, 27 April 1994.

27. 'Shahar ki tang bastiyon mein kichad aur gandagi se rehvasi pareshan' ('Residents in the city's slums fed up with slush and filth'), *Nai Duniya*, 13 June 1994.

28. 'Chabbis lakh ke ghatiya pipe kharide' ('Sub-standard pipes worth 26 lakh bought'), *Nai Duniya*, 29 July 1994.

29. 'Indore ko vishvstariye samman, basti sudhar pariyojna ko safalta' ('Worldwide honour for Indore, success for slum improvement project'), *Nai Duniya*, 23 July 1994.

30. 'Pakistan sahit 14 deshon ke pratinidhi is mah Indore aayenge' ('Representatives from fourteen countries including Pakistan will visit Indore this month'), *Nai Duniya*, 1 November 1995.

31. Diacon, D., *Slum Networking* (Note 3 above), p. 67.

32. 'Videshi pratinidhiyon dwara tang bastiyon ka daura' ('Foreign delegates visit slums'), *Nai Duniya*, 23 November 1995.

33. 'dhyan dal ne ODA karyon ki sarahna ki' ('Study group appreciated ODA'), *Nai Duniya*,

24 November 1995.

34. Diacon, D., *Slum Networking* (Note 3 above), p. 68; 'Indore ki sarahna karte hue laute videshi' ('Foreigners return praising Indore'), *Nai Duniya*, 26 November 1995.

35. 'Shahr ki tang bastiyon mein malaria piriton ka survey' ('Survey of malaria victims in the city's slums'), *Nai Duniya*, 22 October 1995; 'Tang bastiyon mein 11,000 se adhik jwar pirit paye gaye' ('More than 11,000 malaria victims found in slums'), *Nai Duniya*, 19 November 1995.

36. 'Basti vikas mandalon ki gatha chinta janak' ('Worrying tale of neighbourhood groups'), *Nai Duniya*, 14 June 1995.

37. 'Tang bastiyon ke sambandh mein tin-pakshiye anubandh ab tak nahin' ('Still no tripartite agreement regarding slums'), *Nai Duniya*, 17 June 1995.

38. 'India's initiatives for the Habitat II Conference, Istanbul, 3–14 June, 1996', *Shelter* (the official newsletter of HUDCO), January 1996, pp. 18–19.

39. 'Tang bastiyon mein nigam dwara vishesh safai abhiyan shuru' ('Special cleanliness drive in slums by Corporation commences'), *Nai Duniya*, 24 July 1996, 'Varsha ke bad jhuggi vasiyon ki samasyaen badi' ('Problems of slum dwellers increase after rains'), *Nai Duniya*, 11 August 1996; 'Aadhe adhure nirman karyon se kai kshetron mein pareshani badi' ('Incomplete development works increase problems in many places'), *Nai Duniya*, 26 September 1996; 'Ghatia nirman karya' ('Poor quality development work'), *Nai Duniya*, 30 December 1996.

40. 'Pariyojna ke sambandh mein vichar ke liye baithak' ('Meeting to deliberate on the Project'), *Nai Duniya*, 12 March 1997; 'Indore ki ODA pariyojna ko jari rakhne ke prayas' ('Efforts to keep Indore's ODA project going'), *Nai Duniya*, 15 March 1997; 'ODA pariyojna ki avdhi teen mahine aur barai' ('ODA extends duration of its project by three more months'), *Nai Duniya*, 21 March 1997.

41. 'Shahar ki karib 100 bastiyon mein jal sankat utpan hone ki ashanka' ('Danger of water contamination in about 100 slums in the city'), *Nai Duniya*, 4 March 1997; 'Krishnapura jheel mein sandadh, malaria or dengue rog phailne ka khatra' ('Sewage in Krishnapura Lake, danger of malaria and dengue spreading'), *Nai Duniya*, 13 March 1997.

42. The author was the senior consultant for this study.

43. 'Kalalkui...pipe bane pareshani ka karan' ('IDA's pipes cause nuisance in Kalakui'), *Nav Bharat*, 23 June 1997.

44. '...sewer line ke prati nigam ka asantosh' ('IMC dissatisfied with IDA's sewer line'), *Nai Duniya*, 22 October 1997.

45. 'Mahapor ne kaha: takniki drishti se sahi nahin hain tang bastiyon ki drainage lines' ('Mayor says drainage lines in slums not technically sound'), *Nai Duniya*, 12 November 1997.

46. 'ODA...bastiyan vastav mein nigam ki hi hain!' ('ODA slums are IMC's!'), *Nai Duniya*, 15 November 1997.

47. 'Bhraman ke dauran sambhag ayukt ne anek bastiyon mein drainage ki samasya dekhi' ('Divisional Commissioner saw drainage problems in several slums in course of round'), *Nai Duniya*, 14 November 1997.

48. 'Saat crore kharch karke bhi halat nahin sudhri' ('Conditions have not improved even after spending 600 million'), *Nai Duniya*, 9 March 1998.

49. 'Stinking lake shows lack of IDA care', *Free Press*, 18 April 1998.

50. 'Kewal goliyan bantne se dushit jal ki samasya hal nahin hogi' ('The problem of contaminated water is not going to be solved by distributing tablets'), *Dainik Bhaskar*, 26 June 1998.

51. 'Ulti-dast ka prakop phaila, do mrityu aur' ('Water-borne diseases spread; two more deaths'), *Nav Bharat*, 26 June 1998.

52. 'Ulti-dast pe niyantran nahin kiya to mahamari ki ashanka: tang bastiyan adhik badhali

mein' ('Danger of epidemics if water-borne diseases are not controlled: slums in worse condition'), *Nai Duniya*, 27 June 1998.

53. Sen, Pritha, 'Winning Designs', *Outlook*, 19 October 1998.

54. Government of India, *Draft National Slum Policy, 1999*, Para-A, 'Objectives', p. 1, Ministry of Urban Affairs and Employment.

55. Ibid., Para-C-6, 'Resettlement and Rehabilitation', pp. 8–9.

56. Ibid., Para-C-15-g-iv, 'Financing Shelter Upgradation/Targeting EWS/LIG Housing Schemes', p. 36.

57. Ibid., 'Monitoring and Evaluation', p. 39.

58. Ibid., Para-C-1, '"Inclusive" Approach to Definition of Slum/Informal Settlement', p. 3.

59. Government of India, *Draft National Slum Policy, 1999*, Ministry of Urban Affairs and Employment. The section on 'Granting of Tenure' says 'Land for in-situ upgradation projects should be designated as high density mixed use' (Para C-5-d, 'Land Use Classification', p. 7). This is reiterated in the section on 'Planning for Integration', which speaks of ensuring that 'all Master Plans and Land Use plans allow for high density, mixed use (for micro-enterprise) land occupation in all slums/informal settlements.' It goes on to add that 'All plans and other regulatory instruments must provide sufficient flexibility to modify layouts and building regulations in line with more realistic density/ mixed use requirements' (Para-C-7-a, 'Modify Existing Planning Framework', pp. 10– 11). Once again, in the section on 'Shelter Upgradation' the entire discussion on 'Land for Affordable Housing' (Para-C-15-a, p. 32) and nearly the entire discussion on 'Rationalization of Norms and Standards' (Para-C-15-c, p. 33) is about high-density mixed land use.

60. *Draft National Slum Policy, 1999*, Para-B, 'Governing Principles', #4, p. 2; Para-B, 'Governing Principles', #6, p. 2.

61. In fact the discussion on 'Land for Affordable Housing' (Para-C-15-a) is limited to just this suggestion; Para-C-9-b-i, 'Primary Education', p. 18; Para-12-a-iii, 'Role of Private Sector', p. 23.

62. *Draft National Slum Policy, 1999*, Para-B, 'Governing Principles', #5, p. 2.

63. Ibid., Para-B, 'Governing Principles', #5, p. 2; Para-C-7-a-ii, 'Planning for Integration…', p. 11.

64. Ibid., Para-C-8, 'Environmental Improvement', p. 12.

65. Ibid., Para-C-9, 'Improving Access to Social Services', pp. 16–17.

66. Ibid., Para-C-7-a, 'Modify Existing Planning Framework', p. 10.

67. Ibid., Para-C-2-a, 'Comprehensive Listing of Slums/Informal Settlements', p. 4.

68. Ibid., Para-C-2-b, 'Registration of Slum Dwellers', p. 4.

69. Ibid., Para-C-2-c, 'Identity Card', p. 4.

70. Ibid., Para-C-2-d, 'Basic Service Eligibility', p. 4.

71. Ibid., Para-6, 'Resettlement and Rehabilitation', pp. 9–10.

72. 'SC fixes civic code: No slums, no littering', *Times of India*, 18 February 2000; 'SC bans slums', *Indian Express*, 18 February 2000; 'SC bans slums in Delhi', *The Statesman*, 18 February 2000; 'Litterbugs to be fined Rs 50', *Hindustan Times*, 18 February 2000.

73. 'Good news about garbage', *The Hindu*, 19 March 2000.

74. 'Housing and dignity: Universal rights', *The Statesman*, 10 April 2000.

75. 'Thank God the Supreme Court is in Delhi!', *Times of India*, 21 February 2000.

76. 'Dirty Delhi: Our roads are giant trash bins', *Times of India*, 24 February 2000; 'Watch your step, litterbugs', *Times of India*, 24 February 2000.

77. 'Delhi is still dirty: MCD, NDMC bugged with problems in nabbing litterbugs', *Times of India*, 23 February 2000.

78. 'Govt will set up mobile courts to punish litterbugs', *Hindustan Times*, 24 February 2000; 'Watch your step, litterbugs' (Note 76 above).

79. 'MCD to have own system to follow SC directive on city clean-up', *Hindustan Times*, 26 February 2000.

80. 'MCD staff to clean city on holidays too', *Hindustan Times*, 29 February 2000.

81. 'Day 1: Litterbugs thumb their noses at MCD', *Hindustan Times*, 4 March 2000; 'Dirty Delhi: Why the city is never clean', *Times of India*, 27 August 2000.

82. 'First day of drive: MCD focusses on awareness building', *Times of India*, 5 March 2000.

83. 'Govt to appoint 100 executive magistrates to rein in litterbugs', *Hindustan Times*, 5 March 2000.

84. 'Shopkeepers mainly being fined for littering', *Times of India*, 3 May 2000.

85. 'Garbage smears Clean Delhi dream', *Asian Age (Delhi Age)*, 7 August 2000.

86. 'SC castigates govt, DDA, NDMC over solid waste disposal', *Daily Pioneer*, 25 August 2000; 'Supreme Court tells lazy MCD to clean up city', *Asian Age (Delhi Age)*, 25 August 2000; 'SC directive to DDA on waste disposal', *The Hindu*, 25 August 2000; 'MCD to generate electricity from garbage waste', *Daily Pioneer*, 25 August 2000; 'Clean up Delhi, SC tells MCD, DDA', *Times of India*, 25 August 2000; 'Start door-to-door garbage collection', *Hindustan Times*, 25 August 2000; 'SC directs "lethargic" MCD to start door-to-door collection of garbage', *Indian Express*, 25 August 2000.

87. 'SC castigates govt' (Note 86 above).

88. 'MCD begins door-to-door garbage collection', *Times of India*, 31 August 2000; 'Door-to-door garbage collection extended', *Hindustan Times*, 31 August 2000.

89. 'Waste piles up as MCD faces trolley truck crunch', *Times of India*, 23 September 2000.

90. Para 4.4 of edited draft of NEERI's study report on 'Solid waste in Delhi' for DDA (unpublished), 1998.

91. Ibid.

92. Ibid., Para 5.3 and Para 6.3.

93. 'MCD to set up new compost plants for management of solid waste', *Hindustan Times*, 25 February 2000; '10 new compost plants for the city', *Times of India*, 25 February 2000.

94. 'MCD facing landfill crunch', *Hindustan Times*, 27 February 2000.

95. 'Govt decides to manage colossal city waste', *Daily Pioneer*, 5 June 2000; 'Garbage collection rickshaws to be introduced in city today', *Asian Age (Delhi Age)*, 5 June 2000.

96. 'High court seeks records on order for the removal of slum clusters', *Asian Age (Delhi Age)*, 1 April 2000.

97. Ibid.

98. 'I will not allow uprooting of slum dwellers, says V.P. Singh', *Asian Age (Delhi Age)*, 25 March 2000; 'VP opposes eviction of slum dwellers', *Times of India*, 25 March 2000; 'VP vows to thwart move to demolish jhuggi cluster', *Hindustan Times*, 25 March 2000.

99. 'VP Singh saves 30,000 jhuggis at Wazirpur', *Times of India*, 26 March 2000; 'Change attitude toward slum dwellers, says V P Singh', *Hindustan Times*, 26 March 2000.

100. 'Demolition delay victory for poor: V.P.', *Asian Age (Delhi Age)*, 27 March 2000.

101. 'VP stir pays off, squatters of Azad Colony to be given alternate sites', *Hindustan Times*, 28 March 2000.

102. 'Rlys not liable to compensate uprooted slum-dwellers', *Hindustan Times*, 29 March 2000.

103. 'Breather to govt on rly land slums', *Indian Express*, 16 May 2000.

104. 'Govt pulled up over rly encroachments', *Times of India*, 5 April 2000.

105. 'Life for Mumbai railway shanties', *The Statesman*, 5 May 2000.

106. 'Slum demolitions to put trains on fast track', *Times of India*, 4 April 2000; 'Life for Mumbai railway shanties', *The Statesman*, 5 March 2000.

107. 'Railways' slum demolition drive faces derailment', *Times of India*, 2 July 2000.

108. 'Rlys pull down hutments along Harbour line', *Times of India*, 1 March 2000; 'Life for Mumbai railway shanties' (Note 106 above).

109. 'Slum demolitions to put trains on fast track'(Note 106 above).
110. 'Railways' slum demolition drive' (Note 107 above).
111. 'Life for Mumbai railway shanties' (Note 108 above).
112. 'Govt pulled up over rly encroachments' (Note 104 above); 'Life for Mumbai railway shanties' (Note 106 above); 'Railways' slum demolition drive' (Note 107 above).
113. 'Survey to identify slum dwellers near rail tracks', *Times of India*, 13 March 2000; 'Slum demolitions' (Note 109 above).
114. 'Role of charitable trust in rehabilitation questioned: Citizens speak out against halting of demolition drive', *Times of India*, 9 March 2000.
115. 'Govt pulled up over rly encroachments' (Note 104 above).
116. 'Role of charitable trust questioned' (Note 114 above).
117. 'Govt pulled up over rly encroachments' (Note 104 above).
118. 'Slum demolitions' (Note 109 above).
119. 'Railways' slum demolition drive' (Note 107 above).
120. 'Rlys, state clash in HC over encroachments', *Indian Express*, 29 June 2000; 'Railways' slum demolition drive' (Note 107 above).
121. 'Rlys, state clash in HC' (Note 120 above).
122. 'Central Railways' demolition drive begins', *Times of India*, 31 October 2000; '300 hutments along Harbour line demolished', *Times of India*, 2 November 2000.
123. 'Govt told to clear Sanjay Gandhi Park of encroachers by March', *Times of India*, 3 March 2000.
124. 'Slum-dwellers vandalise BJP office in Mulund', *Times of India*, 10 March 2000.
125. 'Angry slum-dwellers bundled out of court', *Times of India*, 14 March 2000.
126. 'National park slum-dwellers watch film for a "rebirth"', *Times of India*, 17 March 2000.
127. 'Lack of transparency raises doubts about motive behind rehabilitation', *Times of India*, 27 March 2000.
128. 'Census of slum-dwellers proposed', *Times of India*, 19 April 2000.
129. 'HC questions govt stand on slum removal', *Times of India*, 30 April 2000.
130. 'V.P. Singh takes up cudgels on behalf of slum-dwellers', *Times of India*, 25 April 2000.
131. 'HC stays demolitions at Carvallo Nagar', *Times of India*, 30 April 2000; 'Demolitions to continue at Sanjay park', *Times of India*, 1 May 2000.
132. 'Demolitions go on amid tight security', *Times of India*, 4 May 2000.
133. 'Slum-dwellers move apex court', *Times of India*, 8 May 2000.
134. 'SC rejects Borivli park dwellers' plea', *Indian Express*, 10 May 2000.
135. 'Slum dwellers must have a say: VP', *Times of India*, 31 March 2000; 'VP Singh's political sanyas ends, rally planned on May 16', *Hindustan Times*, 31 March 2000.
136. 'Wield lathis for your right, VP exhorts jhuggi dwellers', *Hindustan Times*, 17 April 2000.
137. Singh, Vishwanath Pratap, 'Sheltering sky', *Hindustan Times*, 28 April 2000.
138. 'Slum-dwellers to take out rally on May 22', *The Hindu*, 20 May 2000.
139. 'V.P. Singh in favour of a policy for urban poor', *Asian Age (Delhi Age)*, 20 May 2000; 'VP Singh calls for national slum policy', *Daily Pioneer*, 20 May 2000.
140. 'Make right to house a fundamental right: VP', *Hindustan Times*, 22 May 2000; 'Don't bulldoze slum-dwellers: V.P. Singh', *The Hindu*, 22 May 2000.
141. Sajha Manch's letter (dated 3 May 2000, from its convener Dunu Roy) inviting participation for its meeting to discuss the draft national policy on 20 May 2000.
142. 'Maharashtra asked to evolve new policy for slum dwellers', *The Hindu*, 24 April 2000; 'Experts discuss national slum policy', *Times of India*, 29 April 2000.
143. *Draft National Slum Policy*, 1999, Para-C-2b 'Registration of slum dwellers', p. 4.
144. Ibid., Para-C-5a, 'Tenure on Government Owned Land', p. 5.

145. 'Railways, HUDCO sign MoU', *Hindustan Times*, 14 January 2000.
146. Ibid.
147. 'V.P. Singh upstages Cong, BJP in Delhi?', *Hindustan Times*, 26 March 2000.
148. 'Sonia's concern for slum dwellers in flyover function', *Times of India*, 10 May 2000; 'Slum-dwellers must be relocated: Sonia', *Hindustan Times*, 10 May 2000; 'Sonia favours alternate dwellings for slum people', *Asian Age*, 10 May 2000; 'New homes for moved poor a must: Sonia', *Asian Age (Delhi Age)*, 10 May 2000.
149. 'Delhi announces new slum policy', *Asian Age (Delhi Age)*, 11 May 2000; 'Deadline for relocation of slum dwellers extended', *Times of India*, 11 May 2000.
150. 'MCD staff to clean city on holidays too' (Note 80 above).
151. '"Sammelan" of jhuggi residents on new policy', *Asian Age (Delhi Age)*, 29 May 2000.
152. 'Encroachment policy: A wild goose chase', *The Statesman*, 24 May 2000.
153. 'British expertise for Delhi', *The Hindu*, 25 May 2000.
154. 'MPs urge PM to stop "senseless demolitions"', *Hindustan Times*, 13 May 2000.
155. 'BJP MPs urge PM to "rein in" Jagmohan', *Hindustan Times*, 16 May 2000.
156. 'Project for 60,000 displaced slum-dwellers: Jagmohan', *Indian Express*, 11 July 2000; 'Loans, schools and security for Narela families', *Times of India*, 11 July 2000; 'No new slum, says Jagmohan', *The Hindu*, 11 July 2000; 'Jagmohan now targets squatters', *Asian Age (Delhi Age)*, 11 July 2000.
157. 'Walia seeks upgradation of jhuggi clusters', *Hindustan Times*, 21 July 2000; 'Walia demands for JJ Cluster upgradation', *Daily Pioneer*, 21 July 2000; 'Walia demands better deal for jhuggi dwellers', *Times of India*, 21 July 2000.
158. 'Slums born before Jan 1998 not to be demolished', *Times of India*, 7 October 2000; 'Delhi's slum policy awaits Centre's nod', *Times of India*, 10 October 2000.
159. 'Centre to come out with human settlement policy: Jagmohan', *Times of India*, 19 November 2000.
160. Ministry for Urban Development and Poverty Alleviation, *Istanbul + 5 UNCHS(Habitat) Conference 2001: INDIA National Report–Progress of Implementation of the Habitat Agenda (1996-2000)*, p. 9, Government of India.
161. From a note circulated by Almitra Patel amongst a few people for comments.
162. 'HUDCO loan for IMC may be a far cry…', *Free Press*, 5 November 2000.
163. 'Minister to make on-the-spot study of problems of city', *Free Press*, 4 November 2000.
164. 'Khub ghume par kuch na bole Jagmohan' ('Jagmohan roamed a lot but did not say anything'), *Chautha Sansar*, 5 November 2000.
165. 'Bhagdaurh vala raha Jagmohan ka teen ghante ka shahar bhraman' ('Jagmohan's three-hour city trip was very hectic'), *Nav Bharat*, 5 November 2000; 'Uncleji bijli ka bill kam kara dein; keechar bhari sarak par chalkar dikhayen' ('Uncle get our electricity bill reduced; walk on the slushy street and show us'), *Agnibaan*, 5 November 2000.
166. 'Kendriye mantri Jagmohan Indore ki tang bastiyon mein char ghante ghumte rahe' ('Union Minister Jagmohan kept roaming in Indore's slums for four hours'), *Indore Samachar*, 6 November 2000.
167. 'Pehle sunte rahe, phir poochhtaachh ki, madad ke sanket bhi diye' ('First he kept listening, then he made inquiries, he also hinted at help'), *Dainik Bhaskar*, 5 November 2000.
168. 'Minister announces plans for Indore', *HT Indore Live*, 6 November 2000; 'Indore ko diye jane wale sambhavit sahyog ki suchi' ('List of assistance likely to be given to Indore'), *Nai Duniya*, 6 November 2000; 'Indore ke liye anek ghoshnayen' ('Several announcements for Indore'), *Swadesh*, 6 November 2000.
169. 'Vahan ek bhi bal shramik nahin; saare bachche school jate hain' ('Not even one child worker there; all children go to school'), *Agnibaan*, 5 November 2000; 'Indore vikas ke raste nikalenge' ('Will find ways for Indore's development'), *Nav Bharat*, 5 November 2000; 'Nagrik shahron mein anushasan viksit karen va bhu mafia se dat kar ladhen'

('Citizens must develop discipline in cities and fight land mafia'), *Nai Duniya*, 5 November 2000; 'Jan bhagidari se Indore ka vikas karen' ('Develop Indore with citizens' participation'), *Swadesh*, 5 November 2000.

170. 'Perseverance needed to make Indore ideal city', *Free Press*, 5 November 2000.

171. 'Jan bhagidari' ('Develop Indore with citizens' participation' (Note 169 above).

172. 'HUDCO office in city soon', *Free Press*, 5 November 2000.

173. 'Shahron ke vikas ke liye samanvit prayas ki zaroorat: Shri Jagmohan' ('Coordinated effort needed for urban development: Shri Jagmohan'), *Indore Samachar*, 5 November 2000; 'Indore ki vikas yojnaon ko Delhi mein gati denge Shri Jagmohan' ('Shri Jagmohan will hasten Indore's development schemes in Delhi'), *Nai Duniya*, 6 November 2000.

174. 'Shahron ke vikas ke liye' ('Coordinated effort needed') (Note 173 above).

175. 'HUDCO office in city soon' (Note 172 above).

THE GREAT TERRAIN ROBBERY

1. 'Mob gheraos MCD official', *Indian Express*, 18 November 2000.

2. 'Sealing of units: Workers wall up against MCD', *Indian Express*, 19 November 2000; 'Polluting units' workers take to streets in protest', *Hindustan Times*, 19 November 2000.

3. 'Roadblocks to cleaner Delhi: Traders stymie drive against polluting units', *Hindustan Times*, 20 November 2000; 'A day of traffic snarls', *Times of India*, 20 November 2000; 'Traffic held to ransom; Delhi bandh today', *Daily Pioneer*, 20 November 2000; 'Closure of units causing unrest', *The Hindu*, 20 November 2000.

4. 'MLAs promise chaos in House over units' closure', *Times of India*, 20 November 2000. ('The entire city witnessed so many protests that we have to take up the cause now…,' said a BJP MLA.)

5. 'File review plea in SC, DPCC urges govt', *Hindustan Times*, 20 November 2000.

6. 'Khurana seeks PM's intervention to solve problems of units in non-conforming areas', *Hindustan Times*, 20 November 2000.

7. 'Police under pressure to go slow on protesters', *Times of India*, 21 November 2000. ('At scores of places, the police's presence and action at trouble spots seemed more routine than special… Officially, the police say they aren't using force because the violence could spread… But Delhi Police's own record in handling such crises in the past is a potent example of how things are different… Police chief Ajai Raj Sharma said at a press conference that four Rapid Action Force companies had been summoned. In the Seelampur riots last month, geographically a much smaller area, over eight companies of additional forces had been pressed into service… The entire Vikas Marg, for instance, remained closed to traffic for much of the day, even as a handful of policemen looked on…at another trouble spot near Swaran Cinema in east Delhi, the police displayed "remarkable restraint" despite an additional sessions judge being attacked by a mob…')

8. 'Mobs, protesting against relocation, ravage Delhi', *Hindustan Times*, 21 November 2000; 'Who blamed who as Delhi burned', *Hindustan Times*, 21 November 2000; 'Lawless Delhi', *Hindustan Times*, 21 November 2000; 'Industrial workers' stir: All schools closed for two days', *Hindustan Times*, 21 November 2000; 'Agitating mob hold Delhi to ransom; govt refuses to budge', *Indian Express*, 21 November 2000; 'Mobs hold Delhi to ransom over SC order', *Times of India*, 21 November 2000; 'Workers' fury', *Daily Pioneer*, 21 November 2000; 'Delhi protesters go on the rampage', *The Hindu*, 21 November 2000.

9. 'Violent mob ravages MTNL office', *Hindustan Times*, 21 November 2000; 'Vehicles set ablaze, Rs 5 lakh cash, cheques looted', *Hindustan Times*, 21 November 2000;

'Karkardooma court judge's car attacked', *Hindustan Times*, 21 November 2000; 'Rioting workers take over north, west and east', *Indian Express*, 21 November 2000; 'Injured protesters, cops lie side by side', *Indian Express*, 21 November 2000; 'Students caught in middle', *Indian Express*, 21 November 2000; 'Stranded buses leave school children in a lurch', *Times of India*, 21 November 2000; 'Why office-goers got late', *Times of India*, 21 November 2000; 'Delhi comes to a halt', *Daily Pioneer*, 21 November 2000; 'Schools shut down as buses go off the road', *Daily Pioneer*, 21 November 2000.

10. 'Intelligence inputs hint at more violence', *Hindustan Times*, 22 November 2000; 'Disturbed area residents will bear cost of addl. force, warns police chief', *Hindustan Times*, 22 November 2000; 'Day Three of Capital punishment', *Times of India*, 22 November 2000.

11. City page headlines on 22 November 2000 said it all. 'BJP flays Dikshit, Cong targets MCD', *Indian Express*; 'Chief secretary must be sacked: M.L. Khurana', *Indian Express*; 'Mayor is to blame: Cong councillors', *Hindustan Times*; 'Word "polluting" missing from Industries closure notification, Environment Secy blamed', *Hindustan Times*; '"Misinterpretation" of order on units: Khurana, Sahib blame it on Sheila', *Hindustan Times*; '"Operation shut down" disrupts MCD House meet', *Times of India*; 'Assembly adjourned amid unruly scenes', *Hindustan Times*; 'Assembly adjourned amid trading of charges, slogan shouting', *Times of India*; 'House adjourned, MLAs march to PM's residence in protest', *Daily Pioneer*; 'Sheila Dixit leads march', *The Hindu*; 'Cong factionalism evident in MLAs' meeting with PM', *Hindustan Times*; 'Sheila: PM assures of relief measures' , *Daily Pioneer*. There was a feeling in many quarters that the previous day's events had been exaggerated. Police Commissioner Sharma was 'quick to volunteer a detailed list of over 35 spots, where violence had taken place and that more was likely'. He even went to the extent of saying a train engine had been burnt in Shalimar Bagh. Later, when the media went to the spot, only an engine driver had been beaten up. He also said a liquor shop in Farsh Bazar was robbed by the mobs, a detail which normally would have been hidden. ('Police under pressure', Note 7 above.)

12. 'Law and order slightly better; Capital, however, witnesses traffic snarls', *Hindustan Times*, 22 November 2000; 'Commuters on NH-8 have harrowing time', *Hindustan Times*, 22 November 2000; 'Stir impact', *Hindustan Times*, 22 November 2000; 'Intelligence inputs' (Note 10 above); 'Disturbed area residents' (Note 10 above), 'Traffic chaos spills over to Faridabad', *Times of India*, 22 November 2000; 'Some relief for Delhiites on the 2nd day', *Daily Pioneer*, 22 November 2000.

13. 'Day Three of Capital punishment' (Note 10 above); 'Monday violence: Kavir Nagar mourns firing-victim Irfan', *Hindustan Times*, 23 November 2000.

14. 'Injured protesters, cops lie side by side' (Note 9 above); 'Neighbours see "martyr" in accident victim', *Times of India*, 22 November 2000.

15. 'Panicky Delhi govt rushes to SC over riots, gets thumbs down', *Indian Express*, 22 November 2000; 'SC will not yield to stir on polluting units', *The Hindu*, 22 November 2000; 'SC raps Delhi govt for being held to ransom', *Times of India*, 22 November 2000; 'Don't go slow on crackdown on polluting units, Delhi govt told', *Hindustan Times*, 22 November 2000.

16. 'City govt list of hazardous units incomplete', *Times of India*, 2 May 1995.

17. 'CM promises action plan on relocation', *Times of India*, 1 April 1995.

18. 'Nearly half the polluting units may raise objections', *Times of India*, 27 November 1995.

19. 'Midnight knock for eco-unfriendly business in Capital', *Times of India*, 30 November 1996.

20. 'Industrial units contest pollution board's criteria', *Times of India*, 17 September 1997; 'Polluting units say no retrenchment', *Times of India*, 2 December 1996.

168 *Notes*

21. 'Polluting units: SC lands greedy ones in trouble', *Times of India*, 5 December 1996.
22. 'Workers yet to receive compensation', *Times of India (Delhi Times)*, 24 June 1997.
23. 'Delhi Industries Minister Harsharan Singh Balli', *Times of India Q&A*, 27 May 1997.
24. Dasgupta, Nandini, 'Tall blunders', *Down to Earth*, 30 September 1998.
25. 'Labour pains', *Down to Earth*, 28 February 1999.
26. 'Master Plan anarchy', *Down to Earth*, 31 December 2000.
27. 'Delhi govt to petition SC on relocation of industrial units', *Times of India*, 15 September 1999.
28. 'Govt has 6 days for relocation', *Times of India*, 25 October 1996.
29. 'Congress, BJP pass the buck over relocation of industries', *Times of India*, 23 October 1999.
30. Dasgupta, 'Tall Blunders' (Note 24 above).
31. 'Workers yet to receive compensation' (Note 22 above).
32. 'CM promises action plan on relocation' (Note 17 above).
33. 'Delhi Finance Corporation will fund relocation of industries', *Times of India*, 1 October 1997.
34. '25000 industries face closure', *Times of India*, 9 December 1999.
35. 'Govt rethinks on shifting industries', *Times of India*, 5 June 1999.
36. 'Delhi govt yet to get land to relocate industries', *Times of India (Delhi Times)*, 7 December 1999.
37. 'Govt rethinks on shifting industries' (Note 35 above).
38. 'Delhi govt to petition SC on relocation of industrial units', *Times of India*, 15 September 1999.
39. 'Delhi govt yet to get land' (Note 36 above); '25,000 industries face closure' (Note 34 above).
40. '25000 industries face closure' (Note 34 above).
41. 'Reviving the dying Yamuna', *Times of India (Delhi Times)*, 24 May 1999.
42. 'The Delhi stretch of Yamuna is "all sewage"', *Times of India*, 25 January 2000.
43. 'Mater Plan anarchy' (Note 26 above).
44. 'Rs 2000-cr plan to clean the Yamuna', *Times of India (Delhi Times)*, 22 February 1999.
45. 'Reviving the dying Yamuna' (Note 41 above).
46. CAG report, as quoted in 'Delhi water unfit for drinking', *Times of India*, 10 April 1999; 'Delhi's sewage system polluting Yamuna: Ministry', *Indian Express*, 7 September 2000.
47. 'Municipal mess', Editorial, *Hindustan Times*, 28 January 2000; 'City sewage dumped untreated', *Times of India*, 2 February 2000; 'Delhi's sewage system polluting Yamuna' (Note 46 above).
48. 'Rattled govt to foot bill for polluting units', *Daily Pioneer*, 14 September 2000.
49. 'What will industrial units do with solid waste?', *Times of India*, 27 January 2000.
50. '800 units face closure for polluting Yamuna', *Times of India*, 25 January 2000; 'Govt tells units to install treatment plants', *Times of India*, 8 December 1999.
51. 'No norms laid down for effluent treatment plants', *Times of India*, 25 January 2000.
52. 'Govt reopening of industrial units will add to pollution of Yamuna', *Hindustan Times*, 11 January 2000.
53. 'Relocation issue: Panel set up to study industries' pleas', *Hindustan Times*, 1 January 2000.
54. 'Closure of industrial units: Delhi govt on the backfoot?', *Times of India*, 7 January 2000.
55. 'Govt allows 372 units to reopen', *Hindustan Times*, 10 January 2000.
56. 'SC bans effluents' flow into Yamuna', *Hindustan Times*, 25 January 2000; '800 units face closure' (Note 50 above).
57. 'Clean up Yamuna by April 28: SC', *Hindustan Times*, 11 March 2000.
58. 'Yamuna can breathe: Polluting units to be closed', *Hindustan Times*, 14 March 2000.

59. 'SC may fine erring Delhi govt', *Hindustan Times*, 29 April 2000; 'SC talks of fining govt for failure to curb pollution', *Times of India*, 29 April 2000.

60. 'Yamuna pollution: "Excuses! Excuses!" SC slaps Rs 10,000 fine on Delhi govt', *Hindustan Times*, 12 May 2000; 'SC fines Delhi govt over Yamuna', *Times of India*, 12 May 2000; 'Fine slapped on Delhi govt', *The Hindu*, 12 May 2000.

61. 'Stiff penalty if Yamuna is left dirty: SC', *Times of India*, 12 July 2000; 'SC warns Delhi govt on cleaning of the Yamuna', *Indian Express*, 12 July 2000; 'Pollution of Yamuna worries SC', *The Hindu*, 12 July 2000; 'SC: Clean up Yamuna quicker or face music', *Hindustan Times*, 12 July 2000; 'You are cleaning Yamuna at snail's pace, SC to govt', *Indian Express*, 12 July 2000.

62. 'LG, environment dept near showdown over units' closure', *Indian Express*, 9 September 2000.

63. 'Jagmohan's is only sane voice, says SC', *Indian Express*, 14 September 2000; 'SC ruling on hazardous units: Ministry to set up nodal agency', *Hindustan Times*, 14 September 2000.

64. 'Pollution is not a simple matter that can be legislated out of existence', *Times of India*, 11 March 1997.

65. 'Govt rethinks on shifting industries' (Note 37 above).

66. 'Frequent court orders on polluting industries jolt govt into action', *Times of India*, 29 January 2000; 'Water polluting industrial units allotted plots', *Indian Express*, 10 July 2000; '500 polluting units get alternate sites', *Times of India*, 10 July 2000; '500 polluting industrial units to be relocated at Narela', *Hindustan Times*, 11 July 2000.

67. 'Bawana: Site for relocation yet to show signs of any development', *Hindustan Times*, 24 September 2000.

68. 'Shut industries in residential areas: Supreme Court', *Asian Age (Delhi Age)*, 13 September 2000; 'SC damns Delhi on polluting units', *Times of India*, 13 September 2000; 'Jagmohan's is only sane voice' (Note 63 above).

69. 'Balli threatens agitation if master plan is not altered', *Hindustan Times*, 22 September 2000; 'Cong flays Jagmohan's rigidity on Master Plan', *Times of India*, 23 September 2000; 'Amend Master Plan, demands state Cong chief', *Indian Express*, 23 September 2000; 'DPCC wants changes in Master Plan to circumvent SC directive', *Hindustan Times*, 23 September 2000.

70. 'Khurana backs govt stand, for master plan amendment', *Hindustan Times*, 24 September 2000; 'Sheila for a "practical and humane view" of units issue', *Hindustan Times*, 24 September 2000.

71. Jag Parvesh Chandra, 'Where will they go from here?', *Hindustan Times*, 6 October 2000; 'Apply flexible guidelines to Master Plan: L-G', *Hindustan Times*, 30 September 2000.

72. 'Agitating mob hold Delhi to ransom; govt refuses to budge', *Indian Express*, 21 November 2000.

73. 'Closing units an act of bureaucratic terror', *Times of India*, 20 November 2000; 'Revoke industry closure: Khurana tells government', *Indian Express*, 20 November 2000; 'Khurana seeks PM's intervention to solve problems of units in non-conforming areas', *Hindustan Times*, 20 November 2000.

74. 'Cong accuses BJP of indulging in doublespeak', *Times of India*, 18 December 2000.

75. 'Traffic held to ransom; Delhi bandh today', *Daily Pioneer*, 20 November 2000.

76. 'Agitating mob hold Delhi to ransom' (Note 72 above).

77. 'PM house chalo, decides Congress', *Times of India*, 21 November 2000.

78. 'Jagmohan firm on Delhi Master Plan; Tumult in Rajya Sabha', *Hindustan Times*, 23 November 2000; 'Jagmohan bends a little, but won't break', *Times of India*, 23 November 2000; 'Delhi protesters find support in Parliament', *Times of India*, 23 November 2000; 'Jagmohan yields inch, refuses mile', *Daily Pioneer*, 23 November 2000.

79. 'Jagmohan yields inch' (Note 78 above).
80. 'Delhi Assembly passes censure motion against Jagmohan', Hindustan Times, 23 November 2000; 'Assembly says no to proposal; fears fresh stir', Daily Pioneer, 23 November 2000.
81. Interview with Sheila Dikshit, Down To Earth, 31 July 2000; 'Delhi's belly at the click of a mouse', Times of India, 12 July 1999.
82. '15-lakh workers not hooligans: BJP MPs', The Hindu, 23 November 2000.
83. 'Jagmohan bends a little' (Note 78 above).
84. 'Jagmohan yields inch' (Note 78 above).
85. 'Delhi Assembly passes censure motion' (Note 80 above); 'Assembly disapproves Jagmohan stand', The Hindu, 23 November 2000; 'Assembly says no to proposal' (Note 80 above).
86. 'Cong flays Jagmohan's rigidity' (Note 69 above); 'Sheila for a "practical and humane view"' (Note 70 above); 'Khurana backs govt stand for master plan amendment', Hindustan Times, 24 September 2000; 'Where will they go from here?', Hindustan Times, 6 October 2000.
87. 'Where will they go from here?' (Note 86 above).
88. 'Cong flays Jagmohan's rigidity' (Note 69 above).
89. 'Revoke industry closure' (Note 73 above).
90. 'Where will they go from here?' (Note 86 above); '1 lakh industries won't be allowed to shut down', Hindustan Times, 5 October 2000.
91. 'DPCC wants changes in Master Plan' (Note 69 above); '1 lakh industries won't be allowed to shut down' (Note 90 above); 'Where will they go from here?' (Note 86 above); 'Jagmohan yields inch' (Note 78 above).
92. 'Where will they go from here?' (Note 87 above); 'Balli threatens agitation' (Note 69 above).
93. 'Revoke industry closure' (Note 73 above); 'Khurana seeks PM's intervention' (Note 73 above); 'Khurana backs govt stand' (Note 86 above).
94. 'Jagmohan bends a little' (Note 78 above); 'Delhi protesters find support in Parliament' (Note 78 above); 'Jagmohan firm on Delhi Master Plan' (Note 78 above).
95. Delhi Development Authority, Master Plan for Delhi, New Delhi, 1962, p. 6, under (a) Major Policy Decisions.
96. Ibid.
97. Ibid., p. 17.
98. Ibid., p. 8.
99. Ibid., p. 22.
100. Ibid., p (ii) under important recommendations made in the Master Plan.
101. Ibid., pp. 17–19.
102. Ibid., p. 21.
103. Ibid., p. 20.
104. Ibid., p. 46.
105. Ibid., 'Time schedule for non-conforming uses', p. 46.
106. Ibid., p. 45.
107. Ibid., p. 19.
108. Mid-term Appraisal of Delhi Master Plan and Its Implementation, First Report of the Working Group, 14 March 1974, Summary of Recommendations, Para-4. The Working Group suggested speeding up development of industrial plots by DDA and review of sizes and utilization of industrial plots in cooperative societies as these were far bigger than the ones developed by DDA. It said that since light and service industries (many of the ones proposed to be relocated now under the Jagmohan option) are permitted in extensive industrial zones, layout plans for these zones should make due provision for

them. It noted shifting of non-conforming uses had not been successful and strongly recommended a systematic and coordinated approach as well as construction of flatted factories (not one of which had been constructed by then) by the DDA or the DSIDC. It even recommended that a committee to examine in detail the change of land use of some non-conforming industrial units (now proposed in the Sheila option for all units without the benefit of a detailed examination).

109. Seventh Lok Sabha, Estimates Committee (1984–85), *Eighty-fifth Report: Ministry of Works and Housing, Delhi Development Authority–Part-I*, Lok Sabha Secretariat, May 1984, Para-7.

110. Seventh Lok Sabha, Estimates Committee (1984-85), *Eighty-seventh Report: Ministry of Works and Housing, Delhi Development Authority–Part-II*, Lok Sabha Secretariat, August 1984, Para-1.12.

111. Delhi Development Authority, *Master Plan for Delhi Perspective 2001*, New Delhi, 1990, p. 9.

112. Ibid., pp. 13, 56.

113. Ibid., pp. 110–12.

114. Ibid., p. 112.

115. National Capital Region is the larger inter-state region around Delhi whose development had been recommended in the 1962 Master Plan to help keep the population of Delhi within the carrying capacity. See *Master Plan for Delhi Perspective 2001* (Note 111 above), p. 10.

116. *Master Plan for Delhi Perspective 2001* (Note 111 above), pp. 13, 56.

117. Ibid., p. 9.

118. Ibid., pp. 10–11.

119. 'My report's scope is limited: DVB chief', *Hindustan Times*, 25 November 200.

120. The three industrial clusters mentioned are Anand Parbat, Shahadra and Shamapur Badli. See *Master Plan for Delhi Perspective 2001* (Note 111 above), p. 12.

121. 'Minister agrees to declare some more areas industrial', *Hindustan Times*, 23 December 2000.

122. *Master Plan for Delhi Perspective 2001* (Note 111 above), p. 12.

123. There are many more such units in Delhi, as is obvious not only from the inconsistent figures that were being thrown around by the press while the court was hearing the matter, but also because, even after the closure of hazardous industries, hazards have continued. In November 1997 a girl was killed in a blast in a chemical unit. In October 1998 five persons were injured when paint thinner caught fire in a factory. In November 1999 two children died after they fell into a drum containing chemical waste from a factory. In April 2000 two persons were killed in a blast in a rubber solution unit. In July 2000 five persons, including a four-year-old, were injured in a chemical factory fire.

124. *Master Plan for Delhi Perspective 2001* (Note 111 above), pp. 12, 55.

125. In 1962 the Master Plan earmarked 196 acres in then central and 168 acres in then outlying areas (to be developed, respectively, with a floor area ratio [FAR] of 150 and 120) for flatted factories. These would have provided 1,981,901 sq. metres of industrial space. In 1990 again, similar proposals were made for flatted factories and service centres, albeit with somewhat lower FAR.

126. 'DDA says no to DCM plan on mill land', *Indian Express*, 31 July 1991.

127. 'Officers bristle at diktat on DCM', *Times of India*, 23 September 1994.

128. 'Who created the mess that is Delhi today?', *Times of India*, 25 November 2000.

129. 'HUDCO's land allotment for five-star hotel violates Master Plan', *Times of India*, 3 October 1997.

130. 'HUDCO project found violating Delhi Master Plan', *Times of India*, 28 February 1998.

131. 'After units' closure, DDA, industry owners read SC order differently', *Times of India*,

1 February 1999.

132. 'SC tells toxic units to surrender land', *Daily Pioneer*, 4 May 2000.

133. 'Polluting units: SC lands greedy ones in trouble', *Times of India*, 5 December 1996.

134. Dasgupta, 'Tall Blunders' (Note 24 above).

135. 'DDA, industry owners read SC order differently' (Note 131 above).

136. 'SC tells toxic units to surrender land' (Note 132 above); 'Court gives polluting units time till May 28', *Asian Age*, 4 May 2000; 'SC asks hazardous units to give up land', *Hindustan Times*, 5 May 2000; 'Banished units told to cede surplus land', *Times of India*, 5 May 2000.

137. 'Warrants against 9 polluting units', *The Hindu*, 4 August 2000.

138. 'Court issues fresh warrants against 9 units', *Indian Express*, 6 August 2000.

139. *Master Plan for Delhi Perspective 2001* (Note 111 above), p. 10.

140. Ibid., pp. 55, 56.

LITTLE PEOPLE RIGHTS

1. Title of the discussion paper prepared by his Jan Chetna Manch at the end of April 2000.

2. 'Jhuggi fire causes train diversion', *Times of India*, 3 May 2000; 'Over 200 jhuggis gutted in E. Delhi', *Hindustan Times*, 3 May 2000.

3. 'Blackout in S. Delhi due to jhuggi fire', *Times of India*, 11 April 2000.

4. '410 shanties razed in Ultadanga fire', *The Statesman*, 19 January 2000.

5. 'Major fire renders thousands homeless', *Times of India*, 31 January 2000; 'Fire in slum cluster', *Hindustan Times*, 31 January 2000.

6. 'Four-year-old dies in Pushta fire', *Times of India*, 22 February 2000.

7. '600 jhuggis gutted in East Delhi', *Hindustan Times*, 8 April 2000.

8. 'Minor girl dies in Kishan Garh jhuggi fire', *Hindustan Times*, 17 April 2000.

9. '200 jhuggis gutted', *Times of India*, 21 April 2000.

10. 'Fire service outposts in slums to continue till October', *The Hindu*, 5 July 2000.

11. 'No provision for fire safety in slum clusters: Affidavit', *Hindustan Times*, 6 November 2000.

12. Verma, G. D., 'Slum upgrading: Of paradigm shifts and missed lessons', *Architecture+Design*, January 2000.

13. 'As Yamuna swells, it's time for annual exodus', *Indian Express*, 21 July 2000.

14. 'People evacuated from Yamuna banks', *Asian Age (Delhi Age)*, 11 June 2000.

15. 'Sheila launches slum development project', *Hindustan Times*, 31 January 2000.

16. 'Wield lathis for your right, VP exhorts jhuggi dwellers', *Hindustan Times*, 17 April 2000.

17. 'Walia seeks upgradation of jhuggi clusters', *Hindustan Times*, 21 July 2000; 'Walia demands for JJ Cluster upgradation', *Daily Pioneer*, 21 July 2000; 'Walia demands better deal for jhuggi dwellers', *Times of India*, 21 July 2000.

18. The lead NGO in the project Sheila Dikshit had launched had admitted at an NGO meeting just weeks before that it had so far worked in the rural sector and had only just forayed into urban slums and had no completed slum projects, nor any slum projects in Delhi.

19. 'Rain torments Mumbai, entire slum swamped', *The Hindu*, 14 July 2000.

20. 'Poor can't be wished away, Mr. Bhujbal', *The Hindu*, 17 July 2000.

21. 'Sonia to visit victims of landslide in Mumbai', *Daily Pioneer*, 15 July 2000.

22. 'Sonia calls upon NGOs to help Ghatkopar landslide victims', *Hindustan Times*, 15 July 2000.

23. 'Sonia visits landslide-affected people', *Times of India*, 16 July 2000.

24. 'Sonia visits landslip victims', *The Hindu*, 16 July 2000; 'Sonia visits landslide-affected

people' (Note 23 above).

25. 'BMC will soon implement slum sanitation plan', *Times of India*, 7 March 2000.

26. 'Encroachments behind flood fury in Hyderabad: Naidu', *Daily Pioneer*, 1 September 2000.

27. 'Haphazard urban planning leads to disaster' , *Times of India*, 27 August 2000.

28. 'Floods a result of encroachments, says Naidu', *Hindustan Times*, 28 August 2000; 'Drive to remove encroachments on nalas', *The Hindu*, 1 September 2000; 'Encroachments behind flood fury' (Note 26 above).

29. 'Naidu to launch poverty eradication programme', *Daily Pioneer*, 16 June 2000.

30. 'Floods: Rs. 300-cr. sought from HUDCO for housing', *The Hindu*, 3 September 2000.

31. 'City's slums to get face lift', *The Hindu*, 20 October 2000.

32. Ibid.

33. This was told to a social worker who has been working in the slum for several years by the project consultant at his public lecture in May 1999 in response to her question to him about a current threat of eviction.

34. 'British up-uchayukt ne gatividhiyon ki jankari li' ('The British High Commissioner took stock of activities'), *Nai Duniya*, 9 October 1991; 'British uchayukt dwara bastiyon ka nirikshan' ('Inspection of slums by British High Commissioner'), *Nai Duniya*, 24 October 1992.

35. 'Shekhar nagar mein 15 lakh ke vikas karya ka shubharambh' ('Inauguration of works worth 1.5 million in Shekhar Nagar'), *Nai Duniya*, 9 May 1992.

36. 'Jansahyog se basti mein paryavaran sudhar' ('Environmental upgradation in slum through community participation'), *Nai Duniya*, 8 June 1994.

37. 'Jhuggivasiyon dwara shramdan ki anukarniye misal pesh' ('Slum dwellers set example of voluntary work'), *Dainik Bhaskar*, 23 June 1997; 'Chandrabhaga pul ke kshetra ke rehvasiyon ka sarahniye kadam' ('Appreciable initiative of residents of the Chandrabhaga bridge area'), *Nav Bharat*, 23 June 1997.

38. 'Indore ki 174 tang bastiyon ke 50 hazar parivaron ko sthayi patte' ('Permanent leasehold tenure for 50,000 families in 174 slums in Indore'), *Swadesh*, 26 July 1998; 'Indore mein ODA ki 174 bastiyon ko sthayi patte' ('Permanent leasehold tenure for ODA's 174 slums in Indore'), *Indore Samachar*, 26 July 1998; 'ODA project ki 174 bastivasiyon ko sthayi patte' ('Permanent leasehold tenure for residents of the ODA project's 174 slums'), *Nai Duniya*, 26 July 1998.

39. 'People living in degraded and dehumanised conditions', *Times of India*, 28 March 2000; Delhi Development Authority, *Master Plan for Delhi Perspective 2001*, Delhi Development Authority, New Delhi, 1990, p. 3, 45.

40. Mahapatra, Richard, 'Republic quaked', *Down To Earth*, 28 February 2001, p . 43. (The Indian Metereological Department puts the magnitude at 6.9, and France, China and the US measure it at 7.9, later upgraded to 8.1.)

41. In the print media this point was made already on the day after the news first broke. ('When havens turn into hells', *Indian Express*, 28 January 2001.)

42. 'Delhi sees the danger, gets into action mode', *Times of India*, 30 January 2001.

43. '19,000 city buildings vulnerable', *Times of India*, 30 January 2001; '90 per cent new buildings unsafe in Pune, warn experts', *Indian Express*, 31 January 2001; 'Tremor will hit Dwarka, trans-Yamuna the worst', *Times of India*, 31 January 2001.

44. 'Taming the tremors: Better planning can save lives', *Times of India*, 31 January 2001; 'The importance of the structural engineer', *Indian Express*, 2 February 2001; 'Earthquakes don't kill, buildings do', *Indian Express*, 6 February 2001.

45. 'When havens turn into hells' (Note 41 above); 'Who's afraid of earthquakes really?', *The Hindu*, 31 January 2001; 'Spirit is willing, flesh is missing', *Indian Express*, 31 January 2001; 'Earthquakes don't kill' (Note 44 above).

46. Agarwal, Anil, Editorial, *Down To Earth*, 28 February 2001.
47. Agarwal, Anil, 'We can build N-bombs, why not safe houses?', *Times of India*, 4 February 2001.
48. 'Implement building codes to prevent quake disaster', *Times of India*, 5 February 2001.
49. 'Old faults in new Noida township', *Times of India*, 1 February 2001.
50. 'NRI house-hunters ask the obvious question', *Indian Express*, 5 February 2001.
51. 'Quake-proof rules not adhered to', *Times of India*, 31 January 2001.
52. 'BJP blamed for building collapses', *Times of India*, 20 February 2001; 'Cases filed against Ahmedabad builders, contractors', *Times of India*, 3 February 2001; 'Probe against builders may be a non-starter', *Times of India*, 6 February 2001.
53. 'Check all high rise buildings, says Jagmohan', *Indian Express*, 5 February 2001.
54. 'MCH tells builders to examine stability of old structures', *The Hindu*, 30 January 2001.
55. 'Builders' carrot-and-stick to homeless', *Times of India*, 12 February 2001.
56. 'Moolah cements the builder-politician nexus', *Times of India*, 13 February 2001.
57. Ibid.
58. 'Built to collapse', *Indian Express*, 12 February 2001.
59. 'Gujarat govt's answer to illegal bldgs: Regularise them', *Indian Express*, 10 February 2001; 'If the builders were crooks, Gujarat govt was an accomplice', *Indian Express*, 11 February 2001.
60. 'What lies beneath the rubble: Greed', *Indian Express*, 8 February 2001; 'Gujarat govt's answer' (Note 59 above); 'If the builders were crooks' (Note 59 above).
61. 'What lies beneath' (Note 60 above).
62. 'Builders' carrot-and-stick' (Note 55 above).
63. 'Moolah cements' (Note 56 above).
64. 'Committee or calamity?', *Indian Express*, 20 February 2001.
65. 'No more glass houses: Danger ahead', *The Hindu*, 30 January 2001; '90 per cent new buildings unsafe in Pune' (Note 43 above); 'Tap local wisdom to rebuild', *Indian Express*, 31 January 2001; 'Seismic storey: The house that Delhi built', *Times of India*, 2 February 2001; 'Why do we, the super-educated people, ignore basic principles?', *Indian Express*, 7 February 2001.
66. 'Probe against builders may be a non-starter' (Note 52 above).
67. 'Builders explain safety of high-rise flats', *Times of India*, 6 February 2001.
68. 'The importance of the structural engineer' (Note 44 above).
69. 'Shelters examined', *Times of India*, 4 February 2001.
70. 'No more glass houses'(Note 65 above); 'Can Delhi's glass houses shake off a quake?', *Times of India*, 1 February 2001.
71. 'Taming the tremors' (Note 44 above); 'HUDCO to rebuild quake-hit areas: Rs 1,000-cr plan', *Indian Express*, 30 January 2001; 'Jagmohan gets quake-alert, cracks the whip on defaulters', *Times of India*, 30 January 2001.
72. Mahapatra, 'Republic quaked' (Note 40 above), p. 47.
73. 'Who's afraid of earthquakes really?' (Note 45 above).
74. Mahapatra, 'Republic quaked' (Note 40 above), p. 47.
75. 'On Firm Ground', *Times of India*, 4 February 2001.
76. 'Delhi sees the danger' (Note 42 above).
77. 'State of urban infrastructure disconcerting: Jagmohan', *Hindustan Times*, 26 April 2000.
78. Photograph of the same was in a folder with other photographs that was circulated to the press persons taken to Narela in July.
79. 'Resettlement colony turns into a slum?', *The Hindu*, 29 June 2000.
80. 'Notice to govt on lack of schools in Narela', *Indian Express*, 8 July 2000; '5,000 kids fight losing battle for basic right: Education', *Indian Express*, 12 July 2000; 'NHRC help sought to end Narela colony's plight', *Asian Age (Delhi Age)*, 4 August 2000.

81. 'Narela colonies lack civic amenities', *Asian Age (Delhi Age)*, 10 August 2000.
82. 'Jagmohan announces constructive schemes', *Indian Express*, 17 July 2000; 'We've been sent to wilderness: Slum dwellers', *Hindustan Times*, 17 July 2000; 'Resettled slum dwellers hopeful', *The Hindu*, 17 July 2000; 'Jagmohan to MPs: Come, see what I have done for poor', *Asian Age (Delhi Age)*, 8 August 2000; 'MPs to visit resettlement colonies', *Times of India*, 8 August 2000; 'Loans, schools and security for Narela families', *Times of India*, 11 July 2000; 'Narela to be developed into a model colony', *Hindustan Times*, 11 July 2000; 'No new slum, says Jagmohan', *The Hindu*, 11 July 2000; 'Jagmohan now targets squatters', *Asian Age (Delhi Age)*, 11 July 2000; 'Project for 60,000 displaced slum-dwellers: Jagmohan', *Indian Express*, 11 July 2000.
83. Delhi Development Authority, *Master Plan for Delhi*, DDA, New Delhi, 1962, p. 27; Delhi Development Authority, *Master Plan for Delhi* (Note 39 above), pp. 6–7.
84. 'Congress flays MCD for bias in projects', *Asian Age (Delhi Age)*, 6 August 2000.
85. 'Bawana residents protest proposed landfill site', *Times of India*, 10 July 2000.
86. 'Sarita Vihar residents up in arms against slums' relocation', *HT South Delhi Live*, 31 January 2001; 'Slum-glum Sarita Vihar', *Neighbourhood Flash*, 28 January–3 February 2001.
87. 'SMC's relocation plan runs into rough weather', *Times of India*, 16 March 2000.
88. 'Residents protest against slum-dwellers', *Times of India*, 17 October 2000.
89. Delhi Development Authority, *Master Plan for Delhi* (Note 39 above), p. 6. (The Plan recommends gross residential densities of 350–400 ppHa [persons per hectare], which would make overall density of 280–300 ppHa possible. It says 'Still higher gross residential densities increase man–land ratio marginally and should be prescribed only in special conditions'.)
90. Ibid.
91. Delhi Development Authority, *Master Plan for Delhi*, Delhi Development Authority, New Delhi, 1962, p. ii under 'Important recommendations made in the Master Plan'.
92. Government of Madhya Pradesh, *Indore Master Plan (1974-91)*, GoMP, Indore, p. 176.
93. Delhi Development Authority, *Master Plan for Delhi* (Note 39 above), p. 6.
94. 'Resettlement colony turns into a slum?' (Note 79 above).
95. 'Jobless at Narela: Displaced population all set to return', *Indian Express*, 16 July 2000.
96. Singh, V. P., 'From garibi hatao to garib hatao, India has come a long way', *Hindustan Times*, 11 June 2000.
97. Ibid.
98. 'The great divide of Delhi comes to fore, once again', *Indian Express*, 5 June 2000; 'Delhi CM concerned over city migration', *Asian Age (Delhi Age)*, 5 June 2000.
99. Singh, 'From garibi hatao to garib hatao' (Note 96 above); Shourie, H. D. 'Sab ko garib banao, we are Indians', *Hindustan Times*, 18 June 2000.
100. Shourie, 'Sab ko garib banao' (Note 99 above).
101. Government of India, *Istanbul+5 UNCHS (Habitat) Conference 2001–India: National Report–Progress of Implementation of the Habitat Agenda (1996-2000)*, Ministry of Urban Development and Poverty Alleviation, New Delhi, p. 9.
102. 'AIIMS to expand after retrieving land from jhuggi dwellers', *Times of India*, 10 February 2000; 'Slums slow down AIIMS project', *Hindustan Times*, 5 May 2000; 'AIIMS to upgrade transplant facility', *The Hindu*, 23 September 2000.
103. 'AAI, Navy move to tackle squatters, at last', *Indian Express*, 5 May 2000.
104. 'An airport for some, open skies for others', *Indian Express*, 14 October 2000.
105. 'Attachment notice fails to ground AAI', *Hindustan Times*, 12 November 2000.
106. Desai, A.H. and S. Muralidhar, 'Public Interest Litigation: Potential and problems', in *Supreme But Not Infallible*, Supreme Court of India, 2000, pp. 159–92, 162.
107. Chief Justice A.M. Ahmadi, quoted in Desai and Muralidhar, *Supreme But Not Infallible*

(Note 106 above), p. 181.

108. Desai and Muralidhar, *Supreme But Not Infallible* (Note 106 above), p. 181.
109. It might be mentioned here that Justice Krishna Iyer (who had much to do with evolving the concept of PIL in the 1970s) did comment on the Sanjay Gandhi National Park case. He wrote that an environmental group 'initiated a public interest litigation (at whose instance one is left shrewdly to guess, in a heartless megalopolis with builders whose boundless resources and stratagems beat one's imagination in currently-corrupt Bharat). The PIL, I regret, can be a wolf in sheep's clothing or an ineffectual angel espousing the causes of voiceless indigents.' ('Justices and justicing: I', *The Hindu*, 13 November 2000.)
110. 'Jagmohan pulls up DDA officials for negligence', *Hindustan Times*, 24 February 2000.
111. 'Model park inaugurated', *Times of India*, 15 October 2000; 'Andrews Ganj slum area now a park', *Hindustan Times*, 15 October 2000.
112. 'Rohini slums to be relocated', *The Hindu*, 7 November 2000.
113. '500 jhuggis removed from green belt', *Times of India*, 1 September 2000.
114. 'GNOIDA sells forest land as residential plots', *Times of India*, 9 November 2000; 'Cleared slum land will be given to developers', *Times of India*, 15 June 2000.
115. 'Stop demolitions during the rains', *Indian Express*, 17 July 2000.
116. HUDCO/Vastu Shilpa Foundation, *Aranya: An approach to settlement design*, Housing and Urban Development Corporation (HUDCO), New Delhi, 1990; Curtis, W., 'Low-cost housing: Indore', Curtis, W. (ed.), *Balkrishna Doshi: An architecture for India*, Mapin, Ahmedabad, 1988; Das, S.K. and Meera Godbole, 'Urban coherence and architecture of housing' in Singh, K. and F. Steinberg (eds), *Urban India in crisis*, New Age, New Delhi, 1996.
117. Verma, 'Slum Upgrading' (Note 12 above).
118. 'Tap local wisdom to rebuild', *Indian Express*, 31 January 2001.
119. 'LDA's greed shortcircuits "dream" housing project', *Daily Pioneer*, 15 June 2000.
120. 'Thrown out, ex-MPs will soon have govt accommodation', *Indian Express*, 10 May 2000.
121. 'BMC will soon implement slum sanitation plan', *Times of India*, 7 March 2000; 'Condition of toilets in slums to be improved', *Times of India*, 9 March 2000.
122. Ibid.
123. 'Govt departments not using Plan funds', *Hindustan Times*, 11 March 2000.
124. 'Govt-run primary schools: A month after vacations, MCD still to finish repair works', *Hindustan Times*, 3 August 2000; 'MCD primary schools: "All tented classrooms to be replaced by March 2001"', *Hindustan Times*, 12 August 2000; 'After three years, MCD talks education and gets nowhere', *Indian Express*, 22 August 2000; 'Primary education suffers as MCD flunks', *Times of India*, 22 August 2000.
125. 'MCD told to file status report on all its schools', *Asian Age (Delhi Age)*, 25 April 2000; 'HC seeks report on amenities in MCD schools', *Times of India*, 25 April 2000.
126. 'HC wants report on MCD schools', *Times of India*, 18 May 2000; 'Court asks chief secretary to reply on MCD schools', *Asian Age (Delhi Age)*, 18 May 2000.
127. 'Court wants list of girls' schools with broken walls', *Times of India*, 19 April 2000.
128. 'Girls' school walls will be higher', *Times of India*, 12 July 2000.
129. 'Under-construction MCD school building collapses', *Hindustan Times*, 4 July 2000.
130. 'Delhi govt: Back to school, in letter and spirit', *Times of India*, 3 January 2000.
131. Ibid.
132. 'MCD will begin to distribute jerseys to students', *Times of India*, 4 January 2000.
133. 'MCD to replace 2,831 temporary classrooms', *Hindustan Times*, 7 December 2000.
134. 'Delhi: 8 lakh kids in MCD schools to go without uniforms', *Times of India*, 20 November 2000.
135. 'Jerseys for MCD schools: Students will have to wait until summer', *Hindustan Times*,

28 December 2000.

136. 'MCD's class of 2000: On the mat', *Daily Pioneer*, 27 August 2000; 'Increased aid for MCD sought', *Times of India*, 12 September 2000.

137. 'Increased aid for MCD sought' (Note 136 above).

138. 'MCD panel okays purchase of schoolbags', *Hindustan Times*, 26 October 2000; 'Free bags for MCD school kids', *The Hindu*, 26 October 2000.

139. 'Jerseys for MCD schools' (Note 135 above).

140. 'Plan afoot to decentralise mid-day meals', *Hindustan Times*, 28 May 2000.

141. 'MCD's class of 2000' (Note 136 above); 'Schoolkids get mid-day meals for hardly 5 days', *Hindustan Times*, 6 May 2000; 'Plan afoot to decentralise mid-day meals'(Note 140 above).

142. 'Kids throw MCD's midday meal biscuits into the gutter', *Hindustan Times*, 4 May 2000.

143. 'Plan to decentralise mid-day meals' (Note 140 above); 'MCD's better deal for school children', *The Hindu*, 14 November 2000; 'Attendance not enough for promotion to next class', *Hindustan Times*, 14 November 2000

144. 'Govt, aided schools still in the doldrums', *Times of India*, 1 June 2000; 'Don't relegate government schools to the second class', *Times of India*, 5 June 2000.

145. 'Govt-run primary schools' (Note 124 above).

146. 'MCD-run schools are short of 1,000 teachers', *Hindustan Times*, 19 August 2000.

147. 'Sheila opens cyber lab at government school in city', *Asian Age (Delhi Age)*, 2 August 2000.

148. 'Sheila dissatisfied with Education dept', *Hindustan Times*, 21 August 2000.

149. 'MCD to have survey on education', *Indian Express*, 2 September 2000; 'MCD plans survey to increase enrolment', *Times of India*, 2 September 2000; 'MCD survey to identify "out-of-school" children', *Daily Pioneer*, 2 September 2000; 'After a late start, MCD woos children', *The Hindu*, 30 October 2000.

150. 'MCD schools' enrolment figure rises to 80,000', *Hindustan Times*, 16 October 2000.

151. 'After a late start' (Note 149 above).

152. 'Opposition slams shoddy state of municipal schools', *Hindustan Times*, 12 September 2000; 'Increased aid for MCD sought' (Note 136 above); 'MCD has an education target: Squeeze 2 lakh kids in same schools', *Indian Express*, 25 September 2000.

153. 'MCD schools' enrolment figure rises'(Note 150 above); 'After a late start' (Note 149 above).

154. 'PWD to build proper school facilities', *Asian Age (Delhi Age)*, 8 September 2000; 'MCD report presents believe-it-or-not facts', *Indian Express*, 1 October 2000.

155. 'Room with a view for slum kids', *Times of India*, 3 March 2000; 'School still a distant dream for slum children', *Times of India*, 20 March 2000; 'Under the street lights, a quiet revolution in city slums', *Times of India*, 28 March 2000.

156. 'MCD to set up extended schools with people's help', *Hindustan Times*, 22 August 2000; 'MCD plans survey to increase enrolment' (Note 149 above).

157. 'People's effort to nurse MCD school goes waste', *Indian Express*, 3 November 2000.

158. Deenbandhu Samajik Sanstha, *Indore Zila Sarkar's interventions in school education: Betraying our children in the name of decentralisation and universalisation of education*, Indore, 1999.

159. 'Govt's Operation Amalgamation to result in more closed schools', *Indian Express*, 21 May 2000; 'Here, teachers use influence to get posted in city schools', *Indian Express*, 24 May 2000.

160. 'MCD primary schools' (Note 124 above).

161. 'School survives land mafia scare', *Times of India*, 10 May 2000; 'MCD foils builder's school-grabbing move', *Hindustan Times*, 10 May 2000.

162. The following description is based on what was filed before and ordered by the High

Court in and on WP No. 483/1998, Civil Contempt Petition No. 177/1998, WP No. 1816/1998, WP No. 1040/2000, WP No. 1645/2000, M(WP) No. 15/2000, applications for intervention in WP No. 1645/2000, WP No. 2028/2000 and on local newspaper reports.

163. SLP(C) No.159/2001.

BIG PEOPLE RIGHTS

1. 'MCD cracks whip on encroachments', *Hindustan Times*, 5 January 2000.
2. 'Cops, MCD to go after squatters', *Hindustan Times*, 1 January 2001.
3. 'MCD continues drive against encroachments', *Times of India*, 6 January 2000; 'MCD intensifies drive against illegal structures', *Hindustan Times*, 6 January 2000.
4. 'Proposal to bring unorganised sector under pension scheme', *Hindustan Times*, 18 January 2000.
5. 'MCD clears encroachments', *Times of India*, 9 March 2000; 'Delhi govt raises minimum wages', *Hindustan Times*, 10 March 2000.
6. 'MCD action on encroachments; *Hindustan Times*, 6 May 2000; More demolitions in Karol Bagh, GK', *Times of India*, 25 March 2000; 'L-G promises strict action if more encroachments come up', *Hindustan Times*, 6 May 2000.
7. 'Ousted during Clinton visit, 50 street vendors petition', *Indian Express*, 22 May 2000.
8. '14 kiosks razed at Bahadur Shah Zafar Marg', *Indian Express*, 7 September 2000; 'Encroachments on BSZ Marg removed', *Hindustan Times*, 7 September 2000; 'MCD launches demolition drive in BSZ Marg area', *Daily Pioneer*, 7 September 2000; '127 squatters given tehbazaris in city zone area', *Hindustan Times*, 20 October 2000.
9. 'Khairnar strikes at hawkers' stalls at CST', *Indian Express*, 6 May 2000.
10. 'BMC to set up commando force to evict hawkers: Khairnar', *Indian Express*, 10 May 2000.
11. 'Khairnar hawks peace, vendors hail scheme', *Indian Express*, 1 June 2000.
12. 'Hawking to be legalised in Mumbai', *Daily Pioneer*, 7 July 2000.
13. 'New "pay and hawk" scheme mooted for hawkers', *Times of India*, 11 November 2000.
14. 'HC backs PMC move against hawkers', *Indian Express*, 14 July 2000.
15. '"Teh-bazari" rights to squatters protested', *Hindustan Times*, 1 February 2000; 'Shopkeepers at Janpath fight over display of wares on trees', *Hindustan Times*, 29 May 2000.
16. 'Ownership right for shopkeepers in 14 areas', *Hindustan Times*, 1 February 2000; 'Ownership rights for shopkeepers', *Times of India*, 2 February 2000; 'NDMC mum on ownership right for Lodhi Colony Market shopkeepers', *Hindustan Times*, 2 February 2000; 'Cabinet says yes to transfer of ownership in 12 city markets', *Indian Express*, 1 September 2000.
17. STAR News, 8 March 2000.
18. 'Delhi CM concerned over city migration', *Asian Age (Delhi Age)*, 5 June 2000.
19. 'Govt has no figures on slums, will enact laws to stop influx', *Indian Express*, 8 April 2000; 'Bill planned to ban new slums', *Times of India*, 22 March 2000.
20. 'Delhiites have a higher risk of getting HIV infection' , *Daily Pioneer*, 30 May 2000.
21. 'Slum-dwellers feel it's Naidu's manna', *The Hindu*, 21 June 2000; 'Regular power to slums', *Indian Express* (Chandigarh), 25 August 2000; 'Power supply to regularised colonies', *Times of India*, 1 September 2000.
22. Delhi Development Authority, *Master Plan for Delhi Perspective 2001*, 'Informal sector in trade' under 'Annexure-VI: Review of the Master Plan for Delhi 1962 (MPD-62)', DDA, 1990, p. 120.

23. Ibid., 'Trade and commerce: Retail trade' (introduction), p. 13; 'Informal sector' under 'Trade and commerce: Retail trade', p. 18.

24. Ibid., 'Informal sector' under 'Trade and commerce: Retail trade', p. 17.

25. Ibid., pp. 17–18.

26. Ibid., p. 18.

27. 'DVB to step up drive against power theft', *Times of India*, 11 February 2000; '37 DVB employees held for power theft', *Hindustan Times*, 26 February 2000; 'DVB nabs own staff for power theft', *Hindustan Times*, 26 February 2000; '19 more DVB staffers caught stealing power', *Hindustan Times*, 29 February 2000; 'DVB now cracks whip on its officers', *Hindustan Times*, 2 March 2000; 'Rs 2500-cr a year lost to power thefts', *Times of India*, 17 April 2000; 'Power "losses" more in posh colonies', *Hindustan Times*, 30 April 2000; 'Powerful babus stealing power', *Hindustan Times*, 20 May 2000.

28. 'AIDS awareness fortnight to detect possible cases', *Indian Express*, 30 May 2000.

29. 'AIDS awareness fortnight' (Note 28 above); 'Capital to host 15-day anti-AIDS campaign', *Hindustan Times*, 30 May 2000; 'AIDS awareness camps from June 1', *Times of India*, 30 May 2000; 'Delhiites have a higher risk of getting HIV infection', *Daily Pioneer*, 30 May 2000. Indeed, as his AIDS campaign in slums drew to a close, the minister 'held a high-level meeting' to review water-borne diseases and extended the deadline for cleaning drains from 15 to 30 June. ('Health Minister sets deadline for clean-up act', *Hindustan Times*, 14 June 2000.) Obviously the NGOs could not have helped with this larger imperative the previous fortnight because funds flow was for AIDS not to clean drains.

30. 'Walia defends stand: Anti-AIDS campaign', *The Statesman*, 2 June 2000.

31. 'VP Singh upstages Cong, BJP in Delhi?', *Hindustan Times*, 26 March 2000.

32. 'On his birthday, PM gives nation a costly gift', *Times of India*, 26 December 2000; 'Front: New year gift for rural poor', *Daily Pioneer*, 26 December 2000.

33. 'PM's scheme under scrutiny', *Times of India*, 17 January 2001; '21st Century Tughlaks', *Times of India*, 20 January 2001.

34. 'Centre justifies "Antodaya" scheme', *Hindustan Times*, 28 December 2000.

35. 'Antyodaya scheme to start functioning within 2 months', *Hindustan Times*, 30 December 2000.

36. 'Subsidised ration for jhuggi residents', *Times of India*, 21 January 2001.

37. 'Well-meaning but impractical, Anya Yojna may not benefit daily wagers', *Times of India*, 21 January 2001.

38. 'Dole for every jhuggi-dweller in the Capital', *Indian Express*, 21 February 2001.

39. *Dainik Jagran*, 3 February 2001.

40. 'Slum dwellers claim false BPL status', *The Statesman*, 15 February 2001; 'Ration card exercise causing chaos', *Daily Pioneer*, 16 February 2001; 'Dole for every jhuggi-dweller' (Note 38 above).

41. 'Dole for every jhuggi-dweller' (Note 38 above).

42. 'Concrete plan to involve RWAs at last', *Times of India*, 21 January 2000.

43. 'Govt organises meet to empower residents' bodies', *Hindustan Times*, 22 February 2000.

44. 'Govt begins interaction with RWAs', *Times of India*, 2 March 2000.

45. 'Govt to fund RWAs for development work', *Times of India*, 4 March 2000.

46. Ibid.

47. 'Govt launches bhagidari project', *Hindustan Times*, 7 May 2000; 'Government-IIT partnership to transform Delhi', *Asian Age (Delhi Age)*, 7 May 2000; 'Govt ties up with IIT to make Delhi better', *Times of India*, 7 May 2000; 'Identify the areas of cooperation with govt: CM', *Hindustan Times*, 10 May 2000.

48. 'Sheila lauds people's participation in "bhagidari"', *Daily Pioneer*, 15 June 2000.

49. 'Participation of citizens must for progress: CM', *Hindustan Times*, 15 June 2000.

50. 'RWA, govt departments team up for a better Delhi', *Indian Express*, 16 June 2000.

51. 'Delhi: Civic agencies to get "first-hand" feel of city's problems', *Times of India*, 17 June 2000.

52. 'Bhagidari meet: Suggestions will be implemented soon, says CM', *Hindustan Times*, 17 June 2000.

53. 'CM outlines strategy to make city a model place', *Asian Age (Delhi Age)*, 17 June 2000; '3-day Bhagidari workshop concludes', *Daily Pioneer*, 17 June 2000; 'Utilities get 3 mths to incorporate suggestions', *Times of India*, 18 June 2000.

54. 'Sheila renews call for Green Delhi', *Indian Express*, 20 August 2000; 'More role for welfare groups in bhagidari urged', *Times of India*, 20 August 2000.

55. 'RWAs to develop 80 parks', *The Hindu*, 17 August 2000.

56. '3-day Bhagidari workshop' (Note 53 above); 'Bhagidari meet' (Note 52 above).

57. 'DDA flat owners express concern', *Times of India*, 20 June 2000; 'DDA flat owners up in arms', *Hindustan Times*, 21 June 2000; 'DDA flat-owners to stage protest', *Indian Express*, 22 June 2000; 'Vasant Kunj residents to appeal to PM', *The Hindu*, 23 June 2000.

58. 'Jagmohan convenes meeting with Delhi MPs', *Hindustan Times*, 24 June 2000.

59. 'No action in DDA colonies till July 31: Jagmohan', *Times of India*, 26 June 2000; 'Jagmohan sets deadline for DDA flats', *Indian Express*, 26 June 2000; 'Flat owners given 5 weeks', *Hindustan Times*, 26 June 2000.

60. 'What is Bhagidari?', *Times of India*, 3 September 2000; 'People power: How many milestones to go?', *Times of India*, 3 September 2000; 'Bhagidari scheme has not changed anything: RWAs', *Indian Express*, 11 September 2000.

61. 'Water-starved, in boring mode! Bhagidaari, a success?', *Neighbourhood Flash, Vol. III, No. 10*, 28 January–3 February 2001.

62. 'New hospital, college likely in Vasant Kunj', *HT South Delhi Live*, 8 November 2000; 'Vasant Kunj mein haat nirmaan ki prakriya shuru, paryatan vibhag ne manjoori di' ('Process of making haat in Vasant Kunj begins, Tourism Department accords approval'), *Hindustan*, 12 January 2001.

63. 'People power' (Note 60 above).

64. 'Lara Dutta for U.N. meet', *The Hindu*, 30 September 2000.

65. Ibid.

66. 'Private sector can help reduce rural poverty', *Daily Pioneer*, 6 June 2000.

67. Ibid.

68. 'JNU seeks financial assistance from top industrial houses', *Hindustan Times*, 16 April 2000.

69. 'Dear corporates, civic health poor. Help. Love, Delhi govt', *Times of India*, 12 June 2000.

70. 'Govt seeks pvt sector investment in environment', *Hindustan Times*, 14 July 2000.

71. 'Govt to rely on industry for greening AP', *Times of India*, 22 July 2000.

72. Ibid.

73. Ibid.

74. 'Corporates join hands to make city greener', *Hindustan Times*, 30 July 2000.

75. 'Corporates' social focus is narrow, shows survey', *Times of India*, 12 July 2000.

76. Chauhan, U. and N. Lal, 'Public–private partnerships for the urban poor in Ahmendabad: A slum project', *Economic and Political Weekly*, XXXIV (10–11), 13–19 March 1999.

77. 'It's now NGOs' turn to be rated', *Times of India*, 20 January 2000.

78. 'MCD to cancel contract with Sulabh', *Times of India*, 16 March 2000.

79. 'Picking pockets, NGO style', *Times of India*, 26 March 2000.

80. 'Govt asked to submit list of erring NGOs', *Times of India*, 3 April 2000.

81. 'HRD ministry stops grants to 16 NGOs', *Daily Pioneer*, 19 May 2000.

82. 'Maneka to crack whip on errant NGOs', *The Hindu*, 15 September 2000; 'Netted: Maneka

puts bogus NGOs online', *Asian Age (Delhi Age)*, 19 September 2000. By the end of the year, out of 590 NGOs scrutinized by her ministry, ninety had been blacklisted and another 200 faced possible blacklisting. The worst NGOs, the minister said, were from Andhra Pradesh and Madhya Pradesh. ('Blacklist an NGO and MPs intercede: Maneka', *Times of India*, 18 December 2000.)

83. 'Law soon to regulate foreign funds to NGOs', *Daily Pioneer*, 2 October 2000. (The minister said with Andhra Pradesh, Delhi and Madhya Pradesh led in foreign receipts by NGOs.)
84. 'NHRC plans action against fake rights groups', *Times of India*, 11 October 2000.
85. 'Delhi High Court blocks fresh funds to NGOs', *Times of India*, 25 October 2000; 'HC restrains govt from giving grants to NGOs without UC', *Indian Express*, 25 October 2000; 'Utilisation certificate must for grants to NGOs: HC', *Hindustan Times*, 26 October 2000.
86. 'Exaggerate and humiliate', *Hindustan Times*, 10 May 2000; 'A little tact wouldn't hurt', *Hindustan Times*, 7 May 2000.
87. 'A little tact' (Note 86 above).
88. 'NGO shows how not to raise AIDS awareness', *Indian Express*, 9 May 2000.
89. 'Savaging the civilised', *Indian Express*, 10 May 2000.
90. 'A little tact' (Note 86 above); 'How not to raise AIDS awareness' (Note 88 above); 'Exaggerate and humiliate' (Note 86 above); 'Savaging the civilised' (Note 89 above).
91. 'Row over AIDS study: 11 NGO members held', *Hindustan Times*, 27 April 2000; 'How not to raise AIDS awareness' (Note 88 above).
92. 'AIDS booklet leads to controversy in Almora', *Hindustan Times*, 23 April 2000; 'Row over AIDS study' (Note 91 above); 'How not to raise AIDS awareness' (Note 88 above); 'The Sahyog affair', *The Hindu*, 19 May 2000.
93. 'SAHYOG report on AIDS assailed in House', *Times of India*, 18 May 2000.
94. 'AIDS booklet controversy' (Note 92 above); 'Row over AIDS study' (Note 91 above).
95. 'Delhi: Stir held in favour of Sahyog activists', *Indian Express*, 20 May 2000; 'NGOs rally against UP police action', *Asian Age (Delhi Age)*, 20 May 2000.
96. 'A little tact' (Note 86 above); 'Exaggerate and humiliate' (Note 86 above); 'Are NGOs "caring" activists', *Hindustan Times* (Letter), 10 May 2000; 'Savaging the civilised' (Note 89 above); 'Sound and fury in the Hills', *Indian Express*, 12 May 2000; 'Debate the issue', *Times of India* (Letter), 15 May 2000; 'For crying out loud selectively', *Daily Pioneer*, 23 May 2000; 'Role of NGOs', *The Hindu* (Letter), 24 May 2000.
97. Notably, an editorial in the *Hindustan Times* ('Exaggerate and humiliate') and Namita Gokhale's article ('Savaging the civilised') in the *Indian Express* on 10 May 2000. Also, the author's reactions to Harsh Sethi's article in the *Hindustan Times* ('A little tact wouldn't hurt') and Rajeev Dhawan's article ('The Sahyog Affair') in *The Hindu* carried as letters to the editor in those newspapers on, respectively, 10 May 2000 and 24 May 2000.
98. 'The Sahyog affair' (Note 92 above).
99. Ibid.
100. Ibid.
101. Ibid.
102. 'Dikshit wakes up to home truths: NGOs to manage govt-run homes', *Times of India*, 4 January 2000.
103. 'Education policy: NGOs, corporates in govt's good books', *Times of India*, 13 January 2000.
104. 'Engineers will teach people to save water', *Times of India*, 9 March 2000; 'NGO to address potable water problem in Capital', *Hindustan Times*, 9 March 2000.
105. 'Police to seek NGO help in tackling rape cases', *Times of India*, 31 May 2000.
106. 'Census: States urged to utilise NGOs' services', *Hindustan Times*, 28 August 2000.

107. 'Walia urges NGOs to enter health arena', *Hindustan Times*, 28 September 2000.
108. On two separate occasions, the author had informally approached the central government's Council for Advancement and Promotion of Applied Rural Technology (CAPART) and the Central Social Welfare Board to inquire about possibilities of assistance on behalf of, respectively, a group of village boys wanting to set up an enterprise and elderly slum women in need of some social security support. Both times the author was advised to register an NGO.
109. 'Japan has given a grant assistance of $137,208 for grassroots projects to two NGOs', *Times of India*, 8 March 2000.
110. 'Helpage India steps in to fund old age home in Dwarka', *Hindustan Times*, 9 June 2000.
111. 'No kidding, green's the word', *Times of India*, 19 April 2000; '50 young hands to clean our neglected river', *Indian Express*, 15 August 2000; 'Rotary Club to hold discussions on environmental issues', *Indian Express*, 9 September 2000.
112. 'NGOs junk Centre's waste management plan', *Times of India*, 9 October 2000.
113. Singh, Richa, *HIV/AIDS, workers and labour rights: A study of vulnerability of the workers in Wazirpur Industrial Area, Delhi*, Centre for Education and Communication, 1999.
114. Ibid.
115. 'Sheila launches slum development project', *Hindustan Times*, 31 January 2000.
116. Ibid.
117. 'Project TEAM for compulsory education to kids', *Hindustan Times*, 29 April 2000.
118. Ibid.
119. 'City groups come up with alternative Master Plan', *Indian Express*, 20 November 2000.
120. Meeting held at India Habitat Centre (IHC), Delhi, 6 March 2001.
121. Meeting held at the office of Action Aid, Delhi, 13 March 2001.
122. 'A step toward forging closer ties with NGOs', *Times of India*, 3 June 2000.
123. 'NGOs should join hands with govt for development', *The Hindu*, 20 June 2000.
124. 'With eye on govt funds, RSS floats NGO', *Hindustan Times*, 28 October 2000.
125. 'No go NGO', Times of India, 7 November 2000.
126. Aashray Adhikar Abhiyan, *The Capital's Homeless*, New Delhi, 2001, Table 15, p. 54.
127. Khatra Kendra/Sajha Manch, *Dilli Kiski Hai?* ('Who does Delhi belong to?'), February 2001.
128. Mumbai-based architect/urban designer Harshad Bhatia's comment on IIA and CoA, received via e-mail just before the IIA convention in Indore in 1999.
129. GIS: Geographical Information Systems; GIGO: Garbage In Garbage Out.
130. The author was asked to make a presentation on 'Urbanisation, quantity, quality and professional roles'. From the letter that the organisers had sent, I gathered they wanted me to dwell on statistics to show that the scale of the urban problem was huge and argue it was not really the architects' fault that our cities were being taken over by slums. I, on the other hand, was more inclined to try and provoke some soul-searching. Having failed to draw attention to the tragedy of Indore's celebrated project since my 'official' impact study the previous year, I was also deeply dismayed by it having received the profession's highest award a full year after that study. I decided to include in my presentation slides from Indore and to beg the IIA to intervene in whatever manner it saw fit to highlight the truth about Indore.
131. The flier was titled 'Introspection at 2000 before Vision beyond 2000'. It profiled the ground realities of the two AKAA winning projects and suggested how the issues raised could fit into the convention's deliberations on the three sub-themes—Agenda for architecture, Agenda for profession and Agenda for education—being discussed. It appealed to individual architects to join me in insisting that Indore's AKAA winning projects be made central to IIA's deiberations in Indore.
132. *The Statesman* carried reports four days running.

133. 'M.P. HC clears land for IIM at Indore', *Indian Express*, 20 October 2000.
134. Ministry of Urban Affairs and Employment, 'Demand for Health Services', *Draft National Slum Policy, 1999*, Para-9-a-ii, p. 17.

EPILOGUE: WRITING ON THE WALL

1. 'Reform benefits must reach poor: President', *Hindustan Times*, 26 January 2000.
2. 'As workers hide slums, Thailand urges "ambitious" world trade agenda', *Times of India*, 10 February 2000.
3. 'Slum-dwellers vandalise BJP office in Mulund', *Times of India*, 10 March 2000; 'Angry slum-dwellers bundled out of court', *Times of India*, 14 March 2000.
4. 'Wield lathis for your right, VP exhorts jhuggi dwellers', *Hindustan Times*, 17 April 2000.
5. 'AIDS booklet leads to controversy in Almora', *Hindustan Times*, 23 April 2000; 'Row over AIDS study: 11 NGO members held', *Hindustan Times*, 27 April 2000.
6. 'Khairnar strikes at hawkers' stalls at CST', *Indian Express*, 6 May 2000; 'BMC to set up commando force to evict hawkers: Khairnar', *Indian Express*, 10 May 2000.
7. 'An AIDS camp few are aware of', *Indian Express*, 3 June 2000; 'AIDS campaign boomerangs, Walia's apology demanded', *Indian Express*, 8 June 2000.
8. 'Jagmohan discusses illegal constructions, squatters', Indian Express, 30 July 2000; 'Residents' groups to form forum to check squatting, slums', Times of India, 30 July 2000; 'Anti-squatting forum to be set up', Hindustan Times, 30 July 2000.
9. 'Jagmohan to MPs: Come, see what I have done for poor', *Asian Age (Delhi Age)*, 8 August 2000.
10. 'Schools utilise DDA land for commercial purposes', Hindustan Times, 15 August 2000.
11. 'Housing scandal: Eight DDA officials suspended', *Hindustan Times*, 29 September 2000; 'Mafia, middlemen nexus in DDA', *The Hindu*, 30 September 2000.
12. 'DPCC launches "nyaya yudh" for unit workers', *Hindustan Times*, 15 December 2000; 'MCD plans to relocate 30,000 slums', *Hindustan Times*, 8 December 2000; 'DDA housing scam: Seven officials, 2 realtors arrested', *Hindustan Times*, 1 December 2000; 'Jagmohan: DDA illegally acquired land for expanding its golf course', *Hindustan Times*, 22 December 2000.
13. 'Global award for Digvijay govt', *Daily Pioneer*; 19 December 2000.
14. 'CAG: Benefits of growth haven't reached poor', *Hindustan Times*, 26 December 2000.